ALTERNATIVE TO THERAPY

ALTERNATIVE TO THERAPY

A Creative Lecture Series on Process Work

AMY MINDELL, PH.D.

Lao Tse Press
Portland, Oregon

For information contact:
Lao Tse Press
2049 NW Hoyt St., Suite 5
Portland, OR 97209
(503) 222-3395
(503) 227-7003 (fax)
www.laotse.com

Distributed to the trade by:
Independent Publishers Group
814 N. Franklin St.
Chicago, IL 60624
(800) 888-4741
(312) 337-5985 (fax)
www.ipgbook.com

Printed in the United States of America

Cover design: William Stanton
Book design: Heiko Spoddeck
Cover picture: Arnold Mindell
Author photo: Aleksandr Peikrishvili

Mindell, Amy
Alternative to Therapy:
A Creative Lecture Series on Process Work
Bibliography
Includes index.
ISBN: 1-887078-74-6 (pbk.)
Library of Congress Control Number: 2006922666

Table of Contents

Acknowledgments

This book would not be possible without the love, support, and wisdom of my partner, Arny Mindell. It is Arny's groundbreaking discoveries that have inspired the body and soul of the material in this book. His compassionate way of approaching human experiences, and his profound reverence for the wisdom of nature, have always touched me deeply. He has helped me come to grips with every aspect of this work and has given me strength and support to continue when I have felt overwhelmed. I am eternally grateful to him.

I am very thankful to all of the students and colleagues who have studied and tested these ideas over the years from the process work centers of Portland, Oregon, and Zurich, Switzerland, as well as friends and students in Japan, London, and many other countries around the world. I am especially thankful to Randee Cathey, Dawn Menken, Sonja Straub, Jan Dworkin, and Robert King, as well as the many therapists and clients for their very helpful feedback about the details of this book. I also want to thank Margaret Ryan and Mary McAuley for their insightful and detailed editing skills.

Finally, I am indebted to the people I have worked with who have shared their journeys with me, whose lives have touched me greatly, and who have helped me learn about the awesome nature of our existence.

Foreword

by Arnold Mindell

There always seems to be something mundane and something electric and awesome in the air. I have always felt that every moment alone by oneself, every moment in relationship, every group moment is precious. I am happiest when I am in touch with this preciousness. For me, this happiness is the background to working with myself and others; it is the deep background to supervision.

As a beginner, there seems so much to learn, so much to do, so much we can't do, and so much we want to do. As a teacher, at first we feel responsible for explaining the details of things. But with more experience you realize that there is nothing to do. So much happens in life that was never organized by you. After struggling with "doing" things, you slip into the realm of "not-doing." A spiritual person might describe this not-doing as "devotion." In a way, therapy is a form of devotion.

Thus, we begin learning ordinary therapy by studying people, what has been said in psychology, medicine, science, and shamanism. We study people to work with them. We learn, train and get supervision. All of this is crucial. However what really happens when you "work" with someone is unpredictable. You can try to explain working with one another in terms of patterns and the meaning of things. But these explanations do not define what actually happens during the work.

There will never be one single way of defining therapy or its alternative in a manner which is right for all therapists. However we must try. For me, process work is some combination of using your conscious mind, watching closely, following apparent signals and also being open to the magic of the moment. To do that you need to be clear in your awareness about the subtlest things, which happen in and around you. This kind of awareness is very different than programming yourself, different than telling yourself what to do. Programs can be useful, but the healing thing about working with someone is finally being connected with the awesomeness of the unknown, the unpredictable nature of the process, respect for the moment, and the sacredness of the many dimensions of relationship.

Amy's new book, "Alternative to Therapy", is all about the magic of the moment, the magic that she describes in her own creative manner in terms of fairy tale figures. I love this book because her teachers fly through the air to explain their magic. I remember her earliest classes on supervision called "Magical Interventions." The magic she describes is devotion to process, to the Tao as it arises, explains, and interprets itself creating new questions, which it then eventually answers.

I wish the reader an enjoyable journey following Amy's fairy tale teachers into and beyond therapy. Enjoy the journey, but don't forget Amy's pragmatic, concrete tidbits at the beginning of each chapter where she summarizes the salient points describing the essence of interventions. These ideas are like fingers pointing to the moon, so to speak. The fingers show us where the moon is, where that something must be which influences us with its gravitational pull and moonlight, but which is finally almost out of reach. Dona Carletta and Madam Flambé, two of Amy's magical teachers tell us in the next to last chapter, that one must finally realize that the final exercise in learning is dancing, movement, following the rhythm of things.

Arny Mindell
Yachats, Oregon

Introduction

I thought that this book was about therapy and how to become a better therapist. But midway through I realized that it is not. It is about following the Tao (the ancient Chinese term for the *path of nature*) when you are working with and assisting another person. The method I will speak about is called "process work," and it was developed by my partner and husband, Arny Mindell.

In Webster's dictionary *therapeutic* is defined as "(a) serving to cure or heal, curative; (b) serving to preserve health." *Psychotherapy* is defined as "treatment of mental disorder by any of various means involving communication between a trained person and the patient and including counseling, psychoanalysis, etc."

These definitions imply that something is *amiss* and that this difficulty can be healed, cured, or treated. Hence, a therapist is a type of healer who assists another person toward a "healthy" state—*healthy*, that is, as defined by any particular culture. Depending on the therapist's background, she or he may use a variety of methods ranging from behavioral to spiritual approaches, from cognitive to depth psychology.

I do not consider process work in the conventional sense of the term as either specifically therapeutic or a form of psychotherapy per se, even though it can be healing in the larger scale. In essence, a process worker has a different orientation. While she respects and follows an individual's desire for therapy and healing and does her best to meet those goals, her larger focus is placed on what is arising in a given moment and how to follow its unique flow. She doesn't know what is ultimately right or wrong for a given individual, couple, or group. Rather, she places her attention on the flow of experience and discovering its inherent wisdom. While she values and respects momentary cultural ideas about health, illness, and death, her greater emphasis, ultimately, is on the awesome mystery of events and the way in which they unfold. In a sense, nature is her true boss.

Please note that, although such terms as "therapy," "therapist," "client," "case," and "transference" belong to an older paradigm, I use them because they are easy to understand at this point and I have not found more appropriate words. However, I have a new view of all of these terms and future books will certainly change these names to reflect the evolution of our work.

Process work incorporates but also steps outside the medical and therapeutic paradigm and asks, "What is happening? What is unfolding in this moment?" By placing her or his awareness on the flow of experience a process worker sometimes appears as if she is heading in the opposite direction from that suggested by common sense. She finds that the experience that is so disturbing to our conscious minds actually carries the seed of potential wisdom and creativity. In other words, within the difficulty itself lies the solution. Life is full of awesome, and frequently hidden, potential.

Arny's conception of process work emerged from a Jungian orientation in which dreams are seen as meaningful events. Arny then expanded this teleological concept to include such areas as bodywork, movement work, relationship and group work, and near-death and comatose states. To the process worker, experiences arise as much from the ordinary world that we are accustomed to, as from the "invisible" influences of nature. This mixture produces the unfathomable events that we go through from day to day.

The philosophical and practical lineage of process work also includes other predecessors who have sought the patterns and wisdom of nature and the way in which these patterns influence and express themselves in our daily lives. Some of their methods include ancient shamanic practices, alchemy, mysticism, Eastern spiritual practices based on meditation and mindfulness awareness, and Aboriginal beliefs in "the Dreaming." In a sense, process work's "familial heart" includes all individuals, healers, and therapists whose sights are set on the mysterious Tao.

I would be fooling myself if I said that I did not strive to be a *therapist* or *healer.* I have a kind of inborn drive to relieve pain, to bring compassion to people's lives, and to add my two cents to the effort of making things better for humanity. In fact, I've had many sleepless and frustrating nights when I wasn't able to *make* this "betterment" happen!

So, what do I do with this tendency to want to heal? If I were truly a process worker, which I am on occasion, I would use my awareness to notice this tendency and honor it as one of the momentary faces of the Tao. Likewise, when someone asks for "therapy," I would know that this request is an important aspect of the Tao and I would do my best to follow it. At the same time, if I were lucky enough to gain a greater view, I would also notice nature's spontaneous messages about what to do. I would momentarily let go of *knowing* the right thing or *having* to do something and instead learn to follow what naturally unfolds. I would ask, "What is trying to happen?" rather than "What should *I* do?" I would know that it is not me but the whole of nature and our interactions with her that determine our life processes. I would then be able to weave these insights together to address my client's conscious concerns.

In the Boat: The Dreaming Process

When you follow the Tao in your work as a process worker, it is like being in a boat on a river together with your client. Or perhaps you are both in your own boats, paddling alongside one another, trying to get along with the current. The river itself is a unique blend of the processes of the client and therapist and the momentary expression of the Tao, the unfolding of events. Each of you may have an idea about where you are heading, but you both must also adapt to the momentary flow of the water's current, the numinous path of nature.

What fascinates me about this river ride is that the seemingly chaotic movement of the water's current contains a hidden blueprint, a pattern that underlies our everyday experiences. In process work this pattern is called the *dreaming process.* We experience this dreaming process as it expresses itself through various channels, such as our experiences in relationships, the body symptoms we develop, and our nighttime dreams and daytime fantasies. While the dreaming process contains the overall pattern for events, what underlies its moment-to-moment expression is utterly mysterious.

To follow the dreaming process, we need both a scientific and a spiritual attitude: We need the acuity of a scientist who carefully uses her awareness to follow the patterns and signals happening in herself and the other person, and we need the openness of a shaman who can jump into and follow the dreaming process without necessarily knowing where it's heading.

I am not so naïve as to think that this view of life is an easy one to grasp or one that the reader will readily adopt. And yet, as Arny is fond of saying, we all become Taoists, either early in life, because of life experiences, or certainly, at the end of life, when death teaches us to let go. Both the healing and Taoist paradigms are necessary and relativistic; neither one is absolute. They are both significant and complementary aspects of our human experience.

About This Book

I wrote this book to share fundamental and subtle discoveries that have grown out of my studies of case supervision over the past twenty years and that help to illuminate some of the key principles in the process-oriented methods of following the dreaming process. I find myself continually attracted to uncovering the "Tao which has not yet been said;" basic principles which underlie process work but which are as yet unspoken. The book is also a practical guide and workbook of sorts, in which the reader, through many exercises, can explore her own personal psychology and learning. Many of the exercises can be done alone; others require the assistance of a friend or colleague. I also wrote this book because in each client's situation, I see myself: my own struggles and growing edges, my limitations, my fears, my hopes, and my dreams. In addition, I see my reflection in each of the therapists who are struggling to gain greater awareness of, and adjust to, nature's flow. I hope this book will be of help to you in your approach to life and in your work with others.

I focus on the special learning and teachings inspired by case supervision with individual clients. I have narrowed my focus to curb my compulsion to cover everything, which would take many lifetimes and many pages. However, my own mind went on strike more than once as I tried to focus the material on individual work alone, since process work is multidimensional and individual work often overlaps with relationship work and group process.

The book focuses on actual problems in therapy, the real difficulties therapists have; not the theoretical things they were taught but the problems that come up realistically in practice. This book primarily focuses on examples of *interventions* in long-term and short-term cases, not on long-term cases per se. However, short-term issues are viewed in terms of the eternal self as it appears in dreams, signals, and experiences. I also focus mainly on process work, not on its relatedness to and interconnections with other important therapies such as Jungian and Gestalt psychologies. Other authors can do that in the future.

The client-therapist situations that I present are fictional examples I have distilled from the study of hundreds of therapeutic cases. In essence, in order to protect individuals, I have created *generic* situations from them that do not depict actual people but fictitious, generalized examples of both client and therapist. Nothing in this book refers to an actual client or therapist. I provide analyses and practical skills that can be learned from these examples, as well as theoretical constructs that are helpful for understanding and following given processes.

At first, I wrote this book as a manual for students of process work. Then I realized that it really was much broader than that; it gives anyone a glimpse into a process-oriented way of understanding and working with individuals, as well as a query into the deepest questions about life and death. Any therapist who incorporates Taoist principles and feelings in her or his work will benefit from these methods, which are easily adaptable to individual styles of working. However, the usefulness of these methods, including those that have to do with such areas as touch and relationship issues, also depend upon the therapist's particular therapeutic orientation and the system within which she or he is working.

My goal in this book is to stimulate everyone to think further about people working together, trying to help one another to grow. My particular focus is on process work, although, in my heart of hearts, I imagine changes in all kinds of therapy. What I present in this book are not facts or firm procedures. I do not intend this book to be used as a program for training or as a form into which individuals must be pressed. Rather, my interest is to stimulate creative imagination. Theories change, ideas evolve. The principles that I came across seem unchanging though the terms I use to describe them are dependent upon, and limited to, a particular period in time and my personal growth. Therefore, this is a work in progress; it will continue to evolve for years to come. I dreamed recently that I was pregnant and had to give birth right away even though it was quite early for the baby to come out. I, therefore, decided that it was time for the book to emerge in its present form.

The book is structured into five parts based on the flow of case supervision sessions. Part One focuses on intake and overview. Here we explore the kinds of information about a particular client-therapist situation that it is helpful to gather, and we create a chart for mapping the information so that we can discover the structure implicit in it. Subsequent chapters in Part One illuminate specific aspects of this chart.

Parts Two to Four focus on methods for interacting with the client and connecting to the stream of her or his process. Part Two focuses on basic approaches. Part Three explores more advanced approaches related to such areas as dreamwork, pacing, following your feelings, and adapting the intervention to the person's state of consciousness. In Part Three, we see many of the subtleties of the work and realize that even the best method, applied at the wrong time, with the wrong feeling, or without being adapted to the person's state of consciousness, doesn't work very well. Part Four specifically focuses on the intersection between the processes of the client and the therapist.

In Part Five, we turn our attention to the therapist's psychology by exploring the ways in which a therapist is affected by her work, her own development, her fears of failure, her personal therapy myth and style, and her potential to develop into an elder and Taoist. Chapter 32 turns toward the Big Questions: What is our goal? Where are we heading? What is an elder?

I have been fortunate to test all the ideas in this book in my classes at the process work centers of Portland, Oregon, and Zurich, Switzerland, since 1985. I also have given case supervision classes together with Arny in many places around the world and with a wide variety of therapists from different cultures. Our work in countries in which we did not speak the mother tongue helped us realize the cross-cultural applications of process-oriented case control supervision. We were able to do supervision, even though we could not always understand all the verbal content, by watching the person's body movements and their feedback to our suggestions.

The reader may be surprised, or even shocked, by the fairytale-like tone of this book. There will be times when situations sound amazing, outlandish, or shocking. But this is mainly because, for the sake of brevity and generality, I chose not to create a complete context. I also could not avoid spinning my own yarn, which is one of my favorite pastimes: making up stories and funny characters to my mind's delight. After attempting to write in a traditionally academic way, I began to envision fantasy characters that would illuminate the concepts better than myself in a clear and engaging way. The book began to take on a life of its own, full of fantasy characters who have their own voices and stories to tell and who present information in a sometimes lighthearted and humorous way. Even Arny (or my projections onto him) appears as "Eagle," the founder of Process Work as well as speaking at times through the voice of many of the other figures. Aspects of myself appear in most of the characters throughout the book. God help me, this is not a standard text!

I had many inner debates and doubts about this writing style. One side of me (let's call it side A) felt that such humor was blasphemous, that therapy is a serious and often painful business and that this kind of writing has no place in such a deep area. That side of myself said that all of these crazy characters made my whole thesis unbelievable and childish.

Another side of me (side B) felt that this method was the clearest and most comprehensive way of communicating the material. Side B also insisted that learning could be fun and exciting and that even our clients do not always want to be looked upon as poor souls with no humor or joy in their lives. It stated that process-oriented work, and life in general, is full of dreaming and creativity and therefore writing and learning can model these as well. And, the situations could be looked at as short tales of therapy.

Side A worried that people would not learn enough. Side B replied that there are plenty of facts and much down-to-earth material to keep this book solidly grounded. In fact, Side B continued, the lighthearted writing style makes it easier to include more concrete pieces of information and practical methods. Side A said that it would be all right if there were enough rigor and learning, and so it allowed me to continue. The book is really a mixture of these two complementary approaches.

My hope is that the reader enjoys the following book and is delighted by imaginary figures doing the teaching. Some of these "teachers" get into really rigid states, but do not take them too seriously. Even though they become dogmatic at times, and their teachings sound at times more "state" oriented than "process" oriented, the true essence of process work is the appreciation for the flow of events and the ability to continually adapt our methods and feelings to the changes of the Tao. So, first I have to thank Dona Carletta, Rhino, Mary, and all the rest of the gang. Without you, I would have never known that the Tao and some of its principles can be said, yet the mystery can still remain.

Just days before finishing this book, I dreamed that there were three high, snow-covered mountain peaks standing behind the book. For me, these peaks represent the most basic principles of nature, the deep principles that stand behind all of the thoughts and details of this work.

Part One

Finding Hidden Structures by Creating an Intake Chart

Chapter One

Process-Oriented Case Supervision: The Hidden Principles

Over the past twenty years, I have been compelled to search for some of the invisible principles that lie at the root of process-oriented psychology, or process work, as it is called in the United States. Process work is a path that I, as a woman and therapist, have chosen both personally and professionally. It forms the core of my approach to the work I do with others, and it is the spiritual practice that informs my personal view and journey through life.

My book *Metaskills* began as a search for the feeling attitudes that cradle process work's practical skills. At the time, I was plagued by the intuition that there was something more than overt skills that brings process work to life, something that makes it possible to live and model its Taoist philosophy when working with others. My next book, *Coma: A Healing Journey,* developed out of a desire to illuminate the practical and personal skills necessary for working with people in comatose states whom I have witnessed and accompanied for periods of time, together with Arny. And, I continually thirst for more knowledge of, and awareness about, my practice as a process-oriented therapist.

Today, I am fascinated by the key principles and subtle methods I have uncovered by studying case supervision sessions; that is, the presentation of work with clients by therapists and the subsequent feedback from supervisors. These types of sessions have been historically referred to as "case control" or "case supervision," depending on the country and school of therapy. Lately, Arny has called these sessions "process crystallization" to convey the idea that supervision involves the discovery of the crystal-like structure, the unique pattern, that exists within and connects the various details of any particular client-therapist interaction. The change of name also reflects the need for a renewal of the term "case" which can be experienced by many as derogatory. Until now, I have not found a more suitable word and therefore use the word "case," as well as "case control" and "case supervision" in this text hoping that the reader will understand that I am searching for terms that are more generous and applicable.[1]

In particular, I have been inspired by the case supervision sessions conducted by Arny over the past twenty years in various countries around the world and often involving thirty to a hundred therapists. These sessions always had a stimulating atmosphere in which everyone was talking simultaneously, thinking together, meditating together, acting out particular things, and where the focus was turned as much as possible on the development of the therapist and seeing the client as part of that therapist.

In these sessions, I began to realize how important it was to develop a greater subtlety in my work. The vast array of clientele who were presented and the uniqueness of each client-therapist situation demanded much more refinement of my methods and my understanding of myself as a therapist.[2] As I began to study these subtleties, I also unearthed a number of key principles that lie at the root of the work. In *Alternative to Therapy,* I attempt to illuminate these principles. The fictional and generic examples I have created in this book have been distilled from these studies.

Case Supervision Work and the Dreaming Process

There are many different approaches to supervision and case control in therapeutic schools today. Although this book is not about case control per se, I feel that to understand the origins of the basic principles that I present in this book, it is helpful to look at the evolution of our process-oriented type of case supervision.

When Arny first began to give case control classes as a training analyst of the Jung Institute in Zurich, Switzerland, in the late 1970s, each therapist who was going to present a case situation was first asked to write the information on paper. Then in the class, the therapist read that information and Arny and other members of the group gave feedback to assist the therapist in gaining greater understanding.

As time progressed, Arny's emphasis shifted somewhat. While the intake of information ("the content") remained important, Arny's primary focus began to also turn toward learning about the details ("the process") of the interaction between the client and therapist. Arny would ask the therapist to "act out" typical interactions with the client. This behavioral enactment often revealed new, *living* pieces of information about the situation that were previously unrecognized.

With this behavioral information added to the "picture," Arny demonstrated that it is possible to connect the client's presenting verbal information and her or his dreams and relationship situations to the moment-to-moment communication exchange between her or him and the therapist. Instead of *speculating* about the dream or content of a person's past experiences, it was possible to discover how this information arises *in the moment* through sensory-grounded signals such as voice tone, gestures, posture, and the rhythm of speech. Arny has often said that he never feels secure about his dream interpretation, or the understanding of a particular therapy situation, without being able to see how the dream manifests in the moment. This focus created a lively and challenging learning environment.

Arny's shift toward gathering behavioral information about clients was rooted in his discovery of the *Dreambody*—of the mirror that exists between body experiences and dream images. He discovered that dreams do not occur only at night while we sleep but also pop out during the day in our spontaneous motions, sounds, body feelings, and relationship problems and in our interactions with the outer world. The *dreaming process* manifests at any time, disproving conceptions of what constitutes "matter" and "psyche." Instead of relying solely on nighttime dreams or a person's verbal information, he began to observe the dreaming process as it flowed and became evident through our various sensory-oriented channels (such as hearing, seeing, feeling, moving, and relating).

The process work model has a triadic foundation that is scientific and empirical as well as deeply mystical in nature. Its practitioners focus on signals that can be seen and measured, while knowing that these signals emanate from a deep and invisible dreaming process. Like the "Tao that cannot be said," this dreaming process is the mother of all things. We cannot see it directly, but we notice its reverberations in its spontaneous manifestations in our daily lives. In essence, process work is a phenomenological approach emphasizing the perception of, and respect for, the flow of events, as well as the belief that inherent within even the most difficult problem lies the seed of its solution. Therefore, the therapist is an awareness facilitator who notices what is happening, helps the client with her or his awareness, and follows nature as best as she or he can.

With its focus on signal and channel theory, process work uses a set of neutral terms that are culturally unbiased. Therefore, it is possible to work with a wide spectrum of people, from little children who do not talk to people from other countries, from individuals in extreme states of consciousness, such as near death, to groups of people or organizations. Process work theory does not value one view of reality over another but focuses instead on *the relationship between our various parts and processes*. It follows experiences rather than holding fast to any culturally determined standards.

Case Supervision Discoveries

Over the years, this process-oriented form of case supervision has yielded a number of discoveries that have been central to my studies. One of these is that there is a common discrepancy between a therapist's verbal description of her client's issues and problems and the client's actual behavioral signals. Sometimes, when the therapist acted like her client, the client looked *very* different from the person previously described! This discrepancy most frequently occurred as a result of the therapist being confused about the client's situation and therefore unable to see her or him clearly. Playing the role of the client frequently brought to the surface tangible information that the therapist had not yet consciously realized.

Another discovery from this type of case supervision is that sometimes, when the therapist verbally describes her client, she is not describing *that person* but instead *herself and her own problems!* In fact, there are moments when the client seems to be doing well, compared with the therapist's inner struggles! In these cases, the case supervision frequently turns toward the therapist's inner work.

Case supervision brings with it many challenges. One of these has to do with discovering the dreaming process, the underlying structure that lies behind and connects verbal and behavioral information. Methods and suggestions about how to proceed in any given therapeutic situation must be suited to the individual client, the particular therapist's style, *and the special moment in time.* Of great importance is ascertaining the therapist's *metaskills.* Without the right feeling-attitude, in particular, a good deal of heartfulness and feeling for those we work with, even the best method will sink into the sea like a ship with holes.

Where's the Mystery?

Much of process work is based on following the mysterious ever-winding Tao—without necessarily understanding it ahead of time—with an open mind and heart. I worried whether writing about the details of this work might take some of the mystery and beauty out of it. I feared it would create the "Tao that *can* be said" and therefore not the *real* Tao! Would the written word and detailed explanation destroy some of the beauty of its nature? Would it create strict, linear, and inflexible dictums in people's minds instead of fostering process work's basic Taoist approach, which is *open to the moment and its teaching?* Would the methods become more important than the people themselves? Is all that I dread inevitable?

Of course, the answer is "yes," to some extent. Yet, I realized that what happens in any given therapy session is a piece of magic and mystery that no one can analyze or disturb. No book or written word can address the beauty and diversity we find in nature itself. Although there are patterns that can be seen and studied and methods that are helpful, the special way that a process unfolds is a piece of magic. The intimate interaction between a client and a therapist is something that can be both studied and, to some extent, understood; at the same time, it is utterly sacred and unpredictable. And, as Jung said, the therapist's methods have to be adapted again and again, ever anew, to the momentary situation. We must learn to swim before we jump wholeheartedly into the water. It is hoped that starkly defined techniques and methods fade away as we become aware of our immersion in the river of life.

I also realized that, although studying something may destroy it, studying also has the potential to help us learn to open up even *more* to the Tao and its mysteries. A map and a few guideposts make it possible to find our way into aspects of our lives that might ordinarily remain obscured. Special methods serve as the rudder and sail with which we can negotiate the unique and frequently neglected current of the river. The therapist as an *awareness facilitator* helps to bring attention to the details of nature's flow. I hope these chapters will bring clues to the depths of process work and a glimpse into the vastness of our human experience.

Notes

1. Thanks especially go to Susanne Roessing for her encouragement in finding new names.
2. For more on process oriented case supervision, see Alan Richardson and Peter Hands, "Supervision using Process-oriented Psychology Skills," in *Supervision in the Helping Professions: A Practical Guide* (edited by M. McMahon and W. Patton. Melbourne: Pearson Education Australia, 2001).

Chapter Two

Creating an Intake Chart

Therapists may be shy to speak about their cases to a supervisor because of such factors as blocks in perception, therapeutic style, or personal psychology. An intake chart can help provide an overview of and appreciation for the various aspects of an individual's process.

Mary

As we set out on our journey to explore some of the key principles behind case supervision and process-oriented psychology, let's meet our hypothetical therapist, Mary. She will accompany you and learn alongside you, throughout the book. Think of her as a friend, a learner, and a companion on the path. Mary has only been in practice a year and still has a beginner's optimism, though she is frequently plagued by self-doubt and inner criticism. She is anxious to do a good job with her clients.

Mary was always a dreamer and never quite felt at home in the ordinary world. As a child she had a desire to connect to the deeper parts of people and assist them with their lives. People recognized this gift and spontaneously called on her for advice. However, day-to-day, she felt quite overwhelmed by normal life.

During the first year of her work as a therapist, a particular client came to work with her. After meeting with him for the first time, Mary was stricken with inexplicable anxiety. Something about this man made her feel quite nervous. Mary knew that she should talk to her supervisor about this client, but she was so upset that she worried she would be too unclear about how she perceived the situation. She feared that her supervisor would be critical of her lack of awareness. However, she mustered the courage to call a meeting anyway.

Dona Carletta

Let's meet Mary's somewhat unusual, dreamtime supervisor, Dona Carletta. Mary had been aware of Dona Carletta's presence since she was a child but never quite knew what to do with this wise inner figure. Dona Carletta appeared in a multitude of forms in Mary's dreams and either gave her helpful advice or, alternately, appeared as a terrifying dragon that chased her. In any case, it was clear that Dona Carletta was not from this planet.

Over the past few years, Dona Carletta revealed herself as a supervisor of Mary's therapeutic work. Dona Carletta said she had been schooled in the art of process work for many years and had been a therapist for more years than she could remember. She trained directly with Eagle, the founder of process work, and over time, she taught and supervised many hundreds of therapists from this planet and elsewhere.

Eagle

The upcoming series of classes (chapters) that Mary and her fellow students attend are taught by Dona Carletta and some of her colleagues. The information in these classes is inspired by and derived from Eagle's case supervision sessions. Alas, at the time of these classes, Eagle had flown off into hyperspace to process the other dimensions. Therefore, he does not teach any of the individual classes, although his spirit is always present.

Mary and Dona Carletta's First Meeting

Mary called a meeting with Dona Carletta to discuss her situation with her new client. However, Mary was so nervous she could hardly speak. Her thinking was muddled. Dona Carletta understood Mary's dilemma because she had felt this many times herself when she has been a supervisee and has seen this in many other therapists as well. She reassured Mary that a therapist may be nervous or hesitant to talk about a case and vague about the details of that situation for a number of reasons. She mentioned some of these:

- Because we are limited beings, there are always aspects of our work with people that lie outside of our awareness; there is always information that we do not see or are unconscious of. If this were not the case, a supervisor would probably not be needed. Therefore, the therapist is nervous because she is revealing an area (or areas) in which her awareness is lacking.
- The therapist's knowledge may be limited and she may simply need to learn from someone who has more experience.
- A most obvious reason for a therapist's confusion or foggy awareness is that she does not have the detachment that would allow her to gain an overview of the situation. She is steeped in the momentary interaction and needs someone on the outside to help her gain a clearer overview of what is happening.
- The therapist might be missing pieces of information because she is not aware of her therapeutic style. A therapist's style may block her ability to notice particular aspects of the client-therapist situation.
- The therapist may be "dreamed up," which means that she has unconsciously become one part of the client's process. This obscures her vision and makes it difficult to gain an overview.
- The therapist may be attempting to get the person to change in a particular way but it is not working. Her

sights are set on a particular path, although *the process* may be moving in a different direction.

- To make things even more difficult, when the therapist is presenting her case, the most unconscious part of herself—and some of her own deep issues—may surface and complicate her understanding.
- Dona Carletta said that one of the most interesting discoveries Eagle made many years ago is that the therapist frequently gets stuck with a client in just the same place where the *therapist* is growing. In other words, the client and therapist are oftentimes working on a very similar area of development. This mixture of processes makes it hard for the therapist to see clearly what is happening.

Dona Carletta told Mary that she would discuss many of these instances in greater detail at a later point. Mary was not sure which of these reasons applied to her situation, but she was relieved to know that other therapists frequently go through similar experiences.

Dona Carletta assured Mary that each client's process is like a jewel with a crystalline structure at its core, although this structure is not always apparent in the beginning. She remembered one of her favorite artists, Michelangelo, saying that the artist's job is merely to chip away pieces of stone in order to uncover the form that lies within. Similarly, Dona Carletta said that she and Mary would try to discover this basic form or structure, to understand Mary's feelings, and most important, to use this information to be of greatest assistance to this particular client. She then asked Mary to describe the situation with her client as well as she could.

Waldo

Let's meet Mary's client, Waldo. (The reader should know that the description that follows is hypothetical and simplified, as is each client-therapist situation in this book. It is meant as a humorous example that is exaggerated in order to help all of us enjoy the process of learning. In reality, the details of any particular session are much more refined and intricate.) This is the information that Mary related at first, about her initial meeting with Waldo.

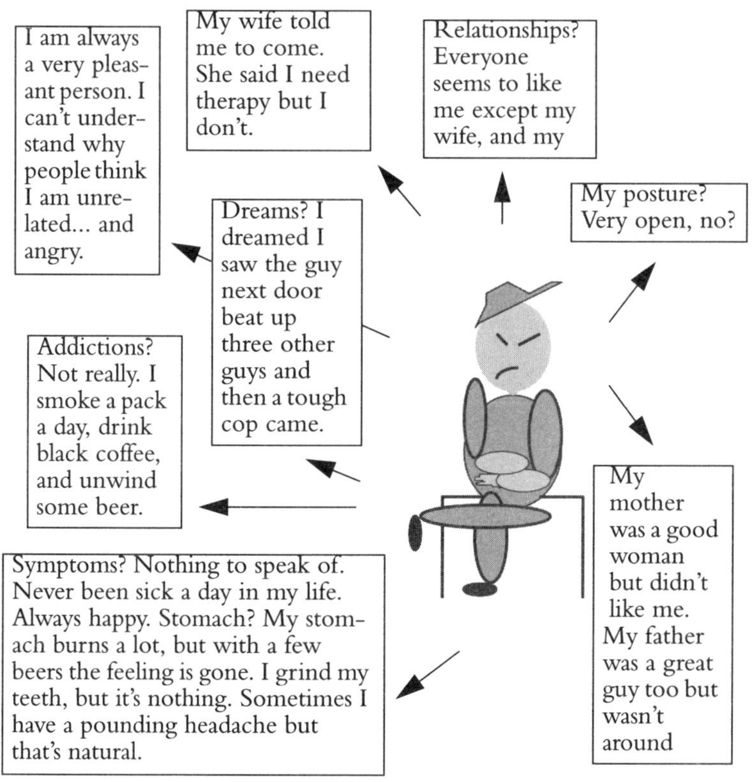

Mary's New Client, Waldo

The Intake Chart

Before talking more directly about Mary's situation with Waldo, Dona Carletta explained that one of the most important feeling qualities (or *metaskills*[1], as she called them) of the process worker are openness and appreciation toward the individual and the various aspects of his or her process. (See Chapter 12 for more on metaskills.) However, the therapist's view is often obscured because of various issues mentioned earlier. Therefore, Dona Carletta explained to Mary that, to gain this openness and clarity, and to truly appreciate the uniqueness and depth of the client's process, it is important to step back for a moment and gain an overview by gathering specific types of information about the client-therapist situation. Dona Carletta used an intake chart to draw together and organize the bits and pieces. Before focusing with Mary specifically on her questions about her work with Waldo, Dona Carletta introduced Mary to the chart.

Dona Carletta developed the intake chart after years of studying the types of information that was important to know about when getting supervision. She chose the image of a wheel with many spokes and sections, all connected to a central hub. This hub symbolizes the *process structure* or underlying pattern that unites the seemingly disparate pieces of information. The chart looks like this:

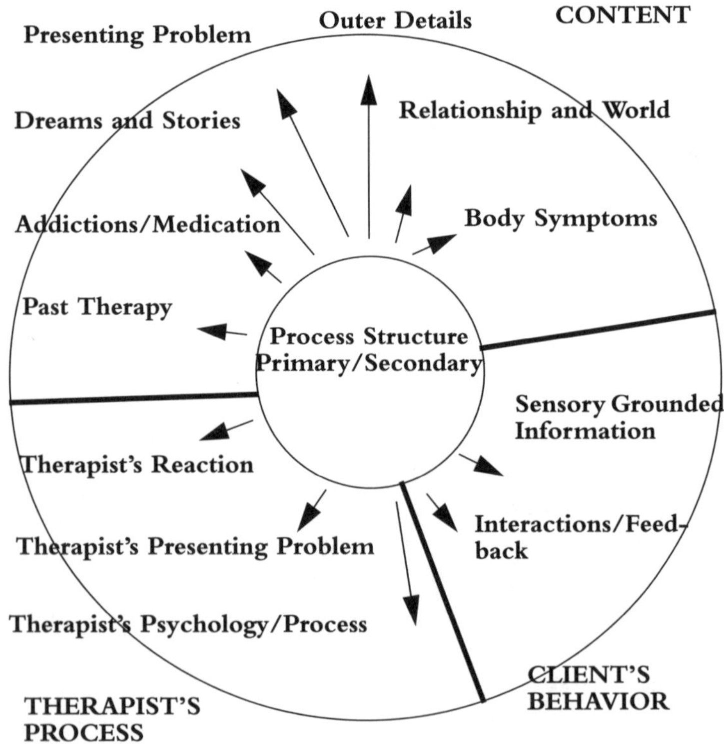

Dona Carletta said that, although this chart with the categories she describes is a good beginning, depending on your therapeutic paradigm and the client's process, particular areas would be stressed, broadened, emphasized, or deleted or other areas included.

The chart has four components. The first is the "content," the general information about the person's life, dreams, history, and so forth. You can gather these details from the person's description of his or her life experiences.

The second section concerning "the client's behavior" refers to the person's momentary behavior; how he or she talks, sits, walks, and speaks, as well as how the person interacts with the therapist (e.g., the types of feedback and responses he or she has to your interactions). You can gather this information by asking the therapist to "act like" her client.

The third area summarizes "the therapist's process" and feeling reactions, as well as problems about the particular case situation ("the therapist's presenting problem") and the way the client situation relates to the therapist's therapeutic style or personal psychology, or both.

The fourth—and central—section is the "process structure," which contains the pattern or dreaming process that integrates the various pieces of information in the chart. The process structure provides an overview and gives insights into the momentary and also long-term perspectives about the person's life.

Dona Carletta said that she herself ordinarily does not actually fill in this chart when she works with someone, but instead keeps it in the back of her mind while interviewing her client. She frequently does use the chart after she has seen someone, to deepen her understanding of a particular case. She added that some therapists do benefit from filling in the chart while speaking with their clients. And she said that in some therapeutic schools, a specific intake chart is a crucial part of the initial therapy process.

Dona Carletta assured Mary that she would discuss each section in greater detail later. Now, she wanted to mention seven different reasons why the Intake Chart is of use to therapists. Mary could tell that Dona Carletta was really gathering steam. She sat back, notebook and pen in hand.

1. If you are blocked with a particular client and do not have a clear overview—and if you do not have a supervisor to go to—attempting to fill out this chart yourself and pondering its details can provide many *helpful insights and a greater overview* of what is occurring.
2. The chart is a good way of keeping track of *the kinds of information that may be important for you to know about your client and the client-therapist interaction.* If you want to bring your case to a supervisor, these details will be important keys to understanding the situation.
3. The chart reveals *what kinds of information you tend not to know about your client or do not ask about.* Perhaps you will notice that you never ask your clients about dreams. Perhaps you are totally unaware of how the person dresses or behaves. Instead of a punitive attitude about this omission, it is more interesting to explore the meaningfulness behind *why* you are not aware of, or do not ask about, particular information.

   One reason for these omissions may be that you simply need to go back and ask about details or observe what your client does. Another possibility is that your process does not allow you, for example, to *see* what your client is doing. For example, you may discover that your inner process is trying to get you to trust your *feelings* to sense what is happening, rather than gain insight solely through using your visual or auditory abilities. This can be explored further through your own inner work and will be discussed in chapter 31.
4. Another reason for the chart is that it will *help you interconnect various elements of the process.* As you look at the chart, you begin to see that many of the elements are not simply isolated or chaotic. One of Eagle's fundamental discoveries was that there is a dreaming process, a flow of process, which reveals itself not only in our nighttime dreams but through all of our various modes of experi-

encing the world. He called these modes or pathways "sensory-grounded channels" such as visual and auditory channels, proprioception (body feeling), and movement, and also the channels of relationship and the world. Therefore, the same pattern can reveal itself through such areas of our lives as our addictions, relationship issues, body symptoms, and dreams. With this in mind, we begin to see connections in the chart.

Instead of feeling submerged in confetti-sized bits of information, with the help of the intake chart you begin to uncover the unifying stream that weaves its way through the various experiences in a person's life. Dona Carletta said that sometimes she looks at the intake chart as if it were an astrological map of a person's life, a picture of the momentary constellation of the stars.

5. The intake chart can *help make sense of your own feelings* and how they may fit into the larger scheme of the client's process, as well as point to inner psychological work of your own.
6. Once you have pondered various aspects of the person's life and experience and have begun to find the structure, the intake chart will help give you insight into helpful *methods of proceeding with your client.* However, Dona Carletta told Mary that, ultimately, it is the specific moment in time and the clients' feedback that determine the usefulness of our methods.
7. Once you have gathered some of the information, it is possible *to guess about elements of the chart that are unknown.* (See *ghostbusting* and *extrapolation* methods in Chapter 3.) Dona Carletta said she learned from her teacher that, although people are utterly amazing and unpredictable and we can never know exactly how events will appear, there is a certain amount of predictability.

Mary was aghast at this remark, yet curious. Dona Carletta said that she would discuss all of the concepts in the chart in greater detail shortly. First, though, she wanted to discuss Waldo's case.

Notes

1. For more on the feeling attitudes of the therapist, see Amy Mindell, *Metaskills: The Spiritual Art of Therapy* (Portland, Oregon: Lao Tse Press, 2003).

Chapter Three

Waldo's Example

The intake chart helps the therapist differentiate and assemble the information she receives from her client into a coherent structure and discover the dreaming process that unites the various elements.

Dona Carletta and Mary went through the intake chart step by step in reference to Mary's interactions with Waldo, though Dona Carletta said they might not have enough time to explore every detail of Waldo's situation. She stressed once again that the intake chart is merely a tool for helping the therapist appreciate the depth and beauty of an individual's process. Mary felt more relaxed and could offer further detail about Waldo's situation.

Content

Presenting Problem: Waldo said he came because his wife told him he needs therapy. He does not agree. He said he could not understand why people think he is insensitive and gruff. He considers himself a pleasant guy.

Past Therapy Experience: He hasn't had any previous therapy and, in fact, he hates the idea of it. He feels he doesn't need it.

Outer Details: He is a salesman but has lost a number of jobs because, he says, he keeps having bosses who are "insensitive." In reference to his past he says his mother didn't like him. He said his father was OK and wasn't around much, and dropped that discussion. This led Dona Carletta to believe that there may be important information about that relationship that we do not yet know.

Dreams: Waldo dreamed that he was walking down the street and saw the man next door beating up people. Then some tough policemen came and interacted with the man.

Body Symptoms: At first, Waldo said he has no symptoms. Yet, he seems to have a stomach ulcer that burns, he grinds his teeth and sometimes has a pounding headache. He is certain that beer will take care of these things and that they are nothing to worry about.

Addictions: He says he doesn't have any addictions, but he does drink a lot of beer and coffee every day, and he smokes cigarettes. When Mary asked him what he experiences when he drinks beer, he says he doesn't experience anything, he just takes it easy.

Relationships and the World: In the course of their discussion, Mary found out that Waldo is unable to tell his wife he doesn't like the green beans she cooks every night. But, he brushes it off and says this isn't really a problem.

He says that everyone likes him but also mentions that just about everyone in his vicinity does not, including his wife, his boss, and the neighbors! You have to wonder why such a pleasant guy who has no problems would be such a problem for others! He says that his bosses have been insensitive and that his wife tells him that he is rough and aloof and she is fed up with him. He can't understand what she is talking about.

With all of this in mind, Dona Carletta and Mary filled in the content section of the chart as follows.

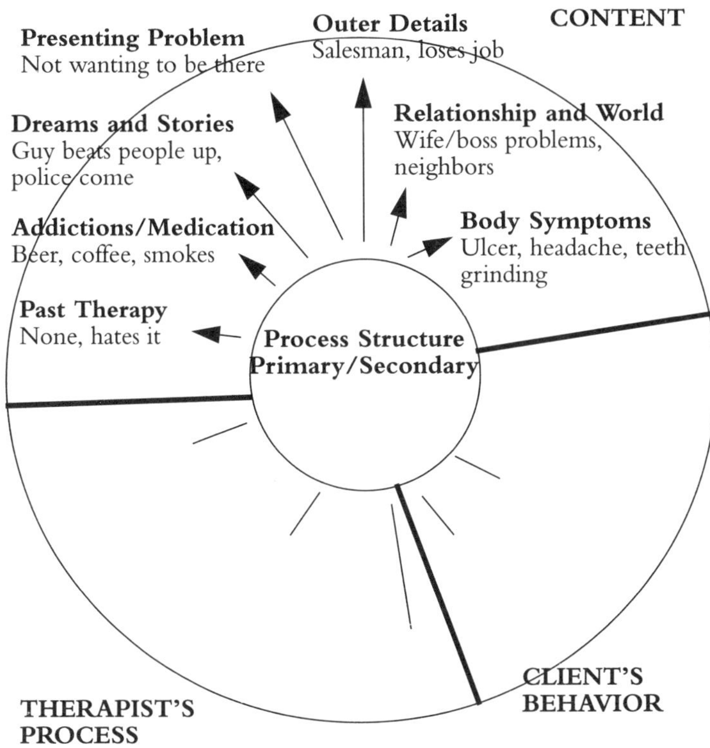

Behavior-Observation

Sensory-Grounded Information: Dona Carletta said that, in addition to the content description (see intake chart above), she needed sensory-grounded details about how Waldo behaves when he is with Mary. This information would help her see how Waldo's verbal content was related to, and revealed itself in, Waldo's momentary behavior. These details might also yield new pieces of information.

Dona Carletta clarified that "sensory-grounded" information includes such pieces of information as how Waldo sits, talks, moves, and gestures. (See Chapters 4 and 12 for more on this topic.) To discover this information, Dona Carletta asked Mary to *act like* Waldo. Mary giggled and was shy to do this but made a valiant attempt.

Dona Carletta acted like Mary, the therapist. As Waldo, Mary sat in somewhat slumped, relaxed-looking way. At the same time, "his" legs and arms were crossed and his body was turned about forty-five degrees away from Dona Carletta. His shoulders looked a bit drawn in and tightly held, and he rarely looked at Dona Carletta. His face had a slight scowl on it, and he tapped his foot in a kind of agitated way from time to time.

Interactional Level: Dona Carletta explained that she also needed to see the dynamic flow of interaction between them as they spoke with one another. How did he greet her? How did Waldo respond to Mary's suggestions? To observe this, Dona Carletta asked Mary to continue to "act like" Waldo, and she, as Mary, would interview "him."

As Dona Carletta attempted to interact with "Waldo," she noticed the following about his behavior. Waldo looked like he was attempting to accommodate her questions, but his body remained turned away, his shoulders appeared to stiffen a bit more and draw in even further, and his voice had a gruff quality about it. Although Waldo managed a faint smile when she suggested something, he didn't seem to listen to, or follow, any of her recommendations. From time to time, a faint groan escaped his lips, which gave the impression that the therapist's suggestions were utterly stupid and ridiculous.

Dona Carletta noticed that in spite of Mary's earlier hesitations, she now seemed to really enjoy acting like Waldo. Dona Carletta said she would speak about this shortly but for the moment, encouraged Mary to join her in filling in the behavior section of the chart.

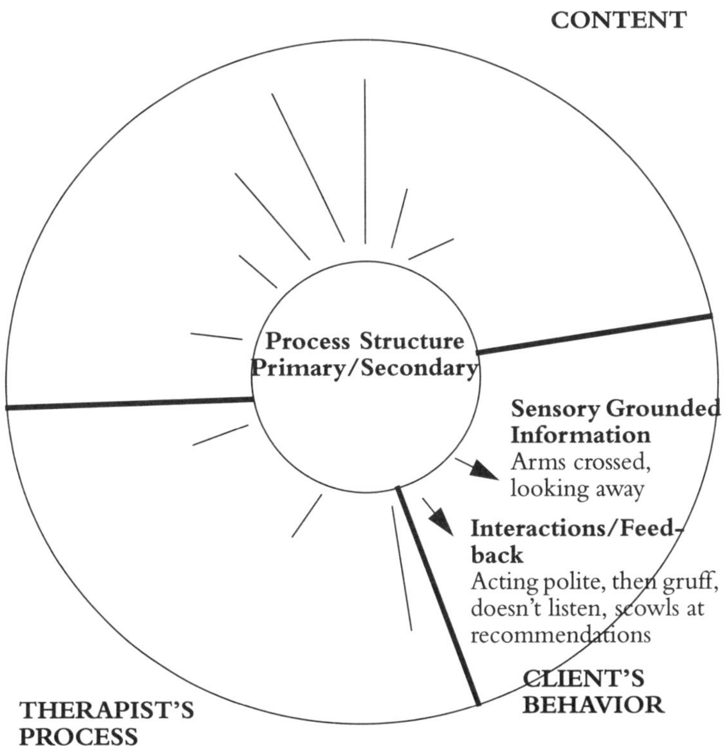

Therapist's Process

Therapist's Problems: Dona Carletta thanked Mary for acting like Waldo. She said that now she needed to find out more about Mary's difficulties with the situation. Mary quickly said that Waldo makes her feel quite nervous, and because of that, she loses track of her skills and overview. She is at a loss as to what to do with him. She also said she feels insecure because Waldo's wife told him to come but she senses that Waldo doesn't really want to be there.

Therapist's Reactions: Dona Carletta wanted to know more about Mary's feelings. She asked Mary, "What stands out to you about Waldo? What upsets or disturbs you about him?" Mary was surprised by these questions. Dona Carletta explained that strong reactions to a client sometimes provide some of the most important keys for understanding that person more deeply and one's self. (Much more will be said about this in Chapter 8.)

After thinking about this for a while, Mary said that what upsets her most about Waldo is that he won't follow anything she says! And, she added, he is "pretty rough." She just can't seem to budge him, even though her suggestions seem like good ideas—at least, to her. She is also sure that if he would just soften up and have more feeling, he would have a better life. But he doesn't seem to pay attention to her insights at all. Mostly she feels intimidated by him. Mary was even shy to admit that she began to wonder whether it wouldn't be better if Waldo saw one of her colleagues instead of herself!

Therapist's Psychology or Process: As Mary continued to talk about her difficulties with Waldo, Dona Carletta noticed that Mary was getting agitated. Mary said that her feelings about Waldo continued for days after he left her office. She said that she even wakes up in a cold sweat in the middle of the night worrying about this situation! Contrary to her ordinarily compassionate feelings, she started to dread the day she would have to go to her office and see Waldo again.

When Dona Carletta questioned Mary further, she discovered that Waldo reminds Mary of her own father. Mary's emotions stretched further than this particular case seemed to deserve. Mary alternated between wanting to get Waldo to be a more feeling person and wanting to get him to like *her* more. Dona Carletta realized that Mary might have been hoping to change Waldo so that she would finally gain the love she never had in her own life. Therefore, instead of focusing solely on methods that might be of help to Waldo, Dona Carletta suggested that Mary take time to work on her feelings about her own father.

Another problem for Mary in this situation concerned her therapeutic style and personal development. At first, when Dona Carletta asked Mary to act like Waldo, Mary was shy to be so "gruff." Mary's normal identity, and also her primary therapeutic style, was gentle and feeling-oriented. It was hard for her to open up to this gruff behavior. However, Dona Carletta noticed that, once Mary got over her initial shyness, she seemed to enjoy the gruff energy so much that she didn't want to stop! In fact, she seemed more animated and energetic than normal. Her shyness about this side of herself was, in part, also at the core of her discomfort with Waldo.

Dona Carletta worked further with Mary on her personal experience of this gruff energy. She told Mary to once again act "gruff," to place her awareness on her body sensations and feelings, and to find out what this behavior is really expressing. Mary tried it again and, after some time, said that actually, for her, it was a kind of earthy and spontaneous way of expressing herself. Mary realized that while this energy now felt very natural to her, she rarely believed in or followed her spontaneous feelings and intuitions in her own life or with others. She recalled being at ease with this type of energy as a child, but this way of being was not supported in her family.

Dona Carletta recommended that Mary take time to focus on, appreciate, and become more conscious of her gentle style and then notice when the earthier, more spontaneous side of her emerged and try to use both in a way that was useful in her life and in her work with people. (See Part V for more on the therapist's style and psychology.) She added that Mary's access to this supposedly gruffer part of herself might help Waldo feel more understood. She said that the disavowal of aspects of ourselves could be one of the reasons why we, as therapists, have difficulty relating to or understanding particular clients.

Now Mary and Dona Carletta filled in the part of the chart dealing with the therapist's process.

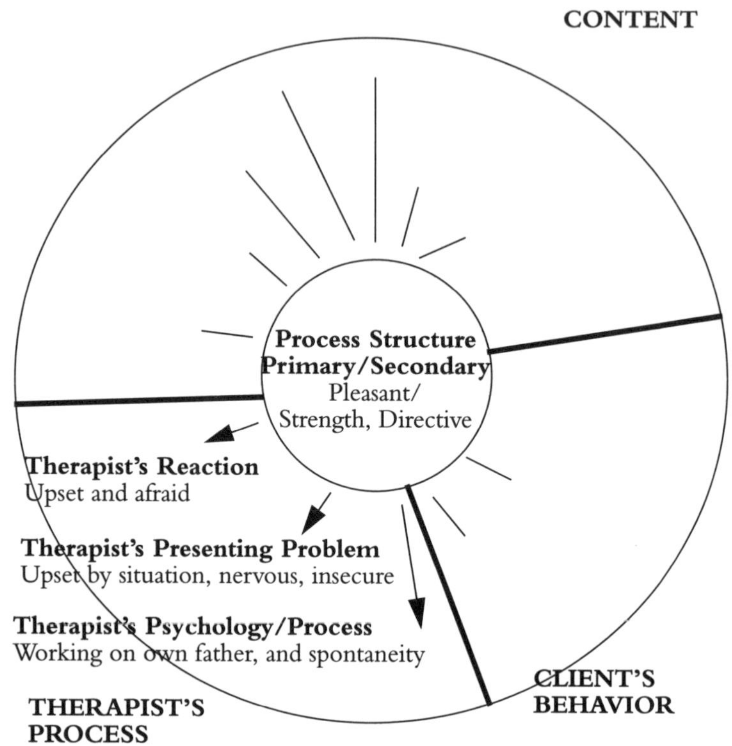

Process Structure

At this point, Dona Carletta drew Mary's attention to the center of her chart, the process structure. She explained that the process structure helps us see the patterns inherent in the various pieces of information in the chart by organizing the material into two categories: aspects of the client's process that he or she *identifies more with* and aspects that he or she *identifies less with*. Qualities with which the client is more identified are aspects of his or her momentary identity or *primary process;* qualities that are further away and trying to come into his or her awareness are the person's *secondary process*. She said that, in essence, process work is based on the appreciation of the whole process. Therefore, it is important to differentiate the various aspects and to open up and bring awareness to those things we identify with and those experiences that are disavowed or further from awareness. She said that this structure changes over time and therefore Mary should not get too attached to any particular description, but that understanding the momentary structure can be of help in her work with Waldo. Dona Carletta begins with Waldo's primary process.

Waldo's Primary Process: How does Waldo identify himself? What does he say about himself? He says that he is *a pleasant, easy-going, and happy guy*. He says he has *no symptoms* and that *everything is OK. He is unable* to tell his wife he doesn't like her cooking.

This primary process can be seen in his behavior in the way that his body is half-turned to the therapist, and when he tries to smile pleasantly and accommodate the therapist's questions. Dona Carletta noted that Waldo's primary process or identity as an easy-going man with no troubles who is shy to tell his wife when he doesn't like something seems to go along with one of his addictions, beer, which *cools things off* by helping him to forget everything and be easygoing.

Waldo's Secondary Process: Again, a secondary process refers to experiences that seem to *happen to us,* those things we experience but with which we do not identify. Waldo has *grinding, pounding, and burning* symptoms that happen to him. *Other people* don't like him. His *bosses* have been *insensitive*. He drinks lots of *coffee*, although he primarily feels he is laid back and relaxed. He dreams about a *next-door neighbor* who beats up others and about *tough* policemen. All of these are indications of his secondary process.

What are secondary aspects of his behavior? Waldo sits with his *legs and arms crossed and turned away* and his voice is *gruff*, although he says he is quite pleasant. He seems to *resist* everything the therapist does, although he doesn't say this directly. Eagle calls these kinds of signals "double signals." They co-occur with the primary signals.

Mary was really surprised by this perspective. She was sure that Waldo's primary process was being nasty and tough and that his secondary process had to do with being more sensitive and feeling! Mary saw him as a bully who doesn't do anything she tells him to do. He is resistant and irritates others.

Dona Carletta explained how, if you asked Waldo if he is rough, he would probably look shocked and sputter, "Oh, no, I'm not like *that*. I'm very pleasant." He does not *identify* with this rough and powerful demeanor. Therefore, *others* complain about this part of him. He tends to encounter such gruff people in his life and in his dreams—and they certainly aren't *him*. You, as the therapist, are intensely aware of, and troubled by, this gruff and resistant behavior. Dona Carletta added that we might speculate that Waldo's father was rough in a way that hurt Waldo and therefore he does not want to be that way himself. However, this gruff behavior seeps out in his secondary behavior, as if this secondary signal is beckoning our awareness, asking to be recognized, explored, and unfolded.

Ghosts and a Beginner's Mind

Perhaps because of her interest in other worlds and spirits, Dona Carletta sometimes describes the search for the secondary process as "ghostbusting"! (See Chapter 9 for more on this.) She inherited this term from Eagle, who is fond of talking about ghosts, particularly when it comes to large group processes. Dona Carletta describes a "ghost" as an experience that the person talks about but does not identify with, so the experience hovers in the atmosphere like a ghost. In Waldo's case, the ghost has various manifestations such as the "nasty" figures that appeared in his dreams, his mean boss, his gruff voice, his pounding and burning symptoms, caffeine, and his body posture. He does not identify with any of these, so they have a "ghostlike" presence.

At this point, Dona Carletta reminded Mary of the importance of maintaining a *beginner's mind*. She explained that if we were to work with Waldo, we would need to find out more about *his* body experiences and addictions and exactly how he describes and experiences them. A hallmark of this work, which she has learned from her studies with Eagle, is following each person's individual experience. Any two people with the same symptom may experience it in very different ways. Furthermore, the person's experience of his or her signals is frequently quite different from what we have imagined is going on for him or her. Dona Carletta reminded Mary to let the person explain his or her process to her. For the sake of this simplistic and short example, however, let's assume that Waldo's body symptoms, his use of caffeine, and his secondary body posture are expressions of some sort of strong and intense behavior of which he is unaware.

Dona Carletta reiterated the idea of a beginner's mind, stressing that it is a pitfall to get attached to the words that describe these processes. They are only our first attempt to *name* a process that is just beginning to *unfold*. They are only the surface descriptions of experiences in the midst of flux. We do not know, until we begin to get inside of and unfold these signals, exactly what they are trying to express. When Mary became "gruff," the "gruffness" then transformed into a sense of earthiness and spontaneity. Dona Carletta also reminded Mary that this information reveals one slice of Waldo's life, which will certainly change and transform, depending on the moment.

Extrapolation

Dona Carletta told Mary that, once you know the process structure, you can use it to help fill in areas of the intake chart you do not know about. She called this extrapolation. (See Chapter 11 for more on this.) You extrapolate from the information and process structure that you do have and imagine from this knowledge what the other elements might be! For example, if you did not know about Waldo's addictions, you might guess that he uses some kind of substance to cool things off, to make himself feel relaxed and easygoing, like beer. You might also guess that there is another substance that supports his intensity, energy, and strength, such as coffee. If you didn't know anything about his body posture but knew the other aspects of the chart, you might guess how he would appear: that he would sit in a relaxed way, yet also reveal secondary signals such as a clenched jaw or folded arms.

Short- and Longer-Term Views

Dona Carletta concluded the discussion of the hub of the chart by taking a look at the short- and longer-term views of Waldo's process. She said that, in general, the person's primary process defines "where he or she is at" in the moment, while the secondary process reveals something about his or her future development and longer-term path. She said she would explain later (see Chapter 17) how you can also learn about a person's short- and longer-term paths by studying dreams.

Consider Waldo. In the short term, Mary will be learning how to interact with him, how to help him become aware of his overall process. She will try to follow his feedback concerning how far he would like to go and what direction to take. He may need more reassurance and praise for his attempt to be a kind-hearted man before approaching this "gruff" behavior.

Where might he be going in the future? What can we imagine in his future if he is able to follow and unfold his process more fully and in a useful way in his life? Dona Carletta said, "Let's imagine that his "gruffness," when used consciously, is a kind of intensity and directiveness that is trying to come into his everyday awareness and be part of his life more fully. Perhaps Waldo might be able to use this strength and directiveness in useful ways to create better relationships with his wife and others. He might be able to use that strength in a loving way by integrating both the pleasant and the powerful processes together. He might also draw on that strength to deal firmly with his addictions and to be more effective in his work. Utilizing that energy consciously in his life could be the way in which he integrates the power of the "police" who appear in his dream."

Here's the full chart created by Mary and Dona Carletta.

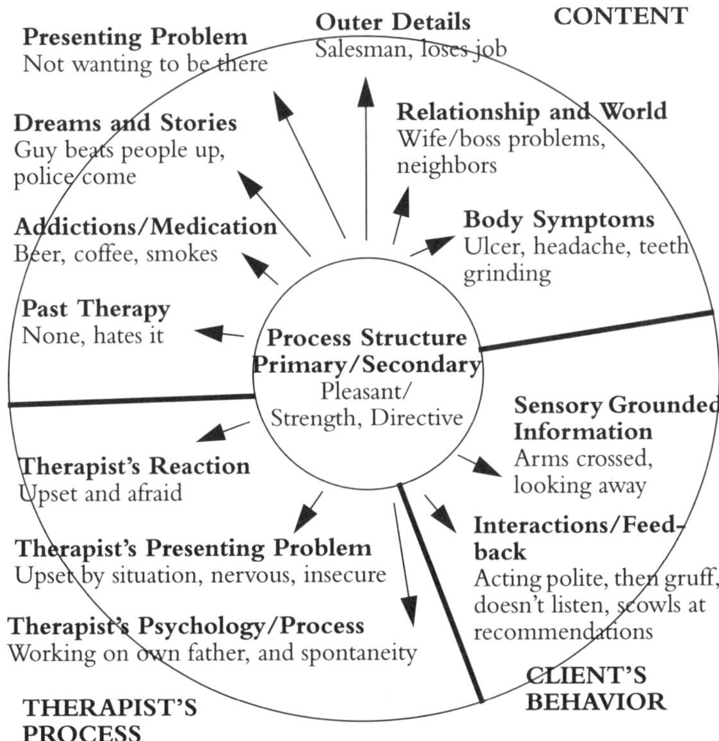

Next, Dona Carletta wanted to discuss details of the intake chart in a more general way.

Chapter Four

Unfolding the Intake Chart

It is important to gather information from three levels of the client-therapist interaction: the verbal content, behavioral signals, and the therapist's feelings and experiences.

Mary was intrigued by the idea of the intake chart and wanted to study it in greater detail. Dona Carletta said that she would explain a bit about each of the areas, and that further amplification would occur in subsequent classes. She reminded Mary that the intake chart was not simply a technical tool but a vehicle for appreciating and gaining greater understanding of the client-therapist process. The following are Mary's notes from their conversation.

The Verbal Content

Presenting Problem: Why is the person coming to you? What is his or her goal? Does the person need help with a relationship problem? Is she or he lonely, depressed, exhausted? Is she looking for a job? Is the person feeling spiritually malnourished? Does he or she need help with a creative project? Does the person have specific long- and short-term goals?

Did the person's partner, the courts, or some other person recommend that he or she come to see you? Does the person *want* to be there? Realize that if someone else was the referral source, whether voluntary or mandatory, this other person or organization is a ghost figure that may play a crucial role in the work.

Outer Details: The information you ask the client to give about her or his everyday life depends very much on your individual style, your particular school of therapy, and the particular client. For example, you might focus on different pieces of information if you are working with a child than with an adult. The following are details that Dona Carletta considers important.

Personal and social characteristics such as gender, age, race or ethnicity, sexual orientation, country of origin (if this is not the person's native country, how long has she or he been in this country? what about her or his parents?), educational level, job, economic level, religion, relationship situation, current lifestyle and living situation.

Past and family of origin information such as details about childhood and historical information that seems important to the person in relationship to family of origin. Has the person suffered from any kind of abuse? Has she or he ever been institutionalized?

If your client is a child, you may have a completely different set of questions, such as the following: How does the child get along in school? Does he or she have siblings? Friends? How does the child behave at home?

Answers to these questions provide important fundamental information. For example, being adopted can have a great impact on a person's feelings about life. Childhood experiences and parental relationships frequently play a central role in therapy. Knowledge about someone's social rank may reveal cultural discrimination because of economic class, sexual orientation, race, or age—pieces of information that are crucial to understanding the overall context of a person's life and experiences.

What information does the person *not* speak about? For example, not mentioning one parent while emphasizing the other parent could be a significant piece of information to keep in mind. Recall that Waldo mentioned but then quickly dropped the topic of his father.

Relationships and World: Is the person currently in a relationship? What kind of relationships has he or she had in the past? Does the person want to be in a relationship? Does he or she complain that it is hard to find the right partner? Does the person mention what *other* people say about him or her?

How does the person interact with the world around him or her? For example, what kinds of synchronicities or disturbances happen *to* him or her in the environment? For example, do the neighbors continually upset him or her? Is the person always being asked by communities to lead meetings even though he or she has given that up a long time ago? Do animals always show up at his or her doorstep?

Dreams and Stories: This category includes nighttime dreams, as well as other visual and "dreamlike" material, such as recurrent stories, fantasies, drawings, and sandplay activities. Dona Carletta said that these types of information create maps of the flow of the person's process. (For more on dreamwork see Chapter 17.)

Dreams

Recent Dreams: What dreams has the person had recently? These dreams relate most closely to the person's momentary life situation.

Childhood Dreams and Memories: What is the earliest dream the person can remember? Was it a recurrent dream? (Childhood dreams reveal long-term patterns that shape the person's life.) If he or she does not remember a childhood dream, what is his or her earliest memory? This memory is equal to, and can be understood in the same way as, the childhood dream.[1]

First Dream in Therapy: Did the person have a memorable dream just before starting therapy, or a dream just after the first session? This dream will give clues about the pattern of the therapy.

Stories

If the person does not remember dreams, recurrent stories can also be viewed as dreamlike phenomena. What stories does the person tell and retell about his or her life? Such stories stay with us over time and contain deep life patterns. The story might be about a heroic act, a terrifying event, or an amazing experience. Sometimes a story may be retold because the person is seeking a conclusion or a sense of closure has not been found yet.

Mary was intrigued by the idea of stories. She thought it likely that most people have some story that they repeat about their life. Dona Carletta recommended that Mary try the following inner work exercise.

Exercise
Stories that Repeat

1. Think of a particular story that you find yourself telling over and over again about something that happened in your life.
2. Retell that story to yourself in detail.
3. If there was something incomplete in the story, how might you complete it today? If there was something amazing and wonderful that happened, recall the details of that amazing experience.
4. Whether it is a happy or a painful story, consider what possible significance that story might have for your life today, and potentially, for your future.

Recurrent Fantasies

Dreamlike material also appears in the form of recurrent fantasies. Mary's common childhood fantasy was that a talent scout would discover her while she was singing in the yard. These "statements" can be treated in much the same way as nighttime dreams.

Drawings or Sandplay

Other visual material includes drawings or sandplay arrangements.[2] Again, these images can be viewed in the same way as dreams, as visual representations of the person's process.

Dona Carletta reminded Mary that of utmost importance when working with any dream or other visual material is to ask the person his or her *associations* to the important figures or elements of the dream or picture. Eagle always emphasizes that you have to make sure that the associations are not just *intellectual definitions* but have *emotional connections* to the various dream parts.

Past Therapy Experience and First Meeting: Has the person been in therapy before? Did another therapist refer the client to you? If the person has been in therapy before, what was his or her experience like? Why did the earlier therapy come to an end?

Previous therapy experiences, or the way in which an earlier therapy was concluded, may describe patterns that are in need of understanding or completion. For example, if a client said he left his therapist because that therapist did not really understand him, this experience may repeat with you as well, or the person may be seeking completion of what has occurred. Dona Carletta said that, depending on the circumstances, a therapist might bring up such things at some point in the therapy and say, "The same experience you had with your previous therapist might happen between us at some point, though I'll try my best. What will you do if it comes up? Let's investigate that now and not wait until it happens. What happens to you when you feel misunderstood?"

It is also helpful to be aware of any unusual or outstanding experiences that happen before or at the time of your first meeting with your client, such as missing the first appointment, forgetting the time of the session and coming very late or very early, asking many questions about your credentials, and so forth. All of these contribute important pieces of information about the person's overall process.

Body Symptoms: Working with and understanding body symptoms frequently play a central role in process work. Dona Carletta reminded Mary that it is important to find out medical details about the symptom and, if you feel some concern, to suggest that the person get a checkup (or other medical tests) if he or she has not done so. Does the person stay away from Western medicine and choose "alternative" approaches? Why? Before doing any type of movement or symptom work, find out whether the person has such conditions as brittle bones or heart problems that you must be careful about. Ask about medical and alternative drugs and herbs the person may be taking for symptoms, and whether he or she is satisfied with the treatment.

Most important, find out how the person *experiences* the symptom. Find out the person's sensory-oriented description of the symptom. A helpful question is, "If you were to create that symptom on me, how would you do that?" For example, imagine a woman who has a headache. She says that she experiences this headache as a pressure that is pushing out from the inside of her head. To *create* this experience, the therapist simulated a "head" by curving her fingers and hands together. The woman then demonstrated the headache pressure by putting her own hands inside this "head" and pushing outward.

Dona Carletta added that every symptom consists of two different experiences. One of these is closer to our identity (primary process) and one further away from our identity (secondary process).[3] In the example just given, one part of the symptom is the side that is *making* the pressure and the other is the side *receiving* and suffering from that pressure. When the woman further unfolded her "symptom creator," the pressure-maker, she pressed outward even more with her hands and said, "I want to be free! I want to be more creative and not so limited!" The other side, the head that the pressure is pushing against, said that it was afraid to change and open up. Ordinarily, this woman identifies herself, primarily, as rather conservative (indicated by the side of the symptom that receives and suffers from the pressure), and her secondary process is the one who wants to be free (indicated by the side of her headache that is pressing outward).

Addictions and Medications: Does the person have addictions or addictive tendencies? An addiction to a substance means that the use of that substance is dangerous to the person's health and that the person requires more and more of that substance to attain the same effect. A *tendency* toward a substance means that the use of that substance has not yet progressed to the point of being dangerous to the person's health.[4]

Eagle discovered that we have two addictions or addictive tendencies, one connected with our primary process and one with our secondary process. For example, a high-paced business person has a primary addiction to coffee, the intensity of which mirrors her or his primary process drive to be wakeful and *fast*. At the same time, the person has a secondary addiction to alcohol that helps him calm down and relax.[5] Dona Carletta pointed out that this was the opposite of Waldo's situation.

If the person is taking a medication of any kind, find out how she or he feels about that medication? Who prescribes it? What are the effects of the medication? Does the medication seem to support one or the other side of the person's process? For example, for someone whose primary process is nervous and agitated, a sedative could support her or his secondary process of detachment and relaxation.

The Client's Behavior

Dona Carletta moved to the second section of the intake chart, on the client's behavior. Here, she stressed the importance of noticing how the person interacts with the therapist. She reiterated the usefulness of drawing connections between verbal content and the person's momentary behavior. She spoke generally at first, and then went into greater detail.

Sensory-Grounded Information: Sensory-grounded information is based on sensory channels or pathways, the most typical of which are auditory, kinesthetic (movement), proprioceptive (body feeling), and visual. Eagle added the relationship and world channels to these fundamental channels, indicating the way in which we perceive our processes occurring through our relationship situations and our experiences of the world around us. Dona Carletta said that Mary should watch for signals—tiny bits of information in these channels—such as the person's tone of voice, pauses in speech, body posture, the angle and distance from the therapist at which the person sits, the way he or she walks into the room, and so on.

As mentioned earlier, to recall sensory-grounded signals, it is helpful for the therapist to "act" like her client by imitating how the client sits, walks, talks, and gestures. This information may add new elements about the person's process. For example, one therapist verbally described a client who *told* the therapist that he was "depressed" and "unable to do anything" in his life. However, when the therapist *acted like* this client, he had an upbeat, fast-paced speaking tone and smiled from time to time. The therapist had paid attention to the client's verbal content but had not consciously registered the client's voice tone and gestures.

Dona Carletta pointed out another great advantage to "acting like" the client. When a therapist begins to "play" the client, he or she can feel more deeply into the client's world and, it is hoped, understand that person more profoundly—"inside out." If you do not have a supervisor available, "acting like" your client might give you a few new insights into his or her process.

Dona Carletta loves Eagle's use of the Zen phrases *Bare Bones* and *Beginner's Mind* in reference to signals. Having a "bare bones and beginner's mind" attitude toward signals means simply noticing and stating *exactly* what you see, without preconceptions or judgments. For example, instead of labeling someone as depressed, you might try describing *only* what you see and hear: the person's head is leaning toward the side, and the chin is held up by the right hand; the voice tone is low and soft, with frequent pauses between words, and so forth. This avoids interpretation while focusing exactly on the person's sensory-grounded signals and experiences.

Here are questions that help us notice some of the many sensory-grounded signals:

- What is the client wearing? Are the clothes very neat and tidy, or loose and hanging, or tight and shiny, brightly colored or dull?
- What is the person's tone of voice? That is, is it soft? Are the words drawn out, or intense? Does it change or remain steady? Does the person pause while speaking or speak nonstop? Does the person speak slowly or quickly?
- What types of gestures or movements does he or she make with the face or hands? Is one arm and hand propped up in such a way as to support the head? Is one of the hands clenched, shaking, scratching? Are the eyebrows scrunched? Is the forehead taut?
- What postural signals do you notice? Leaning back, sitting up straight and rigidly, slumping down? Is the person holding onto something like a notebook or purse? Are the person's arms folded, legs crossed? Is he or she close to or far away from you? Does the person face you directly, or is he or she turned to the side?
- How does the person walk into the room? Does she shuffle? Does she move quickly and intently? Does she walk toward or away from you? Is she light or heavy on her feet? What kinds of spontaneous motions or gestures happen?
- What does the person do when you get up to answer the phone or get a glass of water? In other words, what does the person do when you are not focusing on him or her? Eagle always says that however a person reacts when your attention is diverted is most often an aspect of her or his secondary process.
- What happens to you physically when you are around that person? How does your body feel? What posture do you naturally assume? What is your tone of voice? Do you feel tense? Do you want to move and can't? Do you feel free to be yourself? Or do you feel a sense of pressure to alter one thing or another (how formal or informal you are, how direct or indirect, and so forth).

Dona Carletta emphasized that you may notice that what the person is *saying is not congruent with* what he or she is *doing*. She reminded Mary that these "incongruencies" are called *double signals*. For example, a person might say that he or she is interested in the conversation while she is simultaneously turning slightly away.

Dona Carletta gave Mary an exercise to do at home, to help her practice gaining sensory-grounded information.

Exercise
Sensory-Grounded Information

1. Recall a situation with a client in which you felt somewhat stuck.
2. Pretend you are watching a videotape of your last session.
3. Describe in a "bare bones" manner what you notice about your client as you watch that imagined "videotape." An example: "Her arms are folded, she is turned about a quarter of the way away, her left foot is slightly extended, her head is down, her hair is tightly bound in a knot, her voice has a soft and quiet tone."
4. Now describe yourself. What do you see yourself doing? Are you sitting forward? Do you look tense? Are you smiling a lot? What is your tone of voice?
5. Do you notice anything new about that situation that you weren't aware of before? What can you learn from this new information about your client and yourself?
6. At another point, try the same exercise, but instead of imagining that you are watching a videotape, "act like" your client. Try to remember the person's posture, tone of voice, and the like. Begin to feel your way into his or her world. What can you learn from this "inside" experience that might help you understand that person more fully?

On the Phone

Some therapists work with clients on the telephone from time to time. How do you proceed then? Perhaps you have never even met the client in person. You can, of course, fill in the content area of the chart, but what about sensory-grounded information? Dona Carletta said that she did not have time to go into this aspect in detail, and in fact, the whole discussion about working on the phone would require a book by itself. However, she did give a few hints:

- Listen to the tone of voice. Is it loud, quiet, muddled, soft? What is the pace of speech (fast, slow, measured)? Does the person pause from time to time as she talks?
- Ask the person to describe her sitting or standing posture. Is she sitting in a chair or on the floor? Is she sitting upright or slumped? Is she lying down? If she mentions a symptom, ask her how she would use her hands to describe that symptom, and then, to describe those hand motions to you.
- Notice changes in subject. Does he or she change the subject when certain topics arise? If so, the person may have gotten to an "edge." *The edge* is a dynamic moment in which something that has been disavowed begins to surface and is quickly ignored or does not complete itself. At this point when this new experience is trying to arise, we frequently change themes or begin to giggle, looking nervous, excited, and shy all at once.
- Find out about the person's momentary body sensations. Is she feeling a pressure in her stomach? A lightheaded feeling? An achy sensation in her back?
- If the person is able to walk, ask the person to get up and move a little bit, within the confines of the telephone cord! Ask her or him to notice and describe—in terms of body feelings and movements—what happens as she or he moves.

Interaction and Feedback: The next important category of sensory-grounded signals is how the client interacts with the therapist. Here you discover how the person deals with relationship interactions, and the kinds of feedback and reactions the client has to the therapist's methods, such as:

- How does the client interact when you say hello? Does he or she shake hands? Avoid contact? Smile ever so brightly? Stay close to you or back away?
- Does the person take the lead in talking, dominate the conversation, or speak only when spoken to? Does the person follow everything you say or nothing at all? Does she or he answer right away when spoken to, or is there a delay?
- What kind of feedback does the client give to various types of interactions? Do some methods gain positive feedback and indicate that it is a good track to pursue, or negative feedback indicating that this is not a track the person wants to follow? Does the person smile when you suggest something but not really follow what you are saying? This is mixed feedback. The person is acting accommodating but actually is not following, or will not follow, your suggestion. Do you also notice *edge* feedback, as stated above—a moment when the person suddenly changes subjects or becomes excited and nervous, tempted and afraid? This is an exciting, growing area of exploration.
- To what feeling qualities of the "therapist" does the client respond best? Worst? Does he or she respond well when you are straightforward, but clam up when you are more casual and receptive?

The Therapist's Process

One of the most important aspects of supervision is to find out the *therapist's* difficulties with the case situation and from this information discern what direction would be most helpful both for the client and also to that particular therapist.

Therapist's Presenting Problem(s): Why are you, the therapist, bringing this case for supervision? Are you confused and in need of an overview of the structure of the client's process? Are there specific pieces of information that you need help with, such as dream material? Are you feeling insecure about the approach you are taking? Do you feel blocked and frustrated because you are unable to be of assistance to that person? Are you feeling intimidated or shy with the client?

Therapist's Reactions: How do you feel about the client? In particular, what really stands out, attracts or disturbs you about the person? This information is crucial because, most often, we react unconsciously to things that either disturb or attract us. Then we simply admire the person or begin to form opinions about how to change whatever disturbs us and promptly lose our overview. One of the central discoveries of Dona Carletta's case supervision studies is that, most often, the thing that really stands out about your client—that either bothers or fascinates you—is often just what the client needs *more access to consciously!* (For much more on this topic, see Chapter 8.)

It is also helpful to ask yourself, "What strong feelings do I have when I am around that person?" Your feelings may reveal to you aspects of that person's overall process of which you and the client are not yet entirely aware. A helpful question is, "What am I experiencing and how is this experience possibly an aspect of the person's process?" (See Chapter 18 for more on this topic.) Dona Carletta said that, of course, these strong feelings could also be related to the therapist's personal process, and continued as follows.

Therapist's Psychology: It may become apparent that it is you, the therapist, who needs help with your own psychological process. (See Part V for much more on this topic.) Dona Carletta reminded Mary, as she mentioned previously, that therapists are often working at the same growing edges as their clients. Therefore, it is not uncommon to feel stuck, lose the overview, and be unable to go forward with the client.

Dona Carletta recalled Eagle telling her once that we frequently end up with certain types of clients because they amplify our inner problems and those areas of ourselves that *we* need to develop. It often becomes apparent that certain things that have happened during a therapy session have tripped off the therapist's own process so strongly that she no longer seems to be describing the client, but instead seems to be lost in her own inner process.

Dona Carletta mentioned a therapist who was trying to get her client to "stand up strongly for herself." The therapist insisted that this was important for the client and was unable to see the client's consistent negative feedback to her suggestions. After further investigation, it became apparent that it was the *therapist* who needed that particular change! It was the *therapist* who needed to stand strongly in her life for things she believed in. Once she realized this, she was able to see her client's process more clearly.

Dona Carletta told Mary that the therapist may also have trouble perceiving certain elements of the client's process because she is blocked as a result of therapeutic style. (See Part V for more on the therapist's psychology.)

The Process Structure: Primary and Secondary Processes

Dona Carletta reminded Mary that after she has accumulated the various pieces of information for the intake chart, she can then look for repetitive patterns. Mary would begin to see the aspects of the client's process that he or she identifies with and those that are further from the person's identity—and how this pattern, the *process structure*, appears in the person's body symptoms, relationships situations, dreams, and so on. She reiterated that knowledge of this structure would give clues as to the person's short- and long-term process.

Dona Carletta said that her next three classes investigate process structures more thoroughly. If you are already well versed in the area of process structures, you might want to skip these classes (Chapters 5 through7) and continue with the next class (Chapter 8).

Intake Chart Exercise

Now Dona Carletta gave Mary an exercise that she has used for many years to help learn more about a specific client-therapist situation. The exercise provides a way of investigating the intake chart, the therapist's process of gathering information, his or her observational skills, the ability to act like a client, and gaps in perception.

Dona Carletta said Mary should not worry if she is unable to recall certain pieces of information about a client. In fact, one of the main points of the exercise is to notice *what types of information you have not noticed* about your client. For example, someone might be shy to ask a client about dreams or certain topics. Do you feel insecure about certain areas of your work and prefer to avoid them? Perhaps the therapist cannot recall what the person looks like. It is possible that the therapist simply needs to go back and find out that information from her client. Dona Carletta was more interested in investigating the meaningfulness of *why* therapists do not gather certain types of information. It could be that the therapist's (unconscious) personal style forbids her from being aware of that particular information.

In one training seminar, Eagle elevated these learning difficulties by saying that each learning problem is really a *gift* that hasn't been noticed. The reason that we miss certain pieces of information or have trouble learning specific kinds of things could be because there is a gift, a deep style inherent in us, which is blocking our awareness and of which we are not conscious. Dona Carletta stressed the importance of knowing as much as you can about your style and how to use it most effectively for yourself and your clients.

Dona Carletta reiterated that the point of the exercise is not to do it well, but to learn from it.

Exercise
Intake Chart

1. Think of a client you are having difficulty with or want to find out more about. If you do not yet have clients, think of someone who is difficult for you, such as a friend or family member.
2. Think about that person and fill in as many aspects of the intake chart as you are aware of, including content, behavior (try acting like the person, to fill in this area), and your reactions and problems with the client, friend or family member.
3. Now look at the chart and notice which areas you tend not to know much about and which areas you know a lot about. How do you feel about the unknown areas? Take a guess as to why this information is absent. Are you shy? Did you not have enough time to find out this information? Do you feel that your own process blocks you from asking about or noticing that particular information? For example, for some therapists it is more important to follow feelings than to pay attention to outer visual cues. Take a guess about this.

Dona Carletta then told Mary that the rest of this exercise is pure dessert. Mary should do it only if she has an appetite for it.

4. Look at the intake chart and see if you notice any patterns emerge in the information? Do you see any patterns between content and behavior? Between your reactions and the client's momentary problems?
5. Take a guess at the process structure—the person's primary and secondary processes.
6. From all of this information, take a guess as to what direction would be most helpful at this time in this case situation. Some possibilities:
   a. Simply go back and find out the missing information.
   b. Get help to see the large overview of the structure.
   c. Focus on your own personal psychology and style.

Notes

1. See Alan Strachan's article "The Wisdom of the Dreaming Body: A Case Study of a Physical Symptom," *Journal of Process-Oriented Psychology* 5 (1993), where he documents this connection between childhood dreams and chronic body symptoms.
2. For more on Sandplay, see Dora Kalff, *Sandplay: A Psychotherapeutic Approach to the Psyche* (Santa Monica, California: Sigo Press, 1980).
3. For more on working with symptoms, see Arnold Mindell, *Working with the Dreaming Body* (Portland, Oregon: Lao Tse Press, 2002); for more on bodywork methods see Amy Mindell, *Coma: A Healing Journey* (Portland, Oregon: Lao Tse Press, 1999).
4. Arnold Mindell, "Process Work with Addictions, Altered States, and Social Change," lecture given at the *11th International Conference on Spiritual Quest, Attachment and Addiction.* (Eugene, Oregon: International Transpersonal Association, 1990). Find transcript of lecture at:
   http://www.aamindell.net/publications_frame.htm
5. For more on addictions work, see Debbie van Felter, "Heroin Addiction: From a Process-Oriented Psychological Viewpoint," (Doctoral thesis, William Lyon University, Zurich, 1987) and Reini Hauser, "A Message in the Bottle: Process Work with Addictions," *Journal for Process-Oriented Psychology* 6 (1994-95).

Chapter Five

The River's "Structure"

Following the process is like flowing down a river and noticing those experiences that are close to, and those far from, our intended course.

During their next meeting, Mary told Dona Carletta that she understood more about the intake chart but she was not sure she understood the idea of process *structures* very well. So, before delving into the details, Dona Carletta began by explaining the idea from a *feeling* standpoint. She said that Mary would learn more about basic methods of process work in a later class. (See Chapter 12.)

A Trip Down the River

To begin, Dona Carletta encouraged Mary to sit back, to take a moment to feel herself inside, and then to go on an inner fantasy. She told Mary to imagine that on a bright, sunny day, she and her client get in a boat and have decided to go downriver for a while, then back again. They put their boat in the water and begin their journey, floating peacefully along, swaying to and fro.

As time passes, however, Mary and her client notice that, while they are paddling downstream, a strong current comes along and tugs in a slightly different direction at their boat. It is hard to tell where this new current is coming from, but they know that it is subtly shifting them off their course.

At this point, Dona Carletta interrupted the story and explained that it is useful to imagine being in a river, to give the sense of process as something that is fluid and changeable. Processes are not static but dynamic and flowing. In fact, the term *process* refers to the *flow* of experience. She said that practicing process work means learning to notice its two streams, the intended current (primary process) *and* the flow of the unexpected current (the secondary process), and to join both. She noted that because of the characteristics of water, the two currents are not entirely separable but intermingle and coexist—but we notice the signals from the main current far more often than those from the unexpected current. The secondary signals are incomplete because their meaning has not yet been unfolded. They are like a sudden splash whose cause is unknown. Secondary processes tend to repeat or cycle until we pick up their messages.

Like the alchemists who stood lovingly over their cauldrons, the process worker meditates over these great mysterious signals. The metaskills of love and patience are needed to focus on and unfold them.

Static Names and Processes

Dona Carletta warned that although we tend to give static names to flowing processes, this is misleading. Names such as kind or gruff or pain are, at best, momentary abbreviations for much more expansive experiences that have just begun to unfold. In fact, the way in which they do finally unfold may be very different from what we had imagined ahead of time.

She gave the following example. A man who is normally quite shy admitted that he felt embarrassed because he had a large scar on the side of his face. He complained that he was unable to have relationships or do what he needed to do in his life because, according to him, his face looked so awful. This so-called "awful-looking" face is an aspect of his secondary process with which he does not identify. Eagle asked the man, "What's the worst thing you think of when you look in the mirror?" The man said that he looked like a monster. Eagle knew that the term monster was a static name, the beginning of an unknown experience. Eagle encouraged the man to explore this monster. The man was shy but started to act like a beast that wanted to devour people. The man seemed to enjoy this energy, but then stopped abruptly and said he did not want anything to do with it.

Eagle said that he was not so sure what that monster experience was all about, and he encouraged the man to have a beginner's mind and let the experience unfold a bit further. The man was hesitant but curious and expressed the monster further through movement; the energy behind it began to transform, and he began to *reach out* to people instead of stomping around. He actually began to make contact in a very heartful way. This was a big experience for him because he is normally quite isolated and hesitant to come close to people. What seemed at first to be a monster unfolded into the desire to reach out and make contact with others.

Relativity

Mary was intrigued by the concept of fluidity but because of her Western upbringing, she had a hard time grasping it deeply. Therefore, Dona Carletta tried to appeal to Mary's rational mind. She recalled Eagle's most recent writings on physics[1] in which he speaks about connections between modern physics and process work and Albert Einstein's theory of relativity. In that theory (stated very simplistically!) Einstein shows that everything in the universe is moving and changing and in constant relationship to everything else. Hence, *everything is relative*; nothing is utterly stable, static, or absolute.

Dona Carletta encouraged Mary to imagine that not only the physical world of matter but also each moment in her day, including the moments when she is working in her practice, are moving and in flux; that the earth is suspended in space and revolving; that there is no fixed point on which to rely. Actually, Mary admitted that a part of her, the dreamer, had known this all along. She had always felt in a kind of suspended and fluid state. At the same time, she wrestled with her rational mind that returned again and again to static concepts of the world. A cup, after all, was a cup! She needed many days and nights to ponder this further.

Why Find the Structure?

Mary returned to pondering process structures. She asked Dona Carletta whether it was absolutely necessary to know the process structure or if it was possible to do without it. She felt it might be difficult to focus on trying to perceive the structure while in the midst of working with someone. In fact, it might go against her personal therapeutic style entirely.

Dona Carletta acknowledged that focusing on the structural aspects is a more analytical way of working and is not everyone's "cup of tea." Some people need to wander more, to dream, to find their unique way. Others work purely intuitively or go into a trance to grasp the structure. In fact, this was Dona Carletta's preferred and natural method of working. She also knew that if you simply follow one signal after another, without knowledge of the larger pattern, the structure slowly becomes apparent by itself—although it may take a while.

She said that finding the secondary process can be quite simple. You could ask the person to simply close her eyes and report on what is happening inside or to scan her body and notice whatever catches her attention. This is a non-threatening method that helps in dropping the content and bringing up dreaming material.

She did stress to Mary that knowing the structure at some point can give you access to, and awareness of, more aspects of the process than you may have noticed otherwise. This access in turn can deepen your work in innumerable ways. And, knowledge of the structure could help orient you when you are lost or confused. If you need a greater overview, the process structure can always serve as your guide. She added that knowing the process structure can also save you time (by noticing edges), although that is not necessarily the most important thing!

The River's Crosscurrents: The Edge

Dona Carletta started jumping up and down and said, "Oh, yes, there is another reason for knowing the structure! It has to do with the ability to recognize the amazing point on our river journey where the deep secondary current begins to surface and becomes a powerful surge. That's where we left off on our fantasy trip!"

She encouraged Mary to return to her inner fantasy and remember the moment when the new current surfaced. Dona Carletta said that Mary might have noticed that this new current was surfacing in small ways earlier and that now it was showing itself more strongly. She told Mary to imagine that this current was gaining momentum and was beginning to pull the boat off its set course. She asked Mary what it felt like to feel that second stream tugging at the boat. Mary said she felt tiny shudders running up and down her spine. She also began to feel a bit disoriented and afraid and wanted to paddle harder to return to their original course.

As she continued to unfold this image, Mary said she had all sorts of spontaneous fantasies about that new current. At one moment, she imagined that it was caused by a huge fish under the water, or by a swirling vortex that would drag their boat under and from which they would never return. She also giggled slightly and said that it raised her curiosity and excitement at the same time.

Dona Carletta said, "*Yes*, what a magical and confusing spot! You have found yourself at the *edge*—the place where your identity is challenged when a new process begins to emerge! You have discovered all of the feelings that occur at the edge!" She said that the natural tendency at the edge is to try to ignore this new stream and continue on your original path.

Dona Carletta interjected that it's important to notice when you are working with someone and a new secondary experience or current surfaces. It is natural to become fearful and worry that you will fall off an abyss into knowing nothing if you go into that new territory. It's certainly easier to stay with known territory (primary process). At that point, you may start to get confused, nervous, feel blocked or stuck or bored. You may feel as though the things your client is saying are cycling like a whirlpool, not going anywhere.

A good process worker notices the convergence of these two currents and brings this dynamic intersection to awareness. She will say that she and her client have come to the edge, an important juncture in the process. She will offer awareness possibilities such as, "We may want to ignore this new information or we may want to venture into the new current and find out what it is trying to express. Or, perhaps we should stay at the edge and meditate there." In any case, if they begin to explore the new process, the process worker will let the client know that, in essence, the waters are not really so disparate. She will help the client sense the old stream even as she and the client become oriented to the new.

Since Dona Carletta was a former dancer, and has recently danced quite a bit throughout the cosmos, she gave Mary an example of the edge in movement work. She told Mary to imagine a woman who began to dance gracefully. The woman's primary intention was to move in an elegant and controlled way. At one point, however, the woman tripped slightly over her feet. Like all of us, the woman ignored this slight deviation and returned to her original movement style. However, this stumbling motion happened again, so Dona Carletta suggested that the woman place her attention on it and try it again, this time consciously and safely, and allow it to unfold.

Although this woman was shy about exploring this new stream, she did want to experiment. As she stumbled intentionally, the woman felt somewhat dizzy and disoriented. Dona Carletta suggested that she experiment with being a bit disoriented. The woman giggled; she was at yet another edge to going further. She wanted to try but was a bit afraid. Dona Carletta appreciated her fear and tried to do the motions for her. The woman enjoyed watching Dona Carletta. Then Dona Carletta said that she appreciated the woman's need for stability and suggested that the woman act disoriented for only thirty seconds and then return to her normal steadiness. The woman agreed. Dona Carletta said that the labels of dizzy and disoriented might be just the beginning of the process and perhaps it would unfold in an exciting way.

As the woman began to move, her gestures unfolded and she began to feel as if she was drifting in space, weightless. She started to laugh and felt free and happy. She said that normally in her life she felt she had to do things in a very exact, linear way. This weightless, detached feeling was something she needed much more of in her life. Dona Carletta pointed out that the initial name of "tripping" was only the very beginning of this deep, weightless experience that was trying to arise.

Three Times at the Edge

Dona Carletta added that if this woman gave negative feedback three times to her suggestions to focus on her secondary process, she would drop the idea and follow whatever else occurred. This meant that the process was going in a different direction. She said that feedback was the central guiding force in determining the direction in which to go. The concept of "three times at the edge" was one of Eagle's basic rules. Try three times and if the person does not pick up on the suggestion, drop it and follow whatever arises.

There are countless reasons why people will choose not to go over an edge. It may not be the right timing; perhaps it is too soon, and the person needs more time to establish a sense of safety and trust with you. Perhaps the person does not yet have enough of a pattern for this new behavior. Others need to go slowly because they were always pushed into things in the past and couldn't defend themselves. In that case, saying "no" to your suggestion could be an important process in itself, a person's way of defending himself or herself and standing up for what he or she wants.

Process Structures Change

Dona Carletta finished her general discussion of process structure by addressing Mary's rational mind. She said, "While we do have long-term aspects of our processes that accompany us throughout our lifetimes, the subtleties of our processes change continually and transform. Therefore, we must be careful about getting attached to *any* process structure. The structure changes as we and the Tao change." She said that for her, the beauty of process work is the ever-evolving attempt to adjust to and follow the river's flow.

Dona Carletta acknowledged that it is easier to talk about flow than it is to actually *be fluid!* She recalled a recent case supervision session of a week ago, when she had given suggestions to the therapist. The next time the therapist met with that client, she tried the suggestions. Now the therapist complained that the methods she had learned did not seem to help her client. Dona Carletta asked what happened with her client. The therapist described a situation in which the client was in a very different mood, situation, and state of consciousness than in the previous session. The Tao had moved and, of course, the suggestions for last week did not fit that particular moment! However, the therapist was so fixed on what she had learned that she did not notice the new process that had emerged. Dona Carletta reminded Mary that any suggestion is only temporarily useful.

Dona Carletta noticed a troubled look on Mary's face. Mary asked if she would ever be so fluid. Could she ever really have a beginner's mind? Dona Carletta consoled her by saying that if Mary did not feel fluid, then that was part of the Tao, too; that she should be rigid *consciously* and follow the process that unfolded out of it. She also reminded Mary of her basic nature; she was a spacey and dreamy individual who had always tried to contain herself within the limits of ordinary reality. Mary agreed that fluidity was a basic part of her nature that she loved but was shy about.

Dona Carletta looked rather at peace. She knew that, ultimately, time and life experience would teach these principles to Mary. She remembered Eagle saying that life and death are the greatest teachers of the Tao. In the end, everyone follows the river.

Notes

1. See Arnold Mindell, *Quantum Mind* (Portland, Oregon: Lao Tse Press, 2000).

Chapter Six

Verbal Statements and Moods

To discover the process structure, listen carefully to a person's verbal content, including the mood in which something is said and the figures or parts that are implied.

Class One

Many of Mary's co-learners, both beginning and advanced, were having trouble identifying process structures.[1] Dona Carletta told them that a lack of clarity about the process structure was one of the central reasons that therapists become confused about their cases and need supervision. Dona Carletta was amazed to discover that, quite often, the therapist has the structure *upside down*! Therefore, she created a class to discuss methods of discovering the process structure by listening to a person's language, by noticing her or his behavior, and by looking for "ghosts." The class was scheduled over a series of two nights. (The second class can be found in Chapter 7.)

At the outset of the class, Dona Carletta gave a warning akin to the type you find on cigarette boxes. She said, "The exact and analytical thinking that we will investigate this evening may be detrimental to the learning and therapeutic styles of those of you with a more intuitive or dreamy way of learning about and working with others." She even said that, in fact, she herself belonged to this category and maybe the best thing to do would be to cancel the class!

These startling comments unleashed a group process. Many people had strong feelings about the subject. The feeling and intuitive types among the students were relieved because Dona Carletta had spoken their hidden thoughts. Actually, just hearing this problem stated gave them relief and the courage to continue. Others said that identifying the process structure was a crucial part of their learning and that this was *the* most important class. A few said they needed this knowledge to fall back on, in case of problems, although the topic was not of great interest to them. There was a small contingent of advanced students who felt that this class was "old hat" and that they would be bored by the material. Others had tried and failed so many times to find the process structure that they had practically given up and declared it hopeless.

What had she unleashed? Dona Carletta had certainly stirred up a lot of emotion. People were so animated about the topic (either in a positive or a negative way) that she decided this was a perfect moment to go forward. Suddenly, with what some felt was an unreasonably gleeful tone, Dona Carletta started to jump up and down and said, "OK, let's begin!" She said that she would start by telling us a verbal statement from a client of hers and ask us to discern the process structure within that sentence.

She prefaced all of this by saying that the examples she would bring in this class were brief, encapsulated statements and generalized interactions that do not reflect the subtlety and intricacy of *real* individual's processes. They were instead meant as a means to help us practice and enjoy learning about process structures. She also reminded everyone that the labels we give to primary and secondary processes are static abbreviations for dynamic experiences. However, she stressed that it was possible to learn a lot just by listening to what people say.

She said a client recently said to her:

> *"I am a very orderly person. I can't stand it when my neighbors make a mess and throw everything around."*

"This is a very simple example," she said. "What process structure do you imagine from this sentence?" She reminded us that the primary process indicates those things the person identifies with, and the secondary process includes those experiences the person does not identify with. Someone piped up and said, "That person identifies with being orderly, so the secondary process is *the neighbors* who *make a mess.*"

Dona Carletta said that was right and explained her thinking a bit more. "If you listen to someone's words, you can discover the process structure from the way in which she or he uses language. Those elements that are associated with "I" are more primary, are part of the person's identity, and are close to awareness. Those elements that "happen to the person"—which are cued by the use of verbs in the passive tense—and those elements that are "not" the person (the "not me") are all more secondary. Aspects of the secondary process are further away from awareness and the person's momentary identity. Some of the students who had been nervous in the beginning were feeling a bit more secure.

Dona Carletta reminded the class that channels are also part of the structure. She said that you can also find out which *channels* are more occupied, or closer to the person's identity, and which are unoccupied, or further from the person's identity. She reiterated Eagle's delineation of six sensory-oriented channels (visual, auditory, proprioception, kinesthetic, relationship, and world) that occur most frequently in practice. Some channels are used with greater awareness and are part of our primary process. For example, in Western cultures, many people occupy the visual channel with their awareness. Other channels, such as proprioception, may be used with less awareness and therefore are unoccupied.

She told the class to think of someone who says,

> *"I saw some dogs racing across the road!"*

In this case, she said, the occupied channel is visual ("I saw"), while kinesthesia or movement is unoccupied ("dogs racing across the road"). The secondary experience happens in the movement (kinesthetic) channel and is therefore unoccupied.

Dona Carletta put the following list on the board to help everyone learn several methods of listening for secondary processes that may arise in someone's verbal communication She distilled this list from one of Eagle's most recent classes on dreamwork:[2]

- Listen for *passive verbs* in the person's speech.
- Listen for words that are *stressed.*
- Listen for the use of *foreign words.*
- Notice *quick changes in the person's voice,* such as sudden high notes after a lot of low notes.
- Listen for *missing words,* moments when people can't find the right word to say, or sentences that the person does not complete.

Eagle called these "dream doors." Dona Carletta said that, once you notice any of these cues or dream doors in someone's communication, you can ask the person to focus on these moments and investigate more fully these dreaming, secondary experiences.

At this point, the "know-it-all" students sat back in their chairs and sighed, saying it was too easy. They looked as though they were sinking into their chairs, preparing themselves for a boring evening. With a sly look in her eyes Dona Carletta asked, "Who can answer this?"

"I don't have anything specific to work on."

Someone said, "This person doesn't want to focus on anything." Another person answered, "This probably means that this person has something specific to work on but is shy about it. It is secondary. The primary process is *having nothing specific to work on.*"

"That's right," Dona Carletta said. She recalled Eagle pointing out many times that when someone says they "don't have" something, this could mean that there *is* "something" specific to work on, but it is disavowed or further away from the person's awareness. One possibility is to say to this person, "What is the specific thing that you *don't* have to work on?"

Reformulation and Moods

Some people were confused and getting a bit agitated. Dona Carletta said, "Great! You are actually the best students in the room! Why? To really understand the process structure, you have to be attuned to the person's behavior. You are smart not to be completely certain when you hear a simple sentence! Without watching the person's behavior and listening to the *way* they speak, you may not be fully sure what is primary and what is secondary. For example, it is possible that, in the sentence just mentioned, the person feels he or she "ought" to work on something but does not want to.

"Therefore," she continued, "you have to pay attention to *how* the person says *I*. Notice what mood is associated with the person's primary process." She said that a very helpful tool in becoming clear about all of this is called "reformulation:" restating the person's experiences in another way, beginning with "*I feel or identify with this or that and this is happening to me.*" Let's examine this statement:

> *(Speaking with worry and fear in her voice) "Oh, I feel like I'm dissolving, I can't define myself anymore!"*

One student jumped in and said that this person obviously needs a greater sense of stability and that this sense of stability is secondary. Another person argued that the opposite was the case.

Dona Carletta pointed out that it is important to notice the *way* or *mood* in which the person is saying that she does not want to dissolve. Someone said that it sounded like the person is afraid and disturbed by this feeling. "That's right," Dona Carletta said, and then she asked the group, "If we were to reformulate this sentence, what do you think the person would associate with *I?*"

One student said, "The person would probably say, 'I want to be solid and clear and know exactly how to define myself.' The student continued and said, "The secondary process, the thing happening to this person, is the unusual sensation of dissolving."

"Yes," said Dona Carletta, "and we might reformulate this as, 'Something weird is happening. I'm dissolving and I don't like it. It disturbs me,'"

She then told the full story of this person's process. She said that when this woman began her work, she was annoyed by her watch and took it off. While working with her therapist, the person seemed to want to stay intently focused on her interactions but she seemed to drift off and inadvertently did not answer her therapist's questions. Dona Carletta said that the woman was *already* in the middle of dissolving (albeit unconsciously) without realizing it. One part of her signal was, "Yes, I'm here to relate," and the other, a more secondary, double signal with which she did not identify, was the experience of drifting off and removing her watch.

Dona Carletta offered the following example to experiment further with reformulation.

> *(A man does movement work and then says in a surprised tone) "I went from one state to another without knowing how!"*

After much discussion Dona Carletta said that this man is describing the pattern of his process; deep states are happening with no bridge between them. We can infer from the feeling quality of his statement that, primarily, he wants to know how he got from "a" to "b." But the surprise in his voice indicates that "not knowing how" is secondary. It happens *to* him. Dona Carletta said that she remembered Eagle working with this person. Following this man's secondary process, Eagle encouraged him to drop his linear mind (primary) for a moment and allow himself to change states spontaneously without thinking.

Dona Carletta gave another example:

> *(A man, talking about his interactions with people he is in conflict with, says) "It's awful, I just give up and don't talk! I hate it."*

Dona Carletta asked everyone to reformulate this sentence. Many were sure that this man needed to find his own strength and not to give up during conflict situations. They were surprised by

Dona Carletta's reformulation: "I am a man who wants to speak up for myself, but I am so stupid, and for some reason, I don't do it. That disgusts me!" Here, the man has a mood against his *giving-up* behavior. *Giving up* and *not talking* are secondary for him; they happen *to* him. Dona Carletta said that if this disavowed experience of *not talking* were unfolded, it might lead to surprising alternatives such as various forms of nonverbal expression, trance states, or meditation.

Example: Being a Mother

To finish the first evening class, Dona Carletta took out one of her "super-challenger examples" that she kept for special occasions. She asked the class to meet in small groups and decide on the process structure. She said that everyone should return in ten minutes. At that time, she would gather their ideas, clarify the structure, and describe more about the woman's overall process.

> *In a large seminar, a woman about forty years old was working in the middle of the group with Eagle. She said that she has three children and added, with a distasteful look and tone, "I'm having trouble being a mother. It's enough!"*

Small groups gathered, and there was a lot of haggling going on. When everyone reconvened, people debated about the structure. Dona Carletta was delighted that everyone was so stimulated. After gathering their ideas she gave her own. "The most natural feeling is to think that the woman's secondary process is to get out of the identity of *being a mother.* She says she is fed up with it. Dona Carletta interjected that she could fully understand what this woman was talking about!

However, Dona Carletta continued, "If we reformulate what the woman expressed, we might say, 'I don't want to be a mother. I want to get out of it!' This is her primary process, the desire to stop being a mother and to be free. Therefore, paradoxically, in this moment, 'being a mother' is secondary for her. It is happening *to* her and she cannot get away from it. At this point some people in the class became dizzy and needed some water to continue!

After a short pause for drinks, Dona Carletta assured everyone that the rest of the details of the interaction between Eagle and this woman would help clarify the situation and everyone would once again feel grounded. She described the situation as follows:

Client: I don't like being a mother. I like being motherly but not mothering. *(Here she is saying that she accepts being motherly, this is closer to her primary process—but does not like "being a mother.")*

Eagle: What is the difference?

Client: Motherly is warm and nourishing. Mother means that everyone has a free pass to take.

Eagle: (*Suggesting that perhaps her secondary process had to do with actually being a mother*) Experiment with giving everyone a free pass! *(The woman suddenly giggled, froze, hemmed and hawed. She was at an edge. After a while she took a big breath and tried to go deeper into the experience of giving everyone a "free pass.")*

Dona Carletta said she knew this went against many of our rational mindsets, but she encouraged us to have a beginner's mind. "What might the wisdom of nature be here? And what is a free pass? We don't know what it actually means until it is unfolded further."

> *The woman began to sense the experience of "giving a free pass" to everyone: she gazed around the room and radiated a sense of openness to whatever needed to happen. In that moment, many of the other women in the seminar spontaneously gathered around her. Noticing this, Eagle said, "There must be something in you that draws people together." As the woman began to speak to these seminar women, she said she felt like a female elder who could be there for everyone and give advice about the meaning of life. She said she experienced herself as a mother to the world, for all people, and especially for women. It was apparent that the women who gathered around her were looking to her for*

> *this teaching. How differently this sense of a "free pass" unfolded than what we might have imagined ahead of time!*

Process Structure and Ghosts

To finish the evening, Dona Carletta wanted to talk about something fun. She said this was one of her favorite subjects—*ghosts.* She said that where she came from, ghosts were an obvious part of daily life, but she understood that not everyone on Earth felt that way. She said that, in terms of process work, ghosts (as mentioned previously) refer to those aspects of someone's experience that are *implied* but not directly represented by the client. Ghosts are secondary experiences that are trying to come into awareness.

Dona Carletta said that you have to have special glasses, in essence, to see ghosts. And for the occasion, she had brought a bunch of silly-looking psychedelic glasses and passed them out to everyone. They looked like those 3-D glasses they used to pass out in the 60s during psychedelic movies. Everyone in the class promptly put them on, happy to move away from structures hidden in sentences. Dona Carletta hoped the glasses would help everyone access their inner magical-power place and see the hidden ghosts in the following example:

> *A woman walks into her therapist's office looking afraid. Her head is down. She looks embarrassed.*

Dona Carletta asked: "Do you see the ghost? What figure can be *inferred* from this woman's behavior—the part that is there but *not quite represented?* If this woman's behavior were part of a story, can you imagine another figure in that story?"

Someone correctly answered, "The ghost here is a critical figure who is looking at her and putting her down." Dona Carletta continued by saying that you can also infer from this woman's behavior that she identifies more closely with the victim of this nasty figure. The secondary process is this critical figure. Perhaps when this secondary element is unfolded further, it could become an empowering element of her own critical-thinking ability.

Someone else said that she imagined another ghost, a warm and loving figure that supported the woman. "Right," said Dona

Carletta. She asked how that ghost might express itself in the person's interaction with the therapist. Someone said that the therapist might have motherly and warm feelings towards the person. Hence, the ghost could appear in the therapist's own feelings.

Dona Carletta said that she has known many feeling-oriented therapists who do recognize ghosts in the subtle feelings they experience when they are working with a particular client. Imagine the following:

> *A therapist said that when he was with his client, he felt like a tiny ant in front of a huge monster.*

The therapist's reactions helped illuminate two parts in the client's field: one part that is afraid and another that is extremely powerful. In this case, the client actually identified with being fearful. His secondary process was a great deal of power with which he was not yet in touch.

Dona Carletta then gave one of her favorite examples that Eagle taught many years ago. It has to do with knowledge about body signals:

> *A woman comes into your office, lies down on the floor, and leans against a pillow that is propped up against the wall. She says that she feels lousy about her life.*

"If you look at her posture," Dona Carletta said, "you will notice that she is lying back; she identifies with feeling lousy and needing to lie back. Where is the ghost in her posture?" Someone answered, "It is *the pillow or the wall*, the thing she is leaning up against!" "That's right," Dona Carletta said. "If the woman explored that experience of being the wall, it might unfold into a part of herself that is supportive and comforting, which she needs but is not yet in contact with."

Ghosts in Symptoms and Addictions

Dona Carletta reminded everyone that there are two parts to every symptom. If you have pain, there is one part experiencing the pain and another part *producing* the pain. One of these experiences will be closer to the person's primary process, and one closer to the secondary process.

Dona Carletta told everyone to imagine having an itch! Everyone laughed and thought this was too easy. She asked them, "What is the anatomy of an itch? What is happening? There is someone who wants to scratch and … What is the ghost part, the invisible force that we cannot see?" Someone said, "Something that is making you want to scratch! The tickler!" Dona Carletta said that was right! Usually, the person is identified with scratching and ameliorating that irritating feeling, but the secondary level is the part *creating* the itch.

She told a story about a shy woman who had lots of itches. When this woman acted out the "tickler," she started to tickle others and even began to disturb people. This was over her edge; she ordinarily felt she should not intrude into other people's private spaces. But the tickler actually wanted to activate people and get them involved in all sorts of activities in which she was interested.

Dona Carletta reminded everyone to be diligent in identifying the process structure around symptoms. It can be very tricky. For example, she described a man who said that he felt "trapped" by his symptoms and wanted to "break out." Most people thought that this man *should* break out as if this was always the most therapeutic thing to do! "If we do not jump to conclusions, however," Dona Carletta said, "we would realize that this man is identified with wanting to break out while the sense of being trapped is secondary. It turned out that when the man unfolded this experience of being "trapped" his secondary process turned into the desire to go deeper inside himself and meditate, seemingly a different energy than his original experience of being "trapped."

Dona Carletta reminded everyone of Eagle's discovery that addictions or addictive tendencies also contain two processes. To help them understand this, she asked everyone to recall one of their own addictive tendencies and the state that the tendency evokes in them. She then surprised them by asking, "What was there before this state occurred? What is this altered state in reaction to? When someone is in this altered state, this earlier state of consciousness that they are getting *away from* is the ghost."

She continued: "Think of someone who drinks a lot of coffee when he goes to work. This person likes the buzz and the energy that it gives him. But this need to ingest coffee implies another state from which the person is getting away. This state of needing coffee may be a reaction to a preceding experience of lethargy, exhaustion, or depression. To work on this addiction means focusing on *both* processes that are in conflict with one another."

Dona Carletta ended the evening by encouraging people to wear their special glasses whenever possible and to discover hidden ghosts in people's speech, behavior, symptoms, and addictions.

Notes

1. See Arnold Mindell, *Working on Yourself Alone* (Portland, Oregon: Lao Tse Press, 2002); *River's Way* (London: Routledge & Kegan Paul, 1985); Joe Goodbread, *Dreambody Toolkit* (Portland, Oregon: Lao Tse Press, 1997), particularly Part III, for detailed explanations of process structures and channels.
2. For more on this topic, see Arnold Mindell, *The Dreammaker's Apprentice* (Charlottesville, Virginia: Hampton Roads, 2001),159-163.

Chapter Seven

Behavior's Mysterious Structure

Observe a person's behavior, including posture and gestures, as well as the most mysterious aspect of her or his experience, to discover the process structure.

Class Two

For the final class on this subject, Dona Carletta talked about the way in which the process structure expresses itself through behavior, double signals, and movement.

Behavior, Double Signals, and Movement

At one time, Dona Carletta had been an amateur actor, and she was anxious to re-ignite this interest once again by acting out a few of her examples. Before beginning, she told the group, as she had in the first class, that the examples are simplistic but that they may be more educational and complex than they seem at first. She did begin to worry that because of her love of details, her explanations would seem too technical and stilted in comparison to her true sense of the work: the openness to our clients and the attempt to follow the flow of nature. She assured us that the details she would present, however, are meant to help the therapist become even *more* aware of the beauty and uniqueness of any individual's process. She also reassured everyone that these ideas would eventually melt into, and become an invisible and fluid aspect of, each person's style.

Then she said that she would play the role of a client and asked someone else in the class to take the role of the therapist. She asked the therapist to stand up and greet her (as she acted like the client). The two acted out the scene, and this is what happened:

> *The client walks into the office. The therapist approaches the person to say hello. The client faintly smiles in the therapist's direction and says she's glad she is there and, somewhat quickly and abruptly, walks past the therapist and sits down.*

No one in the group knew quite what to say. Dona Carletta said, "What is really interesting is that the things people do with their bodies, especially the things that stand out or are surprising, are frequently secondary processes of which the person is not fully aware. (See Chapter 8 for more on this.)

"With that in mind, what might the structure of this client's process be?" she asked. Someone replied, "I would guess that this woman's secondary process has to do with following herself because she walks away quickly and abruptly when greeted." "Yes," Dona Carletta said. "Now, what does this *imply* about her primary process?" The same person said, "She might be a woman who ordinarily follows what other people say."

Dona Carletta again said, "Yes, that's right. In actuality, this woman's primary intention was to get advice or help from the therapist, while her secondary process had to do with gaining access to her own sense of power and direction." If she were aware of her secondary process, this woman might say, "I would like to direct the communication process in relationships but my primary process does not allow me to do that. Ordinarily, I feel that I must follow the other person."

Dona Carletta then acted out another example:

> *A woman says: "I feel my friend always cuts me out" (as she is speaking, she makes a strong cutting or slicing motion with one of her hands).*

Many students knew that her hand motion was a typical double signal. One part of the person, the primary part, is upset about her friend. The secondary element in her behavior is the cutting motion with the hand. In other words, the friend's ability to cut things out is secondary for this woman. When she unfolded this motion, the woman discovered a definitive and incisive part of herself that she did not know very well.

Then, with the help of one of the students, Dona Carletta presented one of her favorite cases:

> *A Western couple works on their relationship together. They are having a lot of problems and fights all the time. At the end of their work, as they are getting up to leave, they spontaneously and briefly bow to one another.*

Dona Carletta explained that this couple is identified with working on their relationship issues and dealing with their problems. Their secondary process, the spontaneous bow, revealed a deep spiritual principal that binds them together and reaches beyond their problems and difficulties. As a therapist you might ask them to try to gain access to this spiritual dimension and be in contact with it as they deal with their problems.

She then presented a typical, but often confusing, situation for the therapist:

> *A man says that he is stuck and needs your help. He says he feels hopeless because he is unable to get anywhere with his problems. You, the therapist, do your best to help, yet nothing you do seems to be quite right; none of your methods seem helpful to this man. Although he smiles at you, on further investigation he seems to be giving negative feedback by subtly rejecting all of your suggestions by looking down when you make a recommendation and not answering your inquiries.*

Dona Carletta said that therapists frequently bring this type of situation to supervision; some therapists begin to feel inadequate but do not know why, and others become irritated that the client does not follow anything they say! In either case, the therapist's overview-mind becomes clouded.

The client in this case is primarily asking for help while rejecting (secondarily) everything the therapist suggests. Yet, this person does not identify with saying "no," with rejecting behavior. Dona Carletta asked how the students might reformulate this process. Here is a possibility: "I am primarily stuck and miserable in my life, and things will never change. My secondary process is saying no to everything and that is where my strength is located, although I don't have access to it consciously. I have a lot of power and ideas about my life that I am hesitant to bring out into the open." (See Chapter 20 for more on this type of process.)

The Lesser Known, More Mysterious Signal

Now Dona Carletta presented another interesting example that contains a helpful tool if you are confused about the structure: try to determine which *nonverbal signals* the person identifies with and which ones he or she does not:

> *A man said that he feels like there is a kind of static that keeps him apart from people. His hands are shaking, seemingly to express the quality of this static. Then he says that sometimes he is centered when he is with people. When he says this, he stands in a centered way, squarely balanced on his feet, and has a satisfied look on his face.*

To understand the structure in this example, it is helpful to ask, "Which signals are more known, more congruent, and more understandable to the client?" Those signals are closer to his primary process. The signals that are less known and more mysterious are aspects of his secondary process.

In this example, the man is more identified with being *centered*. When he stands in a balanced way, his movements seem congruent with what he is saying: he seems to like them, and we readily understand them. His movements are like a completed sentence that we understand, such as, "I am very centered *and happy about that.*" On the other hand, the more mysterious signal is his shaking-hand motion. We do not yet understand what that is expressing. It is like an incomplete sentence that stops in midair, such as "I am shaking and making static because …" Hence, the more unknown, mysterious secondary element is what he describes verbally as "static" and somatically by the shaking-hand motion. When this "static" was unfolded, the man began to dance around as he got in touch with his desire to generate and bring a lot of energy and excitement into his relationships with others.

It is helpful to know how to differentiate primary and secondary body signals and movements. Primary body signals are congruent with what we are intending to express, and complete themselves. We can understand them readily. They are like completed sentences that we can understand. Secondary signals, on the other hand, are incomplete and incongruent. We do not understand them. They do not go along with our primary intent or identity. They are like messages that begin but do not have an ending. Hence, the "static" that this man describes, as well as his shaking hand motions, sort of hang in the air. We do not know what they mean or where they are, whereas his centeredness is more understandable, congruent with what he wants, and complete.[1]

Another way to think about the secondary process is to ask, "*Where is dreaming happening?*" In other words, where is the more mysterious and unknown piece of information occurring? Secondary dreaming experiences might occur just when you aren't looking! You might be focusing on one thing and suddenly something spontaneous and unpredictable happens. Imagine that you greet one of your clients as she comes into the room. She is very briefly distracted by the sound of a bird outside the window, or she trips slightly over a pillow. These can be indications of secondary processes emerging. If you get up to make tea for a moment, the secondary element frequently manifests. The person might look in the mirror or slump down in her chair. These are all pathways into the deeper dreaming process.

Least Represented Part

Dona Carletta said one of the easiest ways to understand secondary processes is to think of them as *the least represented part of the total picture.* Instead of trying to sort out all of the experiences, you can simply look for the aspect of a person's experience that is *furthest* away from his or her awareness—the one we know least about. This is where the dreaming process is manifesting most strongly in the moment.

Try to find the "least represented part" in the following:

> *A woman says excitedly and with surprise in her voice: "I'm so happy, I just can't believe it! (Pause. Then, with a somewhat more subdued tone) I was thinking of working on my symptom. Let's do that. "*

In this example, the person seems to have a plan—to focus on her body symptom. The least represented part, however, the most secondary element, is the experience of happiness. It spontaneously arises and is skipped over immediately. How do we know this? This woman says with delight and surprise, "I can't believe it!" Therefore, there is a part of her who cannot believe that she can be happy. This is an unknown experience for her.

If she were aware of this process, she might say, "I can't believe I'm so happy because I *am* feeling miserable and I think, or have learned, that this is the only way to be. I have to have a problem. It's not possible for me to simply be happy!"

Continuum

At this point, Dona Carletta began to worry that what she wanted to do next would really cause confusion. She feared that she would ruin everyone's mood and blow out "circuits" if she went further. She even said that anyone who wanted to go home should do so now and she would totally understand. She related that the kinds of things she was interested in talking about now still troubled her and that she had stayed up many nights to figure them out. But she said that no one else in their right mind should have to suffer with her somewhat convoluted theories and if anyone wanted to go, she would not be insulted. Of course, very few people left, except a couple of people who had previously scheduled dinner dates.

She said that actually the process structure was more complex than just knowing what is primary and secondary because there are *many* aspects of a person's experience, some of which will be closer and some further from the person's primary identity. She suggested the image of a grand continuum of experience, with one section colored the brightest, indicating the person's identity—some experiences being closer to, and others further away from, this bright section.

She continued with another example:

> *A woman got up to work in a seminar. She said that people hate her all the time and that she felt shy about standing up in the group. She feels she is no good and is afraid others feel that way, too. And she said that she feels there is a witch on her back.*

Before going further with the example, Dona Carletta launched into her theory, which she said was really only helpful when all else has failed. Because of the complexity of any given process (and "the continuum" she mentioned earlier), she asked how we might know whether one experience is more represented than another experience? She presented the following clues for determining whether or not something is well represented and closer to the person's identity:

1. Vicinity to the person's identity. How close is that particular experience to the person's identity? The closer it is, the more primary. The more unknown or disturbing it is to the person's identity, the more secondary it is.

2. Accessibility. How easily will the person be able to consciously experience that aspect of his or her process relative to other aspects? If it is relatively easy, then it is closer to the primary process.

3. Amount of information. If you asked the person to tell you as much information as possible about his or her experience, how much would he or she be able to say? If there is little description or knowledge of that experience, it is more secondary.

4. Spontaneity and unpredictability. Does that experience occur spontaneously? Is it unpredictable and mysterious, or is it more familiar and predictable? The less known and more spontaneous an experience, the closer it is to the person's secondary process.

Dona Carletta returned to the previous example. Here, it turns out, the woman could tell you lots of information about herself as a victim and how bad she feels all the time *and also* how people criticize her. She could tell you hundreds of detailed criticisms of herself and would actually say that she believes them, that she really feels that way about herself as well.

However, she does not know much about the "witch." If asked, she might say that it is a weird experience she senses behind her, on her back. It is a vague and numinous experience and might be hard, at first, for her to experience. While she could easily play the critic or the victim of that critic, it would be harder for her to act like the witch she is imagining on her back. It is even *more* unknown and mysterious than the criticism and therefore further from her ordinary identity.

In this case, the victim *and* the critic are very closely related. Most likely, her identity is tied up with being a victim of this critic, but the critic itself, which is a bit further away, is also quite close to her identity. However, the "witch on her back" (which is a name for an experience that has not yet been unfolded) is the *most* secondary element.

Dona Carletta said that a paradox here is that, although something is far from our identity, it might be just the thing that we seem to be *so* aware of and constantly complain about. She told us to think of a body symptom that bothers us and the way it can preoccupy our attention. We might complain a lot about our stomach hurting or our bones aching. However, we do not know any more information about that experience and do not put our attention on it long enough to experience and unfold it.

Dona Carletta was delighted that everyone seemed to still be conscious at this point! She offered the following exercise to try before leaving for the evening.

Exercise: Process Structure and Least Represented Part (in pairs):

1. One person (the helper) interviews the other for a few minutes about what he or she did yesterday.
2. While the person is talking, the helper tries to discover the process structure by noticing what the person does and does not identify with—verbally and nonverbally. Try to decide what is most secondary and least represented.
3. The helper should then ask the partner to put her or his attention on that secondary experience and amplify it a bit until the person finds out what that experience is expressing.
4. Finally, the helper should try to describe the person's primary and secondary process.

Notes

1. For more on movement signals, see Amy Mindell "The Hidden Dance" (Master's Thesis, Antioch University, Yellow Springs, Ohio, 1986) and "Moving the Dreambody: Movement Work in Process-Oriented Psychology," *Contact Quarterly* 20 (1995).

Chapter Eight

That Big Flirt

The aspect of a person that stands out to you—the quality that you strongly like or that disturbs you—is frequently something to which she or he needs more conscious access.

Meet Huffelia (Huffy, for short), a beginning therapist. Huffelia has always been very opinionated and now, as she is becoming a therapist, her opinions are getting somewhat out of hand. When Dona Carletta saw Huffy walking down the street looking blown up like a balloon one day, she decided it was time to approach her gently about one of the most crucial parts of supervision. She recommended that Huffy join her in a class she was giving that afternoon. Huffy shrugged her shoulders and said, "Why not?"

When the class began, Dona Carletta said that the information she was going to speak about was one of the most helpful pieces of supervisory information of which she was aware. She said it was particularly useful when dealing with therapists who are having a great deal of difficulty about a particular situation and are feeling confused about the structure of the process.

Huffy thought all of this sounded fine, but she was sure she already knew about it, more or less. Dona Carletta caught herself before she reacted harshly to Huffy and reminded herself that her irritation with Huffy was a good example of what she would soon be describing.

The Flirt and the Thousand-Watt Bulb

Dona Carletta said that one of the great causes of confusion in a particular client-therapist situation is that there is something about the client that "flirts" with the therapist. Most people in the class were startled when they heard the word *flirt.* Dona Carletta continued, saying that in this context, flirting means there is something about a person that quickly catches your attention, that flickers with, or grabs, your awareness.[1] This flirt, as Eagle calls it, happens in such a "blink of an eye" that you are ordinarily barely aware of it. You may only realize it when you think about the person and notice yourself emphasizing a particular quality that really grabs your attention.

Dona Carletta said, "Let's think of this flirt as something about the client that either attracts or disturbs you, a strong characteristic about that person that catches your attention. Most often, therapists think this characteristic is so obvious that there is no reason to pay attention to it: it is *just* part of that person's ordinary character or identity. Alternately, a therapist may see this quality as a drawback that needs to be changed or circumvented." Dona Carletta paused for a moment. She thought to herself that Huffy's self-assured manner was a flirt catching her own attention.

She emphasized that, after studying hundreds of cases from supervision sessions, Dona Carletta and Eagle realized that this aspect of the client which so disturbed or impressed the therapist was, paradoxically, something the person frequently needs *more* conscious access to in his or her life. To grasp this concept, Dona Carletta recommended that everyone think about a good friend. She told us to recall a strong characteristic, "X," about that friend. She said that if someone else were to say, "Gosh, did you notice X about Sam?" we might say, "Oh, yeah, that's just Sam. That's just how he is. That's his personality," and leave it at that. We are so used to Sam being that way that we begin to take this characteristic for granted. However, that characteristic is frequently a deep, secondary process of which the person is not totally aware.

This flirt stands out like a thousand-watt light bulb that is trying to catch our attention. The bulb is turned on, but no one consciously turned on the switch! If some characteristic really disturbs or attracts you strongly, it is a light bulb, a signal beckoning to be heard, seen, and appreciated. It is an aspect of the dreaming process asking to be unfolded. Exactly how you unfold this characteristic is a matter of timing and style. And, it is always important to check out your perceptions with your client and follow his or her feedback.

Of course, Dona Carletta remarked, the thing that catches the therapist's attention is often strongly related to her or his *own* process. For example, one therapist was enthralled with a client's expressiveness and creativity. That particular therapist was shy about his *own* creativity that wanted to manifest more fully in his life. Therefore, he was especially "lit up" about the client's expressiveness. This was a signal for the therapist to work on his own process as well. In essence, she said, both client and therapist were working on the same edge.

Dona Carletta also said that if your feelings about a client's "flirt" continue long after the client has left, this is a signal that part of your own process is stimulated and in need of inner work. She said she would focus on the therapist's psychology more fully in later classes (see Chapters 27 and 29). However, she stressed, if the signal affects the therapist strongly when he or she is with that client, that flirt remains a crucial part of, and will give the therapist special insight into, the client's process.

Blocks to Perception

Dona Carletta emphasized that our awareness of the aspect of our client that either attracts or disturbs us is crucial because, otherwise, we have a tendency to turn against or ignore this characteristic and our perceptual abilities become blocked. For example, if you dislike something about a client, you might unwittingly turn against that part of him or her and push to get him or her to change. You won't have any distance from your reactions and might forget that your first priority is to follow your client's process and be of service to him or her. If you like a particular characteristic about a person but take it for granted, you will simply enjoy it and not help the person become aware of it and make it more useful in his or her life. In each case, you run the risk of becoming one-sided and ignoring the hidden process behind this flirt. Do you remember Mary and Waldo? Mary was irritated by his gruffness; that was the flirt. Mary started to turn against his gruffness, but actually, this is what he needed more *conscious access* to in his life. In addition, Mary needed more of this quality herself. A lack of attention to this flirt may ignore the relevance of that characteristic for the therapist's psychology as well.

Dona Carletta reminded us that, as with any signal, it is important to unfold the flirt to know what it is really expressing. In other words, we will need to get to the essence or message behind the signal to fully understand it. Otherwise, as mentioned earlier, we tend to immediately place labels on behavior that are frequently incorrect.

Fly-on-the-Wall Exercises

Dona Carletta wanted to give us an exercise about this flirt, but wanted us to first think about ourselves and not our clients. She said that this inner work exercise might seem deceivingly simple but actually may bring new insights about deep aspects of ourselves that we may normally take for granted. She said that we will need the metaskill of a beginner's mind to do this exercise, but she knew this would be especially difficult to have with ourselves! She led everyone through the following inner work and, after that, gave us an exercise that we could apply to one of our clients.

Exercise
The Fly, the Flirt, and You

1. Imagine that you go to see a therapist. Choose a real therapist or an imaginary one (the therapist is not important just now). You are there and the therapist is there.
2. Now imagine that, while you are with this therapist, a part of you could be a fly on the wall. As this fly, you are stuck to the wall and feeling rather detached. You look back at your original self, sitting with the therapist. From

the fly's point of view, notice your ordinary self's posture, tone of voice, gestures. What is the ordinary you speaking about? How does he or she relate to the therapist?

3. As the fly, notice what catches your attention the most about the "ordinary" you. What stands out about you the most (good or bad)? Identify this characteristic.
4. Now, return to being the "ordinary you." Try to have a generous attitude toward yourself and explore the characteristic that caught the fly's attention. Try to feel it inside of you. Amplify that characteristic in your imagination in any way that you like. As you do that, try to find the essence or basic message within that experience. What is it expressing?
5. Experiment with the thought that you might need to engage this characteristic more consciously in some way in your life. What possible significance could this experience have for you?
6. Now imagine into the future. If this characteristic were to develop in a beautiful way, how might it develop in you? What would this mean for you and your life?
7. Write down notes about this.
8. Discuss this experience with a partner. Were you surprised by it? Do you usually take this aspect of yourself for granted? Are you shy about it?

By the end of this inner work exercise, Dona Carletta noticed that many people were very shy about what they had discovered. Some said that the part of themselves they had focused on seemed like such an *obvious part* that they were embarrassed about it. They said they are usually trying to change themselves and get rid of this part. But many realized that this flirt was a deep part of themselves that just won't go away and is asking to be unfolded and used more consciously in their lives.

One woman noticed that she was always smiling at her therapist and even a bit acquiescent. When she amplified that characteristic it turned into something like a religious figure, a servant and healer. The woman said that this very characteristic was the origin of her desire to be a therapist but that she was always shy about it and never unfolded it fully.

After more people shared their experiences, Dona Carletta encouraged everyone to try the exercise again, but this time applying it to a client. Once again, she led everyone through the exercise as they silently meditated on the questions.

Exercise
The Fly, the Flirt, and Your Client

1. Recall a client who is difficult for you or, alternately, that you like very much. If you are not yet working with clients, choose a friend or family member who disturbs you in some way or whom you love. Imagine that this person comes to see you in therapy.
2. Now pretend that you are a fly on the wall. You are there, stuck to the wall, feeling rather detached. As the fly, look back at this client. Notice how he or she talks. Notice how he or she sits and relates.
3. Ask yourself, as the fly, "What stands out about this person the most? What really catches my attention?"
4. Assume a generous attitude and imagine that this characteristic may be something that he or she needs more conscious access to in some way. Imagine that you could help the person amplify that characteristic to discover its basic meaning. What do you imagine that meaning would be? What possible significance could it have for his or her life?
5. Now imagine into the future. If this characteristic were to unfold in a beautiful way, how might that person develop? What would this new development mean for this person's life?
6. Write down notes on this.
7. Think about what you learned. Were you surprised by what you discovered about that person? Do you usually take this aspect of that person for granted? Does this help

you make sense of any other experiences with that individual?

8. How is this flirt an aspect of your own psychology as well, something you are growing into or in conflict with inside of yourself?

As Dona Carletta led the group through the questions, she thought about Huffy. The thing that stood out to her about Huffy was what she experienced as unabashed self-assurance. When she dreamed further into this characteristic, she felt that its essence was a sense of being valuable and worthy. She then realized that Huffy actually does not feel valuable at all. In fact, Huffy identifies with being insecure and unsure of herself! Dona Carletta could see how Huffy needed this feeling of worthiness much more in her life. She started to feel more empathy toward Huffy and was determined to help her with her lack of confidence. What appeared first as her "self-assured" signal was actually an attempt to connect to this sense of value. She imagined that if Huffy were to consciously feel more valuable, she could do many things in her life that she always felt unable to do. Dona Carletta also realized that while she herself feels quite confident, at time she feels a bit shy about her more flamboyant ideas and theories and is in need, at times, of greater self-assurance.

At the end of the exercise, Dona Carletta noted that, although the flirt is most frequently an aspect of the client's secondary process, this is not always the case. It is possible, for example, that the characteristic upsetting you is an aspect of his or her primary process that he or she may also need to become more aware of and, perhaps, interact or wrestle with.

Using Our Feelings to Understand the Process

Dona Carletta discussed more ways in which knowledge of the flirt could be helpful to the client. She said that our strong reactions to a flirt could be used as a flag for greater awareness. For example, Huffy spoke about one of her cases involving a man who was "very wild." She said that he is always changing the subject and is very intense. The man himself says that he has trouble concentrating and meeting concrete goals he has set for himself. Huffy, too, wishes he would settle down and focus on one thing at a time, and she was quite frustrated with him. She was sure that he needed to be more focused, although when she tried to help him do that, she had no luck.

When Dona Carletta asked Huffy more about this man, it became apparent that he actually identifies with being a very conservative, rational person who is always on an "even keel." In fact, this lack of focus and wildness are secondary processes for him; they *happen to* him! Huffy was surprised by this realization. Huffy countered, however, that if she were to try to talk to this man about this wildness, he would change subjects. Dona Carletta helped her realize that changing the subject *is the wildness* happening *in the moment.* That he cannot be held down is precisely the aspect of him that is asking for more awareness, and Huffy could comment about this phenomenon and explain it to his rational mind.

Dona Carletta commended Huffy for noticing such an important signal. Huffy looked proud. Dona Carletta encouraged her to go further and use this perception for the benefit of the client. She also recommended that Huffy herself be a bit wild and unpredictable with this man. In this way, the man would feel joined and supported and would have a model for this new behavior. Huffy was shy about being a bit unpredictable but excited by the idea. It was one of her growing edges as well.

Further, Dona Carletta encouraged Huffy to think about how there may be many reasons for this man not to focus on something specific. Perhaps the lack of focus is a reaction to his primary process (or a figure from his past), that is linear and analyzes him all the time. If so, one possibility is for Huffy to show the man this conflict by acting it out (or using puppets to play the various parts) and asking the man how he would like to deal with it.

Another therapist described a client who asked for help but was "very rigid and internal." No matter what the therapist did, the client seemed to become more rigid and more deeply introverted. After the exercise, the therapist realized that the client needed to move deeply inside and *not* follow the therapist's suggestions. Dona Carletta remembered one such situation in which she said to the client, "Report to me what's going on inside, in your body. Just go inside and report from there." She then guessed at the larger story behind the client's increasingly rigidified posture and asked, "Did you build up rigidity because you were intruded upon? Are you going inside because you have been forced to come out all the time?"

Someone else in the class spoke about a client who was "the most wonderful, loving, and warm person in the world." The therapist simply loved seeing this person because the therapist always felt so warm and cared for when she was with this person. After doing the exercise, the therapist reported that she realized the client actually feels quite badly about herself and needs more conscious and *self-directed* access to this loving and warm quality. The therapist, in this case, also realized how this connected to her own psychology. She also needed to find this inner love toward herself.

The Flirt in Movement

Dona Carletta said that the flirt can occur in any channel. Here she used an example of how the flirt arose in movement when one of her students, Harriet, gave a movement seminar. As part of that seminar, time was set aside to focus more deeply on processes of individuals in the middle of the group. A woman came to the center of the room and said that she needed help. During part of her work, she began to do a dance. Harriet tried to intervene and help her further unfold her movement experiences, but the woman just ignored her and continued on. This made Harriet feel quite uneasy and, after some time, Harriet became frustrated and irritated that this person was taking up so much time!

Later, Dona Carletta helped Harriet realize that the characteristic that so frustrated her about this woman might be something this woman *needs more consciously* in her life. What could be the sense of taking so much time and not wanting anyone to intervene? Perhaps she needs to take more time in her life for herself. Perhaps she needs to learn to be herself even while others are around.

This clicked for Harriet. She admitted that, actually, after some time, the woman looked at Harriet and said, "Gee, I'm shy. Can I take so much time in front of people?" Dona Carletta suggested that Harriet might have said to her, "You've never taken enough time with yourself when others are around. You may have a tendency to follow other people's programs instead of following your own." Hence, the behavior that flirted with, and disturbed, Harriet was exactly what the woman needed more conscious access to in her life.

Dona Carletta also spoke about a child she had heard Eagle mention a number of years ago. This child was brought to a therapist because the parents said that he was "acting out," throwing things, and disturbing the entire family all the time. Although there are innumerable possible scenarios and processes here, in this particular situation, it turned out that this child wanted to be seen as a powerful person with his own ideas, not as a child who has to always be a kid and listen to others. The essence of his behavior was the need for respect. Eagle encouraged the therapist to tell the child that he is a powerful person and to ask the child for advice.

Getting Help From a Dream

Dona Carletta said that if you are really wound up in your reactions to someone and cannot gain an overview, it could be helpful to look at one of the person's dreams for clarity. One supervisee spoke about a situation in which the client was cold and aloof. The client complained about not getting along with people very well and how he was always getting intertwined in uncomfortable interactions with others. The therapist felt that the client needed to learn more about relating in a congenial way with others.

In one of the man's recurrent dreams there were many skeletons walking around a room. Dona Carletta helped the therapist realize that this man's "aloofness," understood symbolically, could be an aspect of the "skeletons"—a "bare bones," detached, and Zen-like attitude toward life. She encouraged the therapist to help the man to be more detached and to bring that feeling into his relationships in a useful way.

Taking Flirting Seriously

Dona Carletta said that, sometimes, flirting in relationship (in the ordinary sense in which we understand it) itself could be a very serious matter. She gave an example about a client who seems to flirt with you. You, the therapist, get upset and think the person should stop being intrusive. You even complain to your supervisor that this man (or woman) is coming on to you. One day, the person's hand even subtly touched you on the rear end. You feel violated and impinged upon.

When discussed further, it turns out that this person is painfully shy, primarily, and does not have any relationships. This flirting is a way of breaking through the boundaries of shyness, an attempt to reach out. Perhaps the person is trying to be recognized as a loving individual, or to express deep feelings in a way he or she has never been able to before, but it is coming out in an offensive way that he or she is unaware of. This person may be hoping to find a safe place to work on this issue with a compassionate therapist who will be able to go deeper into the essence of what he or she is trying to express. Perhaps this is the person's only hope, the last straw.

If the person could speak about what is happening, he or she might say, "Normally I cannot get to this part of myself, so it appears in a way that disturbs you. But I'm aching for someone, somewhere, to help me bring out what I am really trying to express, so that I can have meaningful relationships." It takes a lot for a therapist to remain open, and yet just that attitude might be extremely important to someone.

Pushing Our Buttons

Dona Carletta warned that if the thing that disturbs you or catches your attention about someone clashes with your personal, political or social beliefs, you could get upset and lose your awareness. We are all human; our own feelings are very important and need to be appreciated and, sometimes, depending on the particular therapeutic direction, might be an important aspect of the therapeutic relationship. She reminded us, however, that, first and foremost, our responsibility is to our client.

For example, if you have fairly liberal political views and your client has more conservative viewpoints, you might get upset by some of the things that she or he expresses. In addition to your own reactions, if this characteristic stands out strongly to you, then it is also a flirt that is beckoning greater awareness. He or she might not be conservative *enough* about something in her or his life. Maybe the person does not hold closely enough to certain basic principles in her or his life and needs your assistance with this.

Dona Carletta said that taking the flirt seriously and finding out its essence might help open our perceptions to the deeper structure behind what is happening. Again she added, however, that if we can't seem to get out of our own reactions to what is happening, this might indicate a need for our own inner work. (See Chapter 29 for more on this.)

Basic Principles

At this point, Dona Carletta summarized a few basic points from this discussion:

The overview. Awareness of the "big flirt" helps us learn how to be clear about our reactions and see how this information fits into the larger picture of the client's life. Although there may be a number of things that attract or disturb us about someone, the big flirt is the one that stands out the most.

Being useful to the client. Awareness of the big flirt helps us gain distance from our reactions and make sure that what we do is useful for our client. It helps ensure that our first priority is being of service to the person with whom we are working.

Staying centered and open in the flow. While in the midst of any given process, a flirt might suddenly appear. Staying open and centered enough to help that part unfold is a big task. It may be that you are caught off-guard and need time to think about what is happening, perhaps getting supervision.

Riding the horse backwards. Very often we have to use the metaskill of "riding the horse backwards" when flirts arise—that is, go in the opposite direction rather than where our logic might take us. We think, "Oh, that is *just* the person," or "That is something that should be changed." Instead, it may be just the thing the person needs more conscious access to!

Beginner's mind. Similarly, if something arises that upsets or attracts us, we might think, "Oh, this is too sexual," or "Oh, this is too brutal," or "Oh, that voice is so loud!" or "Oh, that person is just rigid." But remember that whatever you notice is only the initial *name* of an *unfolding* process. Once explored, the experience may be very different from what you had imagined. To do this requires a beginner's mind, one that does not hold to assumptions but rather allows the experience to explain itself—from the inside out. A critical expression could be the beginning of someone's leadership potential; being distracted and forgetful might be the beginning of losing one's identity and becoming free.

To end the class, Dona Carletta put the following exercise on the board. She recommended that we try it with one another for about 20 minutes before going to dinner.

Exercise
Unfolding a Flirt (in pairs)

1. One person interviews the other about his or her ordinary identity and about issues and problems that are on his or her mind.
2. After a few minutes, the interviewer should notice what it is about the partner that flirts with him or her. What attracts, stands out, or disturbs the most?
3. The interviewer describes this aspect to her partner and tries to help her unfold this experience sensitively, if the partner is willing to do so. The interviewer tries to get to the essence of that experience by asking her partner what is the deepest message this experience expresses.
4. Brainstorm together about the structure of the process. Was the flirt primary or secondary for your partner?

Could she use that energy more usefully in some area of her or his life?

5. The interviewer should investigate how the flirt is an aspect of her or his process as well.

Notes

1. For a detailed description of flirts and the connections between flirts and quantum physics, see Arnold Mindell, *Quantum Mind* (Portland, Oregon: Lao Tse Press, 2000); *Dreaming While Awake* (Charlottesville, Virginia: Hampton Roads, 2000).

Chapter Nine

Ghosts and Holograms

Ghosts in the atmosphere are like holograms, basic patterns, that help us connect various areas of the intake chart.

Dona Carletta was walking one day with a group of students. She said that she couldn't hold back from expounding further on her beloved topic, ghosts, which would deepen and expand aspects of the intake chart. Her favorite movie was *Ghostbusters,* and therapy itself was, for her, like ghostbusting! Everyone thought she was a bit crazy but that the idea was fun. She told everyone they could once again use their 3-D glasses if they so chose.

She reminded the group that the word *ghosts* is another term for the secondary process. A ghost is anything a person talks about which is not yet directly represented, or something that *happens to* the person with which he or she is not identified. She liked the term *ghosts* because they were a frequent occurrence on her planet, although she understood that many Earth people were not familiar or comfortable with them. She said that these mysterious, secondary experiences and figures were like presences that linger in the atmosphere, although they are invisible or unknown to us at first. She said that ghostbusting is one of the central tasks of all therapists and, as we have seen, identifying ghosts can be especially helpful when completing the intake chart.

Dona Carletta explained that the roots of this idea originate in Eagle's group process theory.[1] Eagle identified *ghost roles* in groups as those people, institutions, groups, parts of the environment, and so forth that are talked about in a group but are not directly represented. For example, if a group of employees talks about their boss who is not there, this "boss," or the energy of that boss, is a ghost within that group. Inviting the ghost in, and consciously representing its viewpoint, can further unfold the entire field of the group process.

"So," Dona Carletta asked, "how do ghosts appear when we are working with an individual? Where do they appear?" She first mentioned the most obvious way in which ghosts arise—gossip! "All of us gossip a lot about *someone* or *something* else, other than ourselves! In those moments, our *parents* or those *other people* are ghosts!" She reminded us that ghosts also appear in figures in our dreams, in our double signals, and even sometimes in the behavior of our friends and partners.

Where Is Saturday?

She began to laugh and said that the best way she knew for explaining ghosts was to draw upon the teaching of a guru she had heard speak, some years back.[2] She explained that someone came to this guru and said "I have to go home on Wednesday and cannot stay longer." The guru paused and said, "Wednesday … hmm … Wednesday." The guru mused, then suddenly looked straight at the man and said, "Where is Wednesday? Where is it?" The guru started to look around in the air as if he were searching for "Wednesday" and might find it somewhere in the atmosphere! Dona Carletta started to laugh, though no one else seemed to get the joke.

As she explained, the guru was trying to say that "Wednesday" was not only *in the future* but was also *happening now*; that, in some way, this man had already left! It was already *Wednesday.* Of course, there is a future and a past, and these should be taken very seriously. Dona Carletta said that Eagle has always taught that when something is spoken about in the future or past, it is also a ghost *in the moment*. In other words, you can't talk about something that is not present in some form now.

She said that to notice the past in the moment, it's important not only to listen to the person's words, but also to tune into the person's behavior and signals. What is the person's tone of voice? How is he or she sitting? What is the person's posture? How does he or she interact with you?

Dona Carletta mentioned a man who says he can't quite get anything done in life and is unable to make enough money. He said that at one time he was artistic and had lots of creativity. He had been a hippie who was free and spontaneous but now was trying to make it in the world. Dona Carletta asked us to imagine how this man interacts when he is with the therapist. After some discussion, she said that while this man is talking to his therapist, he seems to continually drift off into dreamy and tangential fantasies. It is hard to get him to focus on any issue. This frustrates the therapist!

Reminding us of the Big Flirt, Dona Carletta said that this *drifting off into fantasies* must be a meaningful aspect of his experience. What could this meaning be? Who is the ghost behind these signals? "Yes," she said, "It's the 'hippie' that he no longer identifies with! Now, what ghost could this be a reaction against?" She said that he might be reacting to a more traditional part of himself that wants him to settle down and get a job. If you help him get in contact with both sides of this process, he might be able to interact with them and find a solution to his everyday problems. Otherwise, this conflict continues unconsciously in the background and disturbs his ability to get along in life.

We identify with some aspects of ourselves and "edge out" others. She reminded us of Waldo. His "gruff" behavior was over the edge of his more accommodating primary process.

Ghosts and Holograms

Dona Carletta said that, as we've learned previously, ghosts appear in many different areas of our experiences and in various channels. Therefore, in various sections of the intake chart, we can begin to see ghosts emerging. A ghost is like a hologram whose pattern repeats itself in many areas of our lives.

Recalling Waldo, his ghost appeared in the form of his *body posture*, in the *other people in his dreams*, in the *gruffness of his voice,* in *the way he shirks off suggestions*, in *what others say about him*, and so on.

She also mentioned a woman who has a pain in her stomach, which she describes as intense and burning. In relationships, she is often involved with people who, she feels, are *too intense.* She also dreams about a *fire* that is out of control.

A Woman's Ghost

She went further and said, "Imagine this situation. A woman comes to you and says: 'My father put me down a lot.' As she says this, you notice that her head is hanging down a bit. The client continues to speak and says, 'I do such stupid things sometimes. Oh, I feel so bad.'"

Dona Carletta said that we can talk about her father in the past or in the future and that could be very helpful. But she also asked, "Where is the ghost of that father now? Can you find it?" She reminded us that this woman identifies as the *victim* of that nasty father. Therefore, we must search for the ghost of her "father" in her secondary body signals, in her speech, and in her dreams. Because of her own propensity for artwork and creativity, Dona Carletta encouraged us to draw a picture of this woman and where the ghost might be. One of the students drew the picture below. The student clarified the following:

Body Posture: "We see that the ghost of the father is *implied* in her body posture. The woman is feeling bad and slumped over, while there is another figure or experience that is *putting* her head and body down." "Right," Dona Carletta said. "A useful concept here is that every posture and movement has two parts: One of

Woman feeling put down by her father

them is more obvious and primary, while the other is more implied and invisible—but we can imagine it if we try hard enough!"

Verbal Language: The student continued, "At the same time, the 'father' also appears in an unclaimed hidden form when the woman says, 'I do such stupid things sometimes.' The woman identifies as the victim of that father, but the father's opinions infiltrate her description of herself—'I do such stupid things.' In fact, the one speaking in this moment *is* the father!" Dona Carletta said this was correct and went on to reveal other areas in which this ghost appears.

Dreams, Relationships, Body Symptoms: She told us that if we were to do an intake chart, we would discover that this woman *dreams* of figures who put her down. She is frequently involved in *relationships* with people who are mean to her and with whom she does not know how to get along. Dona Carletta added that we could guess that the woman might have a *body symptom* that expresses a similar type of energy as the critic—perhaps an intense and pointed pain in her stomach.

Ghost Stories

Dona Carletta always loves hearing ghost stories and said that we can also create them! By listening to one of the person's sentences or by noticing someone's posture, you can imagine the larger *ghost story* in which this sentence or posture is embedded—that is, the larger story surrounding that experience.

For example, in the case of this particular woman, you might imagine a story about a parent who had been hurtful to a child and a child who is feeling downed. Dona Carletta said that, although our stories may not be completely accurate, they do give us a possible understanding of the larger system in which that experience is unfolding, and we can always check this out with our client.

Ghost Hangouts

Dona Carletta said that there are many ways to discover ghosts, depending on our given style. She outlined the following areas in which ghosts can be found:

Verbal Language: Listen to what the person says, and identify the ghosts in those aspects of language that are expressed in passive terms and with which the person doesn't identify, such as: "The *dog bit* me," or "My *partner said* this or that." Watch for ghosts in vocal double signals, such as a person saying he is very depressed while having a strong and upbeat voice. Listen to gossip about *others*.

Sometimes the ghost is an implied figure who is not directly represented in the story. For example, when a client tells a story about someone hurting her as a child, a ghost role might be a loving parent who stood up for and cared for the child. Try to imagine the *implied* figures in stories.

You can also notice ghosts in especially strong or exaggerated expressions or behavior. For example, a man says, "I have to stand up for myself and not let people walk all over me!" His emphatic statement implies that he is being so strong because there is a ghost—someone, or an entire culture—to which he is reacting. The signal is so strong because there is something he is fighting, something that is holding him back. The interaction between these parts will be important.

Posture and Movement: Look for ghosts that are implicit in someone's body posture. Remember the example of the person who is feeling upset, slumps down to the floor, and leans against a few pillows on the wall. The pillows are the ghost role, the comforter.

Watch for ghosts in movement. For example, if a person's shoulders seem tense and occasionally rise upward slightly, there might be another (implied) figure that the shoulders are pressing up against; perhaps someone or something is holding or pressing the person down or in.

Dreams: Notice the secondary figures in dreams, that is, the figures we do not identify with, such as in a dream in which cats are meowing loudly or in which a schoolteacher is giving a class.

Relationships: Listen to the kinds of relationship situations or problems the person tends to get into, such as, "Those other people are really loving to me," or "Those people get on my nerves, they are always asking me to do more than I want to do." The *other* people are ghosts.

Body Symptoms and Experiences: Notice those aspects of body symptoms with which the person does not identify. Remember that there are always two parts to a symptom, one that is closer to and one that is further away from our identities.

For example, a person walks into your office. He is very shy, but he manages to say that he is claustrophobic in such small rooms. Who or what is the ghost? An imaginative mind might realize that there are two parts to claustrophobia. One is the part that *is being closed in,* and the man seems to identify with this part; *the* other part is the *walls* that are closing him in—the walls are the ghost.

Dona Carletta recalled working with someone who said he was claustrophobic. She said to the man that, if it was OK with him, she would very slowly come toward him like the wall that is closing him in. All the while, she encouraged the man, at the same time, to notice his tiny reactions and to follow them. The man agreed. As she very slowly began to approach and close him in, the man realized how often he feels trapped and closed in by societal standards and how he would like to break out more often and be more of an individual. The focus of the session then turned toward the conflict between these two parts, until the man was able to find a satisfying resolution.

Interaction and Feedback: One of the places that ghosts can be found is in the subtle feedback between the therapist and client. Dona Carletta said that we need special feeling sensors to notice ghosts during interactions.

Think of a man who said: "My mother never wanted me. She tried to get rid of me." (He then continues) "You know, I have these amazing experiences and incredible ideas about creative work that I want to do." The therapist tried to intervene and encourage the man to unfold his creative ideas and inner experiences in the moment. However, the client seemed to change the subject. "Where is that (ghost) mother?" Dona Carletta asked and then answered, "She is the one who *changes the subject* and ignores his inner experience and creativity in each unfolding moment."

Imagine that someone dreams about a person who falls into a deeply unconscious state. As you interact with the person, he begins to tell you about relationship issues but pauses between words and does not complete his sentences. If you ask the person to focus on the pauses, you may discover the "unconscious" state from his dream. Perhaps he needs to drop out and follow his inner experiences instead of focusing outwardly.

Your Feeling Reactions: You can find ghosts not only in the signals you see on the outside but also in your own *feeling reactions* while you are with someone. She reminded us of our learning about the Big Flirt. She continued with other examples.

Think of someone who calls you up and says he needs help. He asks you a thousand questions about your qualifications. You start to feel insecure and afraid that you won't be up to working with him. Who could the ghost be? In this case it could be a judge or evaluator, the part of this man that is critical and discerning. In fact, this person normally feels quite fearful of others and does not have access to his own power and critical mind. Instead, these parts appears as a secondary ghost that the therapist notices and reacts to through *her* feelings. Dona Carletta said that this type of interaction has to do with dreaming up, a concept she would speak about more fully in a later class (see Chapter 18). In any case, it's most helpful to ask yourself, "What part of the person's process might I be experiencing?"

To have a sense of how your feelings can help you discover roles and ghosts, Dona Carletta led everyone briefly through the following inner experience:

1. Ask yourself: What strong feelings do you have when you are near a particular client who is difficult for you?
2. Imagine two different roles that make up that experience, such as a fearful person and a powerful person.
3. From your previous knowledge of your client, consider how these two roles may be part of her or his process, or even yours!

Other Ghosts: As mentioned earlier, ghosts also appear in those things a client does when you turn your back or take your focus off him or her. Or, the ghost may appear suddenly as a painting on your wall that catches the person's attention.

Dona Carletta said there are innumerable ways to work with ghosts. For the moment, she is mainly presenting ghostbusting ideas and will speak about methods later. She encouraged us to turn to one another and briefly try the following exercise before closing for the evening.

Exercise
Finding Ghosts (in pairs):

1. One person begins to talk about her or his life, work, problems, and the like.
2. After a few minutes, the helper should try to notice any ghosts from the categories just mentioned that have appeared in the person's language or behavior.
3. Now try to unfold one of these ghosts in any way that you, the helper, and the person choose.
4. Together, relate the process that unfolded back to the person's life situation and problems.

Notes

1. For more on group theory and ghosts, see Arnold Mindell, *The Year One* (New York: Penguin-Arkana, 1989); *The Leader as Martial Artist* (Portland, Oregon: Lao Tse Press, 2000); *Sitting in the Fire* (Portland, Oregon: Lao Tse Press, 1995); and Martha Sanbower, "Deep Democracy: A Learning Journey" (Thesis for the diploma program, Process Work Center of Portland, Portland, Oregon, 2000).
2. H. W. L. Poonja.

Chapter Ten

Symbolic Thinking

Translating symbolic words and behavior into everyday language can be of great help in understanding a person's process.

When everyone returned to class the next day, Dona Carletta said she was a bit worn out from her discussion of ghosts and that she wanted to retreat into the other world for a while. She entrusted us to her colleague Hermonculous Hinkelmeyer. Hermie, as she fondly called him, was an inter- cross-planetary therapist. She said he had cooked up all kinds of important ideas that were crucial to our studies. She said she trusted him completely, and then she took off into thin air.

Standing in front of us was something that looked like a person, but it could also have been an animal. No one was sure. Hermie was pretty hairy looking. It was hard to see his mouth or eyes, but occasionally a glimmer of light appeared from the area where the eyes normally would be, and sometimes a great nose appeared out of the thick matting of hair that surrounded that area of his face. No one ever saw his mouth, but a booming voice emanated from somewhere beneath the nose. At first, his ideas seemed too far out for anyone to believe. However, this feeling changed as he began to deliver clear and detailed concepts.

Translation

Because Hermie heralded from another planet and worked throughout the universe, he was excited about the concept of translation. He said, in fact, that one of the most important faculties a person, or any type of being, could have in the coming millennium is the power of translation. To fully understand one another from different planets, and even to understand an individual coming from *this* planet Earth, a full understanding of translation is necessary.

He said that he was not only referring to the ability to translate from one *verbal* language to another, as the mixture of people from various earthly countries required, but *also,* as we had learned previously, the ability to translate between *different language or channel modalities,* such as *verbal* expression to *movement, movement* to *relationships*, and so forth. He said that we had also already studied how one small pattern of a given individual's process reveals itself in many dreamlike ways, through the various channels. These are all types of translation systems.

Hermie said that another supreme form of translation is *symbolic thinking*. In this and the following lesson (see Chapter 11), he would speak about this vital concept.

Symbolic Thinking

The very basis of symbolic thinking is the ability to *translate* or *interpret* symbolic, dreamlike material into ordinary everyday terms. He said this is one of the greatest cornerstones of case supervision. This tool is well known in many therapeutic forms, particularly in relationship to dreamwork:

Symbolic, dreamlike material → everyday life

Hermie said that there are many books you can read which tell you about the symbolic interpretation of dream figures and images.[1] Some symbols are commonly known, such as a bird representing the visionary or fanciful part of a person. Eagle always said that the best method of interpretation is to get associations from the person with whom you are working. However, Eagle warned, when asking for associations from clients, don't be satisfied with a *definition*—which is a common *description* of a symbol—but strive for associations that have an emotional quality attached to them.

If you hear a dream and don't know any of the dream's associations, collective symbolic understanding may be helpful, insofar as you check out how this information connects with what you know about the person's experiences, the information on the intake chart, and, most important, the client himself or herself. Hermie cautioned that we never forget the basic principle, that no matter what your translation or interpretation, the client's *feedback* is of *primary* importance. In other words, always check out your assumptions with your client to see whether they are right for him or her.

Hermie told us about one of his friends, Marvie, who dreamt one night about water and chocolate. She had been feeling a bit critical of her writing that day and felt pushed to finish a chapter that she was working on for a book. Hermie said that, if you were to translate this dream of water and chocolate in a very simplistic way (without finding out Marvie's associations, and obviously, without enough detail) into ordinary terms, you might say that she needs to get in contact with her fluidity in writing and a loving, sweet attitude toward herself and her work. Hermie told this idea to Marvie, and she gave positive feedback to his interpretation, concurring with that understanding.

Hermie quickly shook his head as if he were trying to get the hair away from his eyes, but the hair didn't move and he simply continued. He told the class that one of the keys of process work is not only to think intellectually about symbols but also to recognize their *living* manifestation in a person's behavior. Hermie said that while Marvie was speaking about her writing difficulties, she slightly stroked one of her hands with the fingers of her other hand. Hermie mentioned this signal to Marvie, but she was not aware of doing it. He explained to us that this was a double signal with which she was not identified. Hermie then encouraged Marvie to focus on her hand motions and discover what these motions were trying to express. After a minute or so, Marvie realized that stroking her hand was a way of caring for herself. Hermie clarified that this was the way the "chocolate" in her dream was manifesting in the moment. As Marvie continued to focus on this comforting feeling, she began to have a more open and loving attitude toward her work.

Hermie then stressed that a process worker, therefore, does not only look at verbal material symbolically, but regards *all* secondary dreaming material (such as body signals, posture, and double signals) as meaningful, symbolic experiences. Everything that is unknown, surprising, incomplete, unusual, or disturbing is part of this dreaming or symbolic world.

Symbolic Interpretation

Before going further, Hermie said that symbolic thinking is important for therapists—or anyone, really—for the following reasons:

1. The ability to understand symbolic material can help us gain an overview of a person's process. In turn, seemingly nonsensical or dreamlike behavior, dream symbols, or symbolic experiences can be more deeply understood by translating and understanding them in the context of the person's overall process and ordinary life.
2. Many people come to a therapist hoping that she or he will be able to interpret symbolic experiences they are having. Therefore, this is an important skill for therapists.
3. Symbolic thinking can be very helpful when working with individuals in extreme states, or with children, because the type of imagery and expressions that the person uses might be hard to understand unless you can use translation and symbolic thinking.
4. The ability to think symbolically can help the therapist notice how dream images also appear in the moment in a person's behavioral signals.

Hermie explained that, to use symbolic thinking, there is one crucial *metaskill* (feeling attitude) that we need. This is the feeling that symbolic information is always meaningful, although it might be hard to understand at first. It is important to approach symbolic information with an open and generous attitude, a feeling that what the person is doing symbolically is something that he or she needs in some form, although it may not yet be accessible to the person's conscious mind.

Creating Symbolic Material

Many in the class squirmed uncomfortably. One brave soul admitted that she had never felt able to think symbolically, and heads nodded in relieved concurrence. Therefore, Hermie developed a fun way to learn symbolic thinking. He was convinced that the only way you could understand it is if you first get in contact with the ability to *create* symbolic behavior and images! If you can create symbolic material, then you will more easily understand it. He said the following examples would also help us sense the way in which symbolic material arises in various channels, not only in our dreams.

Example One

After a brief pause in which he seemed deep in thought, Hermie stroked his matted hair and said, "Let me present a person's experience in life and then ask you to imagine any type of *symbolic behavior* that might express that life experience."

> ***Person's experience → symbolic behavior***
>
> *Pretend that you are a second-grade child. You started school early, have pressure from your parents to grow up fast, and your parents pay attention mostly to your younger sibling. If you were this child but couldn't express your needs directly, how might you express your needs in some other symbolic way? What type of symbolic behavior can you imagine?*

Some answers from the group: "I might begin to smash my toys as a symbolic expression of my anger toward my mother." "I might resist learning to read." All of these behaviors express the need to be loved and taken care of as child. Symbolic behavior expresses an experience that is otherwise forbidden or unable to be communicated directly.

Example Two

Hermie was pleased with our answers. Now he said that he wanted to try a second method. He asked us to *create a dream* in which there are images and events that symbolically express the following:

> *A very sensitive and feeling man feels that he has to be smart and assertive when going for a job interview, that to be successful he must conceal his sensitivity.*

Many people in the group came up with creative dream ideas. One person imagined a dream in which this man is in his high school and has to take a test. As he struggles to answer the test questions, a little kitten crawls up beside him and curls up near his feet. The teacher gets angry with him because this kitten has distracted his attention. Hermie applauded this student's creativity with symbolic material. He then said that, in reality, this man dreamt that he bought a cookbook. Then he went to a lecture in which the Dalai Lama was present. But the Dalai Lama left when a very intellectual woman spoke strongly against him.

The man told Hermie that he loved cooking, that it made him feel very warm and heartful and that he liked to cook for many people. He also said that the Dalai Lama was an impressive, kind, and spiritual leader.

Hermie said that the dream expressed, symbolically, that this man is a very kind and feeling person and that he should value that kindness as an important and spiritual way of being in the world—and that that way of being will have a beneficial influence on others. The dream also shows that the feeling and spiritual part of him gets upset when he tries to be too intellectual and ignores this part of his basic nature.

Hermie said that many people tell this man he is a very feeling and deep person. They see his secondary process. However, he puts himself down because he feels he can't make it if he is this way in the ordinary, intellectual world. He came from a very intellectual family in which feelings and spiritual values were disavowed as unnecessary and even foolish.

Example Three

Third, Hermie continued with the following thought experiment:

> *Imagine that you have been hurt, not cared for, and abandoned. You no longer have contact with your parents. You come to your therapist's office and do something. What might you do?*

One person said, "I pick up a stuffed animal in the therapist's office and start to care for it." Hermie said this was one good guess. The person would be expressing the need for love and caring, which is projected onto that stuffed animal.

Symbolic Translation

Now Hermie wanted to reverse modes and encourage us to try another aspect of symbolic thinking, translation. A sparkle of light flashed suddenly from underneath his hair, in the area that would normally be reserved for the eyes, as he bellowed out, "Now I will give you some symbolic verbal sentences, body signals, behavior, interactions, and dream images, and I want you to try to *interpret or translate* these experiences in terms of everyday life as best you can."

Symbolic, dreamlike material → everyday life

He said that he would only give us a tiny bit of information, just enough to stimulate our thinking, not to represent the fullness of any one person or process. To truly understand symbolic material, you would have to ask the person his or her experience of that material and know the context from which it is coming. Instead, Hermie said to think of these examples as brainteasers to develop our symbolic thinking potential. He stressed that no one answer is right. It was just a fun way to experiment and practice.

Verbal Statements

To begin, Hermie told us to consider the following verbal, symbolic statements and to try to imagine the meaningful purpose behind them. He said that, for the moment, he would not expand on methods and ways of interacting in such situations (he would leave that to other teachers) but simply enjoyed stimulating our thinking. He mentioned that sometimes people come out with funny statements when they are either in consensual, or in altered or extreme, states of consciousness. In any case, the basic point is to try to understand these brief sentences in a symbolic way: to translate them into something that can be understood in everyday terms. These phrases, in other words, are doorways to the dreaming, or what Eagle calls *dreamdoors.* He said that the interpretations that we come up with are simply one possibility amongst many and that their validity depends entirely upon the client's process and feedback.

1. *"I feel I want to take my head off sometimes."*
   One answer: This person feels too intellectual and needs to drop the thinking part sometimes and follow his or her body or feelings.
2. *"I feel I'm just one small point in the universe."*
   One answer: This might indicate a sense of humility, of not taking oneself so seriously.
3. *"I have an altered sense of myself: I saw myself in different books."*
   One answer: The person needs an outside view of himself or herself.
4. *"I have to clean things very exactly."*
   One answer: This person is in the middle of an awareness meditation and needs to appreciate this process, meditating on each experience in great detail.
5. *"I'm Jan, Jill, Sue, and Peter ..."*
   One answer: The person's ordinary identity may be limited. In one such instance, Hermie said to the person, "Don't ever be so limited again!"
6. (Client says to therapist) *"I have no money, but could I still come for an appointment next week?"*

One answer: The person has many needs that she or he is unable to express. You might ask, "What else do you need? Say all the things you need and that you are shy to speak about."

7. *"I feel out of my body."*
   One answer: This could signify that the person experiences himself or herself as out of her ordinary primary experience of her body and is feeling in touch with a secondary, altered-state experience.

Body Signals

Hermie now asked us to try to understand *body signals* symbolically. Here you have to *imagine into* the body signals, seeing perhaps the whole story surrounding someone's posture or gestures, as Dona Carletta outlined in Chapter 9, and translate those signals into everyday terms.

"A helpful method of thinking symbolically," Hermie said, "is to take one signal and go really far with it: to *dream into it.* Where would it go in the future if it were allowed to unfold in a meaningful way? Imagine that it is a symbolic seed of an important process the person is flowing toward."

Hermie anticipated some of our reactions and added, "It may seem strange that all of these symbolic interpretations are so *positive!* In essence, the basic idea is that what a person is doing is potentially meaningful even though it may seem unusual or strange to begin with. Our task is to see the *diamond in the rough*, so to speak." "As always," he concluded, "check out your perception with your client. Once again, the following are simply guesses as to the meaning of certain signals.

He told us to try to interpret the following body signals in symbolic terms:

1. *A person sits up military-straight and is very exact and incisive in the way he uses his words.*
   Symbolic interpretation: This may be indicative of a very dedicated way of being. Perhaps this is the beginning of a Zen Buddhist process of being one-pointed and exact.

2. *A person has diarrhea and worries about death.*
   Symbolic interpretation: This may be an expression of freedom and letting go of what has become passé.
3. *A man talks a lot but does not seem to listen to what you say, even though he is asking for your help.*
   Symbolic interpretation: If you do not merely listen to the words, but also watch the form of communication, his behavior might point to the need to *not* look at or listen to others. He may be *too* open to feedback. You might recommend that he not look at or notice feedback from others and focus intently on himself and his inner experiences.
4. *A person starts tearing at her clothes and ripping things apart.*
   Symbolic interpretation: This could mean ripping away all that cloaks the heart: the need to go deeply and not stay on the surface.

Behavioral Interactions

Hermie continued to quiz us on symbolic thinking, now focusing on behavioral interactions between the client and therapist:

1. *While interacting with a client, you notice that the person is always analyzing you.*
   Symbolic interpretation: The "analyst" and "clear thinker" in this person may need support.
2. *A person is shy and always brings you chocolate.*
   Symbolic interpretation: This person may have a lot of feelings about you and may be shy to express them. Ask more about them.

Your Reactions

Hermie reminded us, as we've learned earlier, that you can also look at your own dreamlike reactions to a client as symbolic behavior that can provide you with a lot of information:

A therapist gets tired every time she sees a particular client; exhaustion is also a major symptom of the client.

Symbolic interpretation: This "tired" feeling of the therapist may indicate a need to lower the mental level of the interactions, dropping out of the mind and perhaps going into dreaming instead of analytical thinking.

To end his discussion, Hermie wanted to throw in a fun exercise that might help ease our fears about symbolic thinking. He said if nothing else, we would enjoy this exercise because it has to do with being a child. Many people were relieved because they were trying so hard to be adults and to learn the material and were exhausted.

Hermie said that this is the best way he knows to practice symbolic thinking because just about everything a child does is symbolic, is part of the dreaming process. He encouraged us to try this with a partner.

Exercise
Symbolic Thinking and Being a Child (in pairs)

1. One person discusses his or her problems or issues with a partner.
2. The same person begins to act like a young child or baby. The partner follows, interacting and playing with that "child" in any way that he or she likes.
3. After five minutes, discuss the type of symbolic play or behavior that the "child" engaged in.
4. Together, try to think symbolically and, assuming that this symbolic material is meaningful, try to:
   a. Interpret what that symbolic experience might *mean* for that person's ordinary life.
   b. Find out whether the symbolic behavior provides some kind of answer or solution to the person's original discussion about problems and issues in his or her life.

Notes

1. See Arnold Mindell, *Dreambody* (Portland, Oregon: Lao Tse Press, 1998). Also, Hermie recommends Hans Biedermann, *Dictionary of Symbolism: Cultural Icons and the Meanings Behind Them* (trans., James Hulbert, New York: Penguin (Meridian), 1994).

Chapter Eleven

The Holographic Bottom Line How Life Comes from One Detail

When you know some aspects of a person's process, it is possible to guess about other elements that are unknown, thereby gaining a greater overview.

Hermie was on a roll. The next evening he appeared, hair and all, but this time with glasses that were placed over his matted hair. Though his appearance was absurd to most, the glasses did give him an air of wisdom and intellect. He said he wanted to extend the whole idea of symbolic thinking to the concept of *extrapolation*. He first spoke about the reason he got so interested in translation, symbolic thinking, extrapolation, and also Dona Carletta's concept of ghosts. One night he was visiting Eagle's case supervision class and a therapist started to talk about a client. After she had presented a few pieces of information, Eagle asked the group, "How do you think this person will appear when he comes in the door? Take a guess." Hermie was shocked. How was it possible to know *anything* at this point, with so little information? Another time, a therapist spoke about and then showed the behavior of one of her clients. After a few minutes Eagle asked everyone to imagine what the client dreamed.

Eagle was using extrapolation, that is, the ability to notice the structure behind one aspect of a person's experience and then imagine how that structure expresses itself in other areas of the person's life. A student asked Hermie why it would be important to do this. Hermie said he would explain this in just a moment.

Connecting the Dots

Hermie reminded us that the intake chart helps us connect elements of the person's life that seem unrelated and thereby gain an overview of the process. He noted how the ability to connect one area of the person's experience to another is like the children's game in the United States called "connect the dots." In that game there are a few dots on a piece of paper. You are supposed to try to connect the dots. As you do this, a coherent picture begins to form.

As therapists, we frequently know a few of the dots (pieces of information), but others are missing. From these pieces of information we can discern the deep structure of the process and then can *guess* about other aspects we do not know about. For example, if you know the person's problems, their relationship difficulties, and body symptoms, that information and the structure of the process contained within them may help you guess what the person is dreaming.

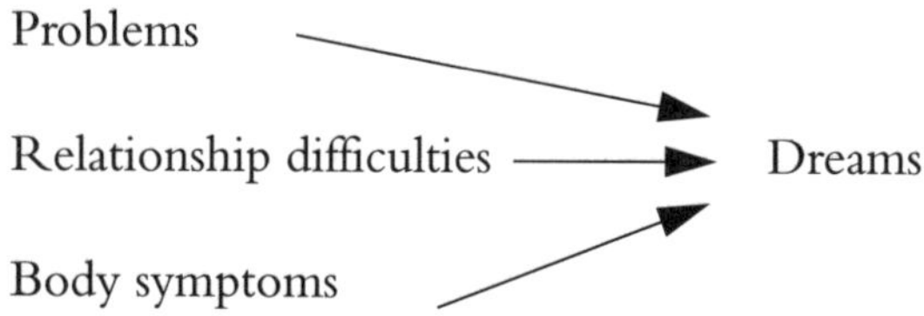

Or, if you know the person's dreams, you can guess how the deep structure behind that dream might manifest, for example, in the person's momentary behavior, symptoms, addictions, or relationships.

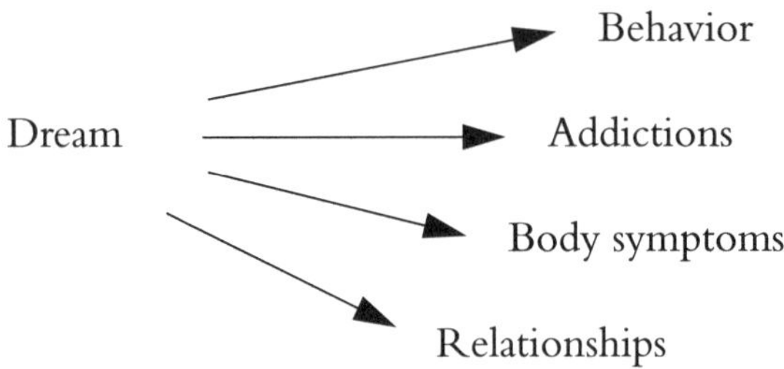

Extrapolating from One Signal

Hermie knew that this sounded a bit mechanical, and of course it is. No human being is that simple, nor should a person be looked at in such a presumptive way! But practicing extrapolation is a good way to develop the ability to imagine the wider context of a person's life situation and can be helpful when symbolic thinking is needed. He said that a long-term, experienced therapist automatically fills in empty elements of the chart because years of practice inform her or him about typical patterns and experiences people go through, but you can also gain this insight through extrapolation practice.

Example: Extrapolating from a Dream

"Enough abstract theory," Hermie said. "Let's look at an example." He told us to imagine one of his clients, a woman who is frequently depressed and feels badly about herself. This woman dreamed that she was lying on a couch, feeling depressed. She reached over, took a pair of scissors, and was going to stab herself. "Wow," someone said, "that's a powerful dream!"

"Yes," said Hermie. "Before extrapolation, let's use our symbolic thinking and interpret the image of the scissors. Why scissors?" he asked. "What is the difference between *scissors* and a *knife*?" After some discussion, we decided that a knife represents the quality of directness and incisiveness. Scissors, on the other hand, are associated with cutting, with cutting something out. Further discussion led to the thought that this woman might be cutting out her inner critic and the depression associated with it.

Hermie said, "Let's say, for simplicity, that this is the case. Now let's begin to extrapolate. Imagine that this woman comes to see you in therapy. How might this underlying process manifest in her behavior?"

One student said that this woman might behave and speak in a depressed way. "What else?" prodded Hermie. After some pondering, another student said that the woman would show some kind of double signal that would express the experience of something being *cut out,* but the student didn't know just *how* that "cutting out" would express itself.

Another student suggested that the cutting-out signal might appear in her suddenly wanting to change the subject and not talk about her depressing state. Another imagined something that might happen when she is at home; she might feel badly and then suddenly have the urge to go to the movies. Hence, the "cutting-out" process would happen unconsciously. Someone else said that while she is with the therapist, she might suddenly forget what she is saying or get distracted by something else.

Hermie said that was actually what happened. During one session, the woman told him that she was feeling badly and just couldn't get away from being so depressed. After some discussion, the woman became distracted by the sound of birds outside Hermie's office window. In a fleeting comment she mentioned how beautiful the sounds were. When Hermie asked her to focus on that momentary distraction, the bird sounds, she started to smile. She loved meditating on the sounds. To her, the tones were innocent and natural. She changed states of consciousness, and with Hermie's help, she began to unfold this experience of innocence and naturalness by feeling it in her body and expressing it in hand motions.

Unfolding this "distraction" gave her a sense of relief, a sense of having no pressure to do anything or perform for anyone. She loved this state and felt she needed it desperately in her life. She said that ordinarily, she was constantly trying to please people and act properly. If she did not live up to these expectations, she criticized herself and became depressed.

Hermie reminded us of the dream and clarified that this woman was now at the point of the dream where she "dies" (stabbing herself), in the sense of dropping her primary identity, altering her state of consciousness, and allowing new experiences to surface.

Hermie encouraged us to now extrapolate and imagine what *other* aspects of this woman's life are like—those we do not yet know about. One student spoke about *addictive* tendencies the woman might have. This person imagined that the woman might tend toward something like alcohol that might help her relax and drop the sense of pressure. Someone else guessed that she might have an addiction to sweets, an unconscious way of loving herself and cutting out her bitter negativity. A great deal of fatigue was mentioned as a *body symptom* that could be the beginning of an attempt to drop out of her ordinary identity. Another person said that she might end up in *relationships* where people are really mean to her (mirroring her inner critic), or with lighthearted people who are fun and loving, or both. Perhaps she really enjoys being with children!

Hermie asked us to guess the *age* of this woman. One person said she was probably middle-aged because it seemed as though she was in the midst of a midlife crisis, a time in which she is beginning to drop her long-worn identity and attachment to the consensual world and allow new experiences to arise. Hermie said that was accurate.

Hermie then challenged everyone to go one more step with extrapolation. He asked us to imagine this woman's *future* and long-term process. "If she is able to pick up this process of *cutting out* her inner criticism and the pressure to perform, and is able to integrate some of that naturalness into her life, what might her future look like?" After brainstorming for a while, one student said that later in life, this woman might be very detached and even shamanic, meaning that she is able to drop her identity, make rapid state changes, and follow her spontaneous impulses. She might be able to do this in the world and be a healer or therapist herself. Hermie thought that was a clever extrapolation.

He adjusted his glasses, which seemed to have fallen down about four inches on his face, and made the following drawing on the board to summarize some of the these extrapolations:

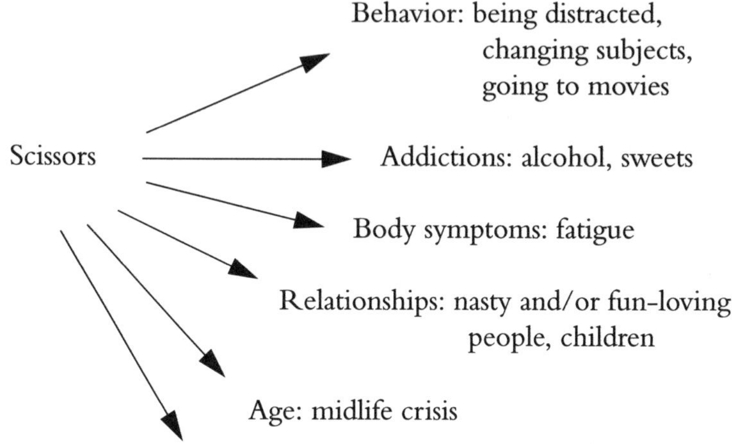

Hermie could not resist throwing one more element into the pot, although it would be discussed more fully in a later class (see Chapter 17). He wanted to focus on a *process-oriented interpretation* of the woman's dream. Process-oriented dream interpretation describes the *flow* of process that is expressed in the dream, rather than producing a static interpretation or prescription. Hermie said that he might interpret the dream to the woman as follows: "You will notice that you get depressed because of inner criticism and pressures to perform. Then notice how something new and spontaneous comes up and cuts out these feelings. If you stay with the distraction and follow it, it will help you change identities and gain access to new experiences, to your free and natural state."

Extrapolating from a Body Symptom

Now Hermie wanted to challenge us with one more example in which we would begin with a body symptom. This example, he felt, revealed the importance of extrapolation and how it can help fill in elements of the person's past and potential future.

In one of Dona Carletta and Eagle's seminars on chronic symptoms, they gave an exercise in which people were supposed to feel their body symptom, express the symptom energy with their hands, and then unfold that experience until they discovered what the symptom energy was trying to express. During the exercise, Eagle helped a woman who said, in an uneasy tone, that she was stuck and didn't know how to go further. She said that she was focusing on a cramp in her stomach. Eagle asked her what this cramp was like, and she made a tight fist with one of her hands. She said, in a distraught tone, that she didn't know what the fist meant and was unable to go further. Eagle realized that she was unable to unfold that experience further and instead he interpreted the experience for her by guessing at its underlying structure. He said, "You are a really powerful woman but have never been supported in it!"

What did he do? Eagle noticed that the woman had an edge to the "fist" experience; she was shy about it and was unable to go further. Eagle put together her tone of voice, which sounded quite distraught, with what he imagined was contained in the fist experience. He imagined that her primary process had to do with being a heartful woman who might sometimes feel incapable of doing things she deemed harsh or tough. Her secondary process, expressed in her fist, he imagined, represented a lot of certainty and strength.

Finally, Eagle extrapolated and put the whole process in a larger framework. He imagined the (ghost) story surrounding this signal and said, "Gee, you normally are a very kind person and may feel a bit weak at times, but part of you is very strong." He continued to imagine into her past, "You probably never had anyone in your family or culture support the strength in you, but I do."

The woman said that he was right, that she is a heartful and loving person and has never been supported to feel like a strong individual who is certain of her beliefs. Eagle imagined further into this woman's future and, trying to be open to both sides of her, said that if she were able to identify with some of her strength, she could be a person who could stand strongly for her principles about love.

Hermie reminded us, of course, that the key is *feedback*. If you get negative feedback, you are off track. In this case, the woman was delighted. She felt seen and understood, even though Eagle didn't know anything at all about her life!

Hermie told us that he was getting hungry and wanted to go home for dinner. Before leaving, he presented the following exercise for us to try, at our leisure, which involves extrapolating into the future.

Exercise
Extrapolation and the Future (in pairs)

1. One person is the "client," one is the "helper." The client talks for a few minutes about herself, about her problems, and about the way in which she identifies herself.
2. The helper focuses on noticing something secondary in the client's verbal content or something that happens spontaneously, such as a quick gesture, change in voice tone, or body symptom. The helper should assist the client in unfolding one of these secondary signals until the client discovers what that signal is expressing.
3. Next, the helper tries to see how that secondary signal relates to the larger context of the person's ordinary identity and life, saying, for example, "Ordinarily, you feel like a person who is [fearful … confident … too passive … assertive, etc.], and this experience, "x," is trying to emerge." Try to imagine the story surrounding these experiences, as Eagle did above.
4. Now imagine the person's possible future. To do this, extrapolate from that secondary signal while incorporating the primary process. If the person could embrace that

signal and realize its message in a useful way in his or her life, while also integrating it with his or her primary identity, what might occur? What future development can you envision for that person?

5. Watch the client's feedback! If your imagination is not quite accurate, ask for the details of how to adjust that future vision so that it feels "on target" to the client.

Part Two

Introductory Methods for Working with People

Chapter Twelve

Basic Methods

Basic methods must always be adapted to the unique moment in time, the individual client, and the therapist's style.

While everyone waited for Dona Carletta to return from her vacation, Esmeeri, one of her colleagues, took over the "Basics" class. Now that we had studied the core concepts behind gathering information and the intake chart, Esmeeri started us out on the fundamentals of process approaches to working with people. Esmeeri was a musician and poet prone to going into deep trance states and looked forward to conveying the artistry beneath what sounds like dull, linear material.

A Few Crucial Factors

Esmeeri said she would go back to the beginning, to basic methods at the core of our knowledge. Once we are sure of these, we can build on them and ascertain more subtle approaches that can be adapted to particular situations. She reminded us that any method must be adapted to the particular client, therapist, and special moment in time, and must be carried out with the right feeling-attitude (*metaskill*). Above all, a sense of heartfulness was a crucial element behind any therapeutic method.

She then said that her overview of the basics would be brief and simple because there are many good sources for this information.[1] She excused those of us from the class who were already well informed about the basics but said we should come back to Dona Carletta's follow-up classes in which she presents more subtle approaches that grow out of these fundamentals. Most people stayed. She added that the kinds of things she will talk about are "*methods* or *approaches* for following the process." She liked these terms better than the term *intervention,* which has a technical and mechanical feeling to it.

She also said that all of the methods we would study in the upcoming classes were not carved in stone, not facts or firm procedures. Instead, they are meant to stimulate all of us in our creative exploration of the flow of process. She added that she is not always able to use or remember all of the many skills that she and others will present, not at all! Most students were relieved to hear this! Esmeeri said that the point is not to remember every single detail, but instead to enjoy the process of learning, to be stimulated by the beauty of process, and to incorporate the various methods we would be studying as they arise naturally in the flow of our work.

Esmeeri began by talking about a strong dream she'd had in the night about a river. She reminded us of Dona Carletta's description of the client and therapist who ride together down the river's currents. The basis of process work is following this stream of nature. As Esmeeri spoke, she seemed to go into a trance. Her arms began to rise up slowly to the side as if she were floating, suspended in the waters of that river, sensing its flow. A deep silence enveloped the room. Then she suddenly snapped out of it and began to speak.

Basic Concepts

"First of all," she said, "I want to reiterate some things that Dona Carletta has already spoken about and then add some new thoughts."

Process work, she said, is based on **sensory-oriented perception**. This refers to the *way* in which someone *perceives* and *experiences* his or her world through various sensory **channels,** the most common of which are the visual, auditory, proprioceptive (body feeling), and kinesthetic (movement). Eagle added the relationship and world channels to these.

She said that some channels are more *occupied* by our awareness and connected with our primary processes, while others are more *unoccupied*. Unoccupied channels are not used with awareness and are associated with our secondary processes. You can notice channels that are occupied or unoccupied by listening to language and descriptions of dreams. For example, one person dreamed that she was looking down a road and then suddenly sank into a swamp. Here, the visual channel is more occupied and the proprioceptive (sinking into the river) is more unoccupied.

Esmeeri said that our secondary experiences appear most often in the channels with which we are least familiar, the channels we use with least awareness. That is, if I am very visually and relationship oriented, my secondary experiences may appear in my body signals and movements.

Esmeeri reminded us that, when thinking about these basic concepts and approaches, it is the **metaskills** which underlie them that determine their effectiveness. Metaskills are the feeling attitudes or qualities that support and bring to life our ordinary skills. She stressed that the feeling with which we interact with clients is the most crucial part of our work. Important metaskills of process work include *compassion*, the sense of openness to, and respect for, all parts of the person; a *beginner's mind* that does not know what experiences mean but allows them to unfold with an open and curious heart; the *fluidity* to follow the unique flow of process; and the perceptual *precision* of a scientist.

She continued to outline basic concepts. A process worker notices **signals**—tiny bits of information in these channels—and attempts to embrace them in their respective channels. For example, a description of a headache as a sensation of heat in one part of the head is a proprioceptive experience. A person who describes a pounding sensation in the head and simultaneously makes pounding movements with her hand reveals that her process is happening in the kinesthetic channel.

The term **double signal** refers to the existence of two signals at once, one closer to, and one further away from, our awareness.

An important aspect of the work is **unfolding** signals that are further from our awareness. Esmeeri said that unfolding was really quite numinous and encouraged us to think of it in this way: "Imagine the way a seed unfolds into a plant, or the way a baby unfolds into a grown person. Unfolding is a natural process that flows from a seed or embryo toward its manifest expression."

She offered analogies from her music background. When writing music at the piano or writing a poem, she has an intuitive sense of the music as it naturally unfolds into a song or poem. She begins with a note or a few words and lets the sounds, the notes, the words, lead her into places she had not thought of before. It is as if the entire piece of artwork existed in embryonic form in the first note or word. Her job is simply to assist it to unfold further. She likened this to playing a role in the theater. A really good actor takes the skeletal lines of her or his part and unfolds them into the breadth and depth of a character.

Likewise, the therapist notices an initial signal, such as a slight, gentle movement of a person's hand. She then tries to follow and unfold that motion, which might express itself more fully as a blooming tree. Esmeeri showed this to us by gently moving her fingers, which were at her sides, and then her hands and arms began rising slowly upward and outward like a tree.

She reminded us that unfolding emerges from the momentary creativity of the client-therapist interaction. It may look very different from one moment to the next. At one time, unfolding may mean chatting with your client. At another, it may mean offering an analytical interpretation of a dream, focusing on an inner body feeling, or even progressing into a dance or storytelling.

A student asked, "How do you know whether you are really *on track* when you are unfolding something?" Esmeeri said, "What a good question. The sense of "being on track" is a very special *feeling,* as though events are generating and unraveling themselves naturally and spontaneously without having to work at it. At the same time, your client gives positive feedback (see "Feedback" later in this chapter) to what is occurring."

Esmeeri said that the main method of unfolding is **amplification**. That means, expanding the signal so that all its details—its full message and expression—can emerge. To understand amplification, she told us to imagine writing a simple musical tune. To amplify or embellish this tune, we might repeat it again, fill in the chords, add other instruments, create a symphony around it, add voices. You can sing the tune in a child's voice or in a rough voice or in the voice of a bear! You can improvise and create a whole new piece by following the "mistakes" you make.[2] There are endless possibilities.

Esmeeri told us to think about the following example of one of her clients, a woman who says in a longing way that she loves being in her garden. She says it is her only place for refuge. Her life is otherwise extremely hectic. When asked how she experiences "being in the garden," she says it gives her a feeling (proprioception) of quiet and peacefulness and a relaxed feeling in her head.

A therapist can further unfold the experience by asking her to feel that quiet and peaceful feeling *in other parts* of her body. This woman felt the experience in her head, then in her jaw, in her shoulders, chest, hips, and legs, and finally, in her whole body. She amplified this further by *adding other channels* to express that quiet experience more fully. She began to make *motions* that mirrored this sense of peacefulness, and simultaneously made humming *sounds*. A helpful question to ask at this point is, "Who is moving in that way? What figure is making these motions and sounds?" This woman said that she felt like a meditator—quiet, centered, peaceful, and loving toward others.

Esmeeri was excited to add one more method of unfolding this experience—storytelling.[3] She asked the woman to tell a story about this meditator: to imagine the context and environment in which the meditator lives, other figures who could be in that story, and how the story unfolds. Esmeeri even jumped in and used her own creativity to help the woman complete the story.

The woman imagined the following story. She was sitting on top of a mountaintop as the meditator. Many people came to her. She was very quiet and every so often, with no stress or tension, she offered a few words of wisdom. The client and therapist acted this out, and the woman felt very much at home and content. Finally, the woman imagined how she could bring that feeling of the meditator into her life, in her relationships and busy work situation.

Esmeeri continued, "If this woman had felt too shy to explore her experience further, we would say that she has gotten to an **edge.** This is the moment when a new aspect of a person's process arises, something outside of his or her identity, and the person is both excited and shy about it. *The edge is the boundary between primary and secondary processes.* At the edge, people frequently giggle and falter."

Esmeeri said that there are numerous ways to work with an edge. "One method has to do with *staying at the edge* and exploring the belief system that is against this new experience, such as, 'I cannot be so peaceful because I have too much to do! My life is hectic.' Another method is to ask the person to experiment with this new behavior as if she were a *child* who has a beginner's mind. You could also act out the new behavior for the person and ask her or him for advice as to how to unfold it further. Sometimes it is helpful to enter into the new state simultaneously with your client, so the person does not feel so alone in this new experience. Another helpful approach is to ask the person to get to the *essence,* the core or seed, of the secondary experience before it became so big. For example, the essence of of this woman's meditator might be a sense of "being-ness" or "presence." She might stay close to this deep essence while engaging in the many activities of her life. Think of someone who is pushing things away that are impinging upon him. When experienced in its most subtle form, this man said the essence of this experience was a very sensitive flower that moves ever so slightly when the breeze blows by. The essence is usually a more palatable form of an experience and is easier for the person's primary process to accept."[4]

She continued with a couple more concepts. As mentioned previously, **dreaming up** refers to the experience when a therapist unwittingly begins to act like an aspect of the client's process that is not yet directly represented. (See Chapter 18 for more on this topic.) In our current example, if the woman were not aware of her quiet, meditative nature, the therapist might suddenly become very peaceful and quiet but not know why.

Feedback is a cornerstone of process work and determines which current to ride on the river.[5] If you receive *positive feedback*, wherein the person looks upbeat and excited about your suggestion, you can trust that this is an open and natural current to pursue. *Negative feedback* means that the current you have chosen is not quite right, at least not in that moment. The person seems to lose energy and is not really interested in what you suggest. You may notice those moments when a client smiles at your suggestions but has a kind of slow and downbeat feeling, indicating that he or she is adapting to your recommendations but is actually saying no to the direction you are taking.

When *edge feedback* occurs, there is a lot of energy and a mixture of positive and negative signals. The person is saying "yes" *and* "no" simultaneously. You may notice excitement as well as fear and hesitation. The person frequently giggles, squirms, and sends out a multitude of conflicting signals. This is a dynamic and important moment to explore.

Esmeeri said that process work is based on the idea of respecting and supporting the *whole* process. This means bringing awareness to those parts of ourselves that we disavow, to the parts that are more known and closer to our identities, and to the relationship between them. The unknown parts rarely receive equal attention and therefore often are experienced as disturbing to our primary processes. Opening up to all of our experiences is a kind of inner **deep democracy**—Eagle's term for the metaskill of having an open and inclusive attitude toward all of the various parts inside and outside of ourselves.[6]

Esmeeri loves the aspect of process work that explores the unknown because it reminds her of her deepest mystic self. She recalled a time when Eagle worked with a woman who described a meditation experience involving a beautiful, silver river. She made gentle, undulating motions with her hands as she said this. She continued to describe other developments in her inner work. Eagle realized that the "silver river" experience was vivid but not complete. It was an aspect of her dreaming that was beginning to unfold but had not yet been explored. The woman said she was mesmerized by the river but didn't know what to do with it. Eagle encouraged her to hold her attention to that river a little bit longer and notice how it unfolds.

As she began to focus on the river, she again made the undulating hand motions and suddenly said, "I don't know where I am!" At that point, Eagle said, "Me either, wonderful not to know. Follow that!" Her primary process was confused because she was in the midst of an unknown experience in the movement channel, one of her unoccupied channels. Eagle said simply, "Don't know. The process will guide you!" As she continued, the woman sensed herself reaching out in time and then began to speak about timeless and eternal things that were very close to her heart, but with which she had lost contact.

It is especially hard to be deeply democratic when the secondary process is experienced as especially undesirable or distressing. Esmeeri mentioned a man who was very kind to others but was plagued by a mean and critical inner figure. After listening compassionately, Esmeeri told us she used her beginner's mind and said that she wanted to meet this awful figure. The man was at an edge, but after a few moments' pause, began to enact this nasty critic. Esmeeri challenged the figure and said that he was not nasty enough! She encouraged the figure to be less shy, and to really be critical and say what he feels is wrong with this man. The critic said that the man was too much of a weakling with people and didn't stand up for himself. At that point, the man started to laugh boisterously and agreed with the critic's suggestion! He needed access to the "critic's" strength and, at its core, inner certainty, just the qualities that seemed so awful in the beginning!

Esmeeri said that she wanted to mention just a little bit about **goals**. What is the ultimate goal of this work? She said there are as many answers to that question as there are people. However, she spoke of two goals: integration and awareness. **Integration** means discovering and then incorporating new aspects of ourselves into our lives. This is a behavioral goal. **Awareness,** the ever-increasing ability to notice and follow what is arising in a given moment, is a process goal. This goal is based on learning to use fluid awareness from moment to moment rather than focusing on specific behavioral change. Esmeeri said, "For example, in the situation I just mentioned, the critic is a momentary aspect of this man's experience. He could notice when this inner sense of strength and inner certainty is emerging while remaining open to other experiences also arising inside of him. For example, in one moment he feels a surge of the critic's strength and tries to open up to that part of himself and then, in a subsequent moment, noticing the compassionate side of him surfacing, he allows this kind part of himself to emerge as well.

Focusing on one goal or the other, or both, depends on the person and the particular moment in time. Eagle says that usually, as people grow older, they become closer to the awareness paradigm, in which they are more attached to awareness than to any particular goal or state.

The Next Chapters

Now it is time to venture forward from this groundwork of fundamentals. Esmeeri said that Dona Carletta had discovered through her case control studies that, although all methods are built on these basics concepts, it is not always possible to use them in their most elementary form. The wide variety of people and situations that we encounter demands the study of more subtle and differentiated means of implementing these approaches. The next class addresses some of these subtleties.

Notes

1. See Arnold Mindell, *Dreambody* (Portland, Oregon: Lao Tse Press, 1998); *River's Way* (London: Routledge & Kegan Paul, 1985); *Working with the Dreaming Body* (Portland, Oregon: Lao Tse Press, 2002); Amy Mindell, *Metaskills* (Portland, Oregon: Lao Tse Press, 2003); Joe Goodbread, *Dreambody Toolkit* (Portland, Oregon: Lao Tse Press, 1997); and various articles in *The Journal of Process Oriented Psychology.*
2. For more on a process-oriented way of working with music and musical "mistakes," see Lane Arye, *Unintentional Music: Releasing Your Deepest Creativity* (Charlottesville, Virginia: Hampton Roads, 2001).
3. For more on dreaming and co-storytelling, see Arnold Mindell, *The Dreammaker's Apprentice* (Charlottesville, Virginia: Hampton Roads, 2001).
4. For much more on the essence and sentient experience, see Arnold Mindell, *Dreaming While Awake* (Charlottesville, Virginia: Hampton Roads, 2000); *Quantum Mind* (Portland, Oregon: Lao Tse Press, 2000).
5. For more on feedback, see Randee Cathey, "The Dreaming Facilitator" (Thesis for the diploma program, Process Work Center of Portland, Portland, Oregon, 1998); Joe Goodbread, *Radical Intercourse: How Dreams Unite Us in Love, Conflict and Other Inevitable Relationships* (Portland, Oregon: Lao Tse Press, 1997).
6. For more on deep democracy, group theory, and practice, see Arnold Mindell, *The Year One* (New York: Penguin-Arkana, 1989); *The Leader as Martial Artist* (Portland, Oregon: Lao Tse Press, 2000); *Sitting in the Fire* (Portland, Oregon: Lao Tse Press, 1995); for more on group and community work, see Gary Reiss, *Changing Ourselves, Changing the World* (Tempe, Arizona: New Falcon, 2000).

Chapter Thirteen

Subtle Transpositions

When it is not possible to focus directly on problematic issues, subtle methods are required.

Dona Carletta returned from her vacation with renewed enthusiasm. She looked refreshed and raring to go. She said that, now that we were well versed in the basic methods, she wanted to discuss subtle aspects of unfolding the dreaming process. She said it is not always possible to follow the general methods of unfolding in the elemental form that her dear friend Esmeeri spoke about; subtler methods are frequently needed. Her fascination with these subtleties, she said, is one of the main reasons she created this entire series of classes.

"If you are unable to unfold experiences in the ways that you have learned until now, there are many other possibilities. Remember that the dreaming process expresses itself in myriad ways and offers many options. The skill and art of process work follows the unique and precious pathway that presents itself in a given situation," she said.

Transposing Music

One of the subtle approaches to unfolding that she liked she called *transposing,* a term she borrowed from the field of music and had learned from Esmeeri.[1] She explained that, if you try to sing a song in a particular key but it is too high or too low for your voice, you can *transpose* the key to be higher or lower in pitch so that it is easier to sing. The notes have the same relationship to one another but are sung in a different register or key. In other words, transposition means focusing on the same pattern but expressing it in a different position or area. She said that the most common method of transposing, which we have already studied, is *channel changing*; that is, transposing an experience from one channel into another channel.

Dona Carletta outlined two large categories of transposition that, because of her love of flying, she playfully called *zooming out* and *zooming in.*

Zooming Out

"For fun," she said, "imagine that your client is a pink flower and this flower has one bright red petal on it. Let's say that this redness is secondary and the flower is shy to identify with that red part of itself. To complicate matters, the flower feels uncomfortable if you look directly at its red petal. If you try to help the flower experience that redness directly, it will be uncomfortable and turn away. What can you do? How might you *transpose* this experience of "redness?"

Dona Carletta said it could be helpful in this instance to create a less threatening environment in which to explore that redness. How? One possibility is to focus on the experience in a broader, more generalized way rather than focusing on it directly. Dona Carletta said this transposition was like listening to a *full symphony* instead of listening specifically to one of its *individual melodies*. She also liked the analogy of a camera. She said that many cameras have wide-angle lenses. Instead of focusing tightly on the given image, you can open up the field of vision, zoom out, so to speak, and view the given image in a larger, more general context.

She said she would now bring out a list of many possible methods for zooming out.

Symbolic Thinking: Symbolic thinking, which we learned about from Hermie, is one of the main methods of zooming out, or generalizing. "Here," Dona Carletta said, "we do not focus directly on or unfold a secondary experience but instead understand and view it in terms of the person's overall life situation. For example, you might say to this flower that she is a lovely and sensitive flower and may have a dynamic part of herself that she is shy about. Here we are giving the flower a greater context within which to understand her experience. We might also look at one of the flower's dreams to gain a larger overview of how this redness fits into the flower's overall process."

Dona Carletta reminded us of an example she had given of this method in her lesson on extrapolation (Chapter 10) in which Eagle worked with a woman with a stomach cramp. In that instance, Eagle interpreted the woman's body experience as embedded in her overall experience of herself and her life situation.

Speaking Generally: Dona Carletta mentioned another way of zooming out in the case of the "redness" of the flower: Speak in general about collective views about how a flower should look and act, as well as other types of flower appearances and behaviors that do not follow that norm, without referring directly to the flower's appearance.

Telling a Story: Another method of zooming out is to tell a story about *another* flower or tree or animal that had this kind of redness or intensity and then ask the client for suggestions about that *other* flower. If the client allows, you might tell a story about yourself and how you have struggled with such issues.

Dona Carletta said it can be very creative to tell a story.[2] You can develop a fairy tale-like story in which a person is in a predicament similar to that of the client, go to the edge where there is not yet a solution, and ask the person to fill in what happens next. You can also weave into that story an amazing incident that happened in the person's past, when something miraculous occurred.

This incident might contain a pattern or solution to the present problem. Dona Carletta recommended that we take some time to focus on ourselves and try the following exercise.

Exercise
Telling Stories with Amazing Events

1. Think of an area in which you feel stuck in your life.
2. Recall an amazing event from your past in which something miraculous occurred. Recall the circumstances surrounding that event.
3. Begin to tell a fairy tale-like story about a person who is at a stuck place in her or his life (the place you described in step 1). Perhaps that person is walking in the forest and gets to a cliff and is unable to go forward or backward. Use your imagination to create a tale.
4. At the stuck place, weave into the story some aspect of the miraculous event that you thought of in step 2.
5. Let the story unfold further, and come to some conclusion.
6. Ponder how this story provides solutions for today's difficulties.

Gossiping: Another way of zooming out is to simply wait until the person (or flower) begins to *gossip* about *someone else* who has this red quality and then *dream together*—that is, gossip about the "other" without having to consciously integrate the process. Eagle calls this "secret dreaming."[3]

If someone tells a dream and is unable to give associations to the different dream parts, you can simply begin to gossip with the person about a particular figure. Like "Yeah, that person, wow, they can do that!" This is another aspect of secret dreaming.

Creating Distance by Acting It Out: Another way to zoom out and take the focus off the flower (or person) is to act out the experience. The client does not have to participate but can watch and direct you. In this case, you could act out a person who has an amazing red quality and allow yourself to dream further into what that redness might be expressing. You might also act out something that could be against this redness coming out. The client can then agree with or correct what you are saying or have an idea about how to deal with that conflict without having to be involved directly.

Switching Channels: Dona Carletta shared more thoughts about switching channels in the context of zooming out. She said, "When you zoom out, you can see the same pattern in various channels. Here is another typical example in which it is impossible to focus directly on a particular secondary experience." Dona Carletta told us to imagine a person who has a lot of power and is shy about it. This power reveals itself in the way that the person continually (but unconsciously) resists your suggestions. If you were to focus *directly* on this resistance and ask the person to notice it, he or she would have to resist! What a bind! What are your alternatives?

An alternative way to zoom out and approach this power is to focus on it in a general way by changing channels. For example, you might ask the person (without reference to his or her resistance and with the permission to interact physically) to arm wrestle or simply lift a chair and feel his or her strength. (See Chapter 28 for more on ethics and body contact.) This may help the person get in touch with the power behind the resistance signals.

When it seems that all roads are blocked and you cannot focus on the secondary experience, it may be that you are in the wrong channel. To further unfold the process, you need to switch *channels*. Dona Carletta mentioned the following example. A man who had widespread cancer said he had severe pain but didn't want to think about it. He said the pain felt as though someone were punching him. But he did not want to focus on the symptoms and did not want to do movement work or visualization. He did say, however, that he was upset with some of his family members (relationship channel). He seemed to have a lot of energy around those interactions. The therapist thought it would be best to work with this person somatically, but this did not work. The open pathway was the relationship channel. Therefore, the therapist thought it best not to focus on proprioception or movement or visualization but to switch channels and focus on his relationships. Together, they focused on difficult interactions with the man's family in which he experienced others as "punching" and hurting him.

Dreaming and Blank Accessing: Dona Carletta continued with her list of methods. She said that another way to momentarily zoom out is to drop what you and the client are consciously focusing on and let yourselves dream. This is particularly helpful when you are stuck or unable to go further with a given issue or secondary experience. With this method you go to a more general way of working and allow spontaneous and otherwise disavowed information to arise.

For example, if the client agrees, you can ask her to drop what she is focusing on and to either look at the wall and notice what image she spontaneously sees or look around the room and notice what catches her attention.[4] Then you can focus on and unfold the experience that has arisen. You can also ask the person to simply follow her body, do sandplay or movement work, and from there unfold whatever process emerges.

Dona Carletta stressed that sometimes a therapist's sense of confusion and cloudiness signals the need to pull back, zoom out, and go to a more general approach. For example, one therapist said she remembered feeling totally confused about what was happening with a particular client. She felt very "foggy" and, with the permission of her client, she went into that foggy feeling. She suddenly had an image of a threatening monster behind, and on the shoulders of, her client! When she told this to her client, it clicked immediately with the woman's internal experience. They were then able to find out more about this "monster" and interact with it.

Dona Carletta said that another way of unfolding an experience when it is not possible to focus on it directly is to use the same channel but in a "blank" way, without focusing on any particular content. Dona Carletta said that Eagle's term for this is *blank accessing*. What does this mean? Let's say a person experiences a pounding headache (kinesthetic channel) but is unable to focus on it. Or, say a person dreams about a dog that is racing up the hill, but cannot focus on it. Both of these experiences occur in the kinesthetic channel but cannot be focused on directly. "Instead,"

Dona Carletta said, "you might suggest general movement work in which the person stands up and begins to walk around the room. While doing so, the client and therapist can notice any spontaneous, secondary motions that occur and then follow them. This is a gentle way of entering and focusing on the movement channel."

Making a Frame: Dona Carletta brought one more method of zooming out when it is impossible to focus on a particular experience. This, she said, was somewhat different from methods mentioned previously. She said that sometimes it is helpful to place what is happening in a special "frame" in which the person can view the process, or experiment with it, in a satisfying or kind way. For example, a client wanted to work on her inner critic. But she was already feeling so bad that, when the therapist suggested focusing on it, the woman said, in a hopeless and resigned tone, "Oh, I guess we have to do this, so, OK, let's do it." When the therapist started to focus on this inner critic, the implied context to the already sensitized client, was, "You are bad person and need to work on this." The framework unwittingly is the world of the negative critic who disavows everything this woman does. Therefore, it can't work! Another possibility is to zoom way out. First, create a warm atmosphere by drinking tea and talking about things that make the person feel well and then, *from this sense of wellness*, begin to explore the more difficult issues. (See Chapter 23 for more on frameworks and atmospheres.)

Zooming In

Dona Carletta continued her photography analogy by describing the opposite approach, that is, "zooming in." She said that when you are focusing on a more *general* aspect of someone's life, it is sometimes beneficial to notice how that experience is happening in a more subtle way in the moment. She returned to her camera analogy and said this is like replacing the wide-angle lens with a telephoto one: zooming in and viewing the process more closely and in greater detail.

Noticing the Past and Future in Present Signals: Dona Carletta reminded us that all of us speak about past or future events. Here, zooming in could mean finding those events *happening in the moment* in the person's signals. For example, as discussed previously, if a client is complaining about a parent who was mean to her, you could notice how that "hurt" is happening in the moment. Perhaps she is criticizing herself just as the parent did.

Going from Bigger to Smaller Signals: Dona Carletta said that sometimes it is helpful to notice how a general process is happening between you and the client in a minute way. Imagine that you feel ignored and hurt by a client. However, if you were to bring this up with your client, you might fall into a deeper struggle with the person and potentially lose your awareness. Eagle says that one protection against loss of awareness is to "catch" emerging signals in a very minute form, before they even have a chance to express themselves in a larger way.

She continued, "Imagine that this client who is upsetting to you walks into your office, sits down, looks out the window when you say hello to her, and seems to ignore what you are saying. Then she looks quickly back at you and seems to be embarrassed that she was looking away when you greeted her." Dona Carletta said, "Instead of waiting for this experience to escalate at a later point in the relationship channel, where you might become upset, feel ignored, and lose your awareness, you could focus on this small signal when it is happening and say, 'The way you looked out the window was interesting. You seemed to negate my presence. We might go back to that. Perhaps there's something meaningful in it.'" Dona Carletta reiterated that each aspect of our process is happening simultaneously at different levels; therefore, the process can be joined at various moments.

Dona Carletta said that, although we have understood symbolic thinking as an aspect of "zooming out," it could also be a useful means of going from the general to the specific. For example, Eagle was working with an elderly woman who was slowly losing her memory. She began to feel that she should sell her blouses but was afraid they wouldn't be worth anything. Instead of only focusing on "her belongings," Eagle focused on her symbolic communication: She was asking, "Do I have any value? Am I worth anything?" Eagle transposed this sense of worth and value from her general possessions to herself. He said to this woman, "You are a valuable person. I buy you. I accept you." Eagle said that this is a typical process that many older people go through: not feeling that they are taken seriously or valued.

Going from Signals to Essence: Dona Carletta said, "A very important method of zooming in has to do with getting to the *essence* of a particular signal, especially those signals that either disturb or attract you." (She reminded us of our learning about the "Big Flirt" [see Chapter 8].) "Here it can be important not to take those signals solely at face value but to try to get to their essence, the root beneath their expression."[5]

She mentioned the following situation. A therapist felt shy about a client's sexual attraction to her. The therapist felt that the client was flirting with her, and she was uncomfortable and did not know how to deal with this situation. Eagle recommended that this therapist try to find the essence of the signals from the client—the *root or core* of the "flirting" signals—before they became more overt. When the therapist meditated on this, she sensed that behind these signals was not simply sexual energy, but a search for kindness and closeness in relationships. She was then able to talk about and connect with the client about what turned out to be a very important issue for that client. In other circumstances, the client might meditate on the essence of his or her signal and discover its essence.

Dona Carletta finished the class with the following exercise. She encouraged us to try it with a co-learner.

Exercise
Transposition (in pairs)

1. Begin to work as a therapist with a partner.
2. Notice something secondary in the person's speech, behavior, or movement that you would like to unfold.
3. Experiment with unfolding and transposing the experience by either zooming out or zooming in, depending on the person's feedback.
4. Discuss the experience with your partner and what effect the transposition had on him or her.

Notes

1. Thanks to Randee Cathey for help with this idea. See Lane Arye, *Unintentional Music: Releasing Your Deepest Creativity* (Charlottesville, Virginia: Hampton Roads, 2001).
2. For a description of a dreamwork method involving weaving a story, see Arnold Mindell, *Dreammaker's Apprentice* (Charlottesville, Virginia: Hampton Roads, 2001),99-110.
3. Mindell, *Dreammaker's Apprentice*, 172-173.
4. Mindell, *Dreammaker's Apprentice*, Chapter 8; Arnold Mindell, *Dreaming While Awake* (Charlottesville, Virginia: Hampton Roads, 2000), Chapter 6.
5. For more on the essence and sentient experience, see Mindell, *Dreaming While Awake.*

Chapter Fourteen

How Process Creates Therapy

The client's process suggests the method he or she needs.

The next day, a person who seemed quite old came into the room and stood in front of the class. He looked as though he was one hundred and twenty years old. Apparently, Dona Carletta had other business to attend to and this was our teacher for the day. She had told us that our next lesson would have to do with discovering the therapeutic direction and method that the client is organically suggesting. In any case, the man standing in front of us constantly sputtered and coughed and spent much of the forthcoming lecture blowing his nose and searching for the tissue box.

His name was Professor T. Frinklash III. He was the descendant of a long line of professors, all of whom had this irritating cough whenever they tried to speak. Many people tried to heal the Frinklash family of this curse, but to no avail. Perhaps it was an indelible part of their genius.

Professor Frinklash had only one subject, which he spoke about again and again. He never seemed to tire of his message.

Ultimately, he felt that this was the *only* topic that really had any significance, and that is why he had not attended any of his colleagues' earlier lectures. He was from the old school ... before the new school came into being. Most of the students were not around during the old school but had heard gossip about his lengthy lectures and tirades on this particular subject.

Professor Frinklash began with a booming voice and fire gleaming from his eyes. He boomed:

> *"The only thing you need to know about the art of therapy is that the client suggests the therapeutic direction! If you are a careful observer, you will notice the method your client (and her or his process) is describing. If you use that method, you will have great success!"*

After he yelled this out, he sputtered and wheezed quite a bit. Some students worried that he might have a heart attack if he continued this way.

It seemed to take a lot out of him; nevertheless, he continued. During the next hour he repeated the exact same thing again and again, with numerous variations. Although many people were irritated by his insistent tone of voice, Frinklash didn't seem to notice. As he spoke, he did not look up at his audience but only down at his notes. In fact, we were not sure whether he cared if we were there at all. He seemed content to give his tirade and then leave. Which is what he did.

While the other students fell asleep or gossiped in the back of the room, Perfidious Doodleberry, the best student in this class, and the only one returning consistently to Frinklash's lectures, took detailed notes. He was spellbound. To save the reader from the worst repetition, here are some of the *summaries* that Perfidious put together from his notes.

A Beginner's Mind

Professor Frinklash said that one of the greatest challenges and tasks of the process worker is to discover the particular method of therapy that the client's process is suggesting. He said that this is quite a paradox. "One thinks that one should be well trained and know what to do, but actually, the less one knows, the better!"

He stressed that the metaskill of the beginner's mind was the only metaskill of any *real* virtue because it made it possible to be totally open, to drop all previous knowledge and actually *notice* the method the client is recommending. He added that this ability is the foundation for a well-known quality of the therapist, empathy. He said that when one truly has a beginner's mind and notices the client's inherent way of working on him or herself, the therapist automatically empathizes in the deepest way.

"One must notice what method the person is suggesting (consciously or unconsciously) and *clothe* your methods accordingly," he emphasized. Frinklash also quoted Eagle once saying that there are so many different therapeutic methods because there are so many different types of people!

Frinklash did acknowledge that attaining a beginner's mind was a great challenge. "It takes a grand amount of flexibility to let go of your particular style of working. If a therapist likes working with movement, but his client feels most comfortable talking, the therapist may be challenged to let go of his or her preferred methods."

Process-Oriented Symptom, Channel, and Dream Work

Frinklash reminded the students that many basic aspects of process work are founded on the principle that the client suggests the type of therapy. He recalled the basis of process-oriented symptom work: "It is the person's individual experience of the symptom that shows you how to work with that symptom! Watch how a person describes his or her symptom, and that will inform you on how to go forward."

He discussed the following example. A woman said she was in the middle of a terrible conflict with a friend. She also said she had a gallstone and that the stone was static—it was not going either forward or backward. This description provided an important approach to the process: staying in the middle and not moving forward or backward! The woman realized that she had been pushing for some sort of solution to the relationship problem but nothing seemed to work. She was relieved to let things be for the moment and to wait for something to happen organically.

Frinklash triumphantly concluded, "The symptom experience showed the way!" He reminded us that if you notice the unoccupied channel in someone's speech, you know that this could be an indication of a good entrance point into the process. He also said that you can discover a person's method of dreamwork when you work on his or her dream.[1] Listen, and watch how the person *tells* the dream. If the person stresses a word, that would be a place to use word association. If they begin to describe parts of the dream by using their hands or in some form of movement, movement work would be interesting at that point. If the person visually focuses on one of the images, visualization would be helpful, and so on. In other words, all the various therapeutic modalities are natural and useful when they appear organically!

The Therapist's Metaskills

Frinklash stressed that people come to us because of our unique personalities, because of our skills, and above all, because of our *metaskills*. Whatever metaskills the person is looking for provide an important hint about the direction to take. For example, a client felt that her therapist had great wisdom. However, the therapist was very shy about this part of herself and did not identify with it. The therapist's supervisor said that the therapist should try to go over her edge and grow into the sense of her own wisdom because that is the metaskill the client is seeking. Then the client can experience that wisdom and eventually find it in herself. The supervisor recommended that if the therapist were unable to find a way to identify comfortably with her own wisdom, and if the situation allowed, then she could talk openly about her difficulties and how she is also stuck at that growing edge. The client might feel understood, and perhaps both would then be able to grow together.

The Client's Metaskills

The client's metaskills could also show you the way! Frinklash reminded us of Waldo. Waldo had a rather gruff metaskill and would have enjoyed Mary using a bit of it as well. He would have felt more understood. Another client is very kindhearted toward others all of the time, which could be an indication that this is the metaskill the person is wanting from the therapist so that he or she can finally feel kindhearted toward himself or herself.

Frinklash talked about one of his own clients from many years back. This man asked Frinklash to tell him what to do. Frinklash then surmised that this man's secondary process was to be a leader. Therefore, Frinklash decided to become that authority and *instructed* the person about *how to find his own leadership potential.*

Frinklash abruptly ended his lecture for the day. He stressed that there are many more areas in which we find the "therapeutic method the person suggests" and that this concept is actually the basis for much of what we would learn in subsequent classes, such as the one on "states of consciousness."

Just before walking out the door he said that we should not fear, he would definitely return. (Some people had no fear at all!) In an afterthought, he came back for a moment to put an exercise on the board. And without another word, he left.

Exercise
The Method the Client Is Suggesting (in pairs)

1. One person is the client and the other the therapist or helper. The client begins to talk about issues that are on his or her mind.
2. As you interact with one another, the therapist should try to discover one of the organic methods or styles of working that the client is suggesting.
3. The therapist should then try to use this method as a way of working with the client. Try this for ten minutes.
4. Discuss the experience and share your discoveries.

Notes

1. For more on this form of dreamwork, see Amy and Arnold Mindell, *Riding the Horse Backwards* (Portland, Oregon: Lao Tse Press, 2002), 35-42.

Part Three

More Advanced Approaches of the Work

Chapter Fifteen

Subtle States of Consciousness

Sometimes a therapist's methods do not work well because he or she has not recognized the client's state of consciousness.

When Dona Carletta returned from her vacation, she brought with her one of her longtime gurus, Terrina. Terrina was a mystic and a deep thinker and lived alone on a distant star. Terrina really did look like an outer-space being. Her body was wiry and translucent. An electric stream of colors seemed to jump out of her head when she was having a good thought.

Apparently, Terrina spent most of her time ruminating about the vast spaces of consciousness in the universe. In previous times, when she was on Earth, she had worked as a therapist and, still today, she considered herself one, although now she described herself as a universal therapist-mystic who could do things at a distance. She'd spent much of her earlier years studying case supervision, particularly the intricacies and fine-tuning of the therapist's methods.

Many years ago, Terrina researched and wrote a paper about "Subtle States of Consciousness." Unfortunately, this paper was lost, never to be found again. It was so subtle she couldn't even trace its footprints. In any case, Dona Carletta told us that Terrina's writings and discoveries were the foundation of Dona Carletta's most interesting teachings. Hence, she had asked Terrina to drop by and expound on her ideas. Terrina was hesitant to leave her planet, but out of love for Dona Carletta, and since the stars were favorable that day, she decided to drop by Earth and share her thoughts. People were quite excited about her visit.

Quiz

Right away, Terrina said she was going to give us a quiz. Most of us were afraid because we had been so traumatized by tests in the past. But her glee made us curious and more open than normal. She told us to imagine a client who says she is depressed but has a glow in her eyes. The client occasionally smiles brightly and is quite expressive; her hand motions wave in the air in an excited manner.

Terrina said that there are many ways to interact with this person depending on your school of therapy and personal style. The vast numbers of approaches for a specific situation would fill an encyclopedia. "If you were a process worker," she said, "you would probably want to support and care for this woman's primary process, and also try to bring her awareness to the double signals of her smile and the movements of her hands."

"However," Terrina said, "this woman is so miserable that she cannot follow your suggestions. She is sure nothing will help. And she becomes shy and embarrassed when you mention her double signals. In this case," Terrina added, "some of the most fundamental methods that you have learned may not be helpful! The woman will not join you in trying to discover what her secondary experiences are about." Terrina reminded us of some of the subtle unfolding methods that we had learned in an earlier class that might be of help here. Today she wanted to discuss another central concept that underlies, and assists with, such situations.

To do this, she wanted everyone to consider another example. "Imagine a client comes to you with a headache and he or she says that it really hurts," she said. "Obviously, I'm not giving enough information for you to really know or do anything! But let's remain simplistic to begin with." Then, with an impish sparkle in her eyes giving the impression that there was much more to her question than she was letting on, she asked, "How might you work with that person?"

A student answered, "I would spend time getting to know the person and find out his or her goals and medical condition. Then, at some point, I would ask, "*How do you know* that you have a headache? Help me to feel it, too, so that I know what you are experiencing." Terrina looked fully pleased and acknowledged that this is a very good method of gaining sensory-grounded information about the headache. The student continued, "Then I might encourage the person to amplify that experience and allow the message behind the symptom to unfold."

"Good!" Terrina said. "Congratulations! You have successfully done what you think you should do! And that's a big accomplishment!" At that point, we all began to wonder what was up her sleeve. She continued, "Now let me tell you something about my studies. After researching hundreds of supervision cases, I realized that while this method, and so many others, are very useful, much of the time therapists bring cases to supervision precisely *because* it is difficult to use the basic approaches they have learned!"

Terrina explained that this difficult situation must contain the keys to special concepts and subtle methods at the root of our work. After staying up night after night studying Eagle's writings, having exciting theoretical talks with him, and twirling around in the sky and throwing fits, she had made a big discovery, which she would now share with us.

Normal State of Consciousness

As her research and discussions with Eagle evolved (they were close colleagues), she realized that a person could be in a number of states of consciousness. Her work extrapolates on and extends

Eagle's previous writings about the subtle differentiation between these states.

She first said that when we work with someone who is not in an obviously extreme state of consciousness, we usually assume that that person has a "meta" position. This means that the person is able to be aware of, and can *talk about,* her or his experiences. The person is also interested in exploring and unfolding the various aspects of his or her experience and perception (primary and secondary) and is able to step outside him or herself and talk about what is happening. A person with a meta position also has *feedback* to outside input and can temporarily alter his or her state of consciousness to explore other realms of consciousness.

"However," Terrina cautioned, "You may be surprised to learn that this meta state is *not* so common! Most people are so closely *identified* with *one* part of themselves that they do not have access to this meta position. When you ask them to talk about or unfold their various experiences, they are not able to do so. In such instances, the therapist may become confused and wonder why his or her methods are not working. "With this in mind, we must consider a spectrum of states of consciousness. In a moment, I will outline the characteristics of this spectrum, which are based on the amount of meta position a person has (as well as other factors)."

She clarified that we might feel blocked with a client because we are trying to relate to that person *as if* she or he were in one state of consciousness when the person is actually in another. "Our great challenge is to adapt our methods to the person's state of consciousness. If we do this, our clients feel respected and more deeply understood. Many therapists do this unconsciously; they have a sense of these different states and somehow know just what to do. Others of us need to study a bit."

Spectrum of Awareness

Terrina then rolled out a bunch of charts she had made that were adapted from Eagle's research. "There are many dimensions that are helpful in understanding consciousness and altered states of consciousness. To make things simple, we'll deal with only two:

The first is the ability of the person to *metacommunicate,* and the second is which reality the person focuses on."

"To begin with, let's explore the first dimension." Terrina said Eagle had outlined a spectrum of consciousness in which the person is closer to, or further from, a *meta position.*[1] Again, a person with a great deal of ability to metacommunicate is someone who can *talk about* his or her states of consciousness and experiences, regardless of the condition that she or he is in. A person with very little ability to metacommunicate cannot speak *about* experience but is *immersed in it* instead. She or he is *identified* with the experience. Terrina said that people are somewhere along this spectrum at any one moment.

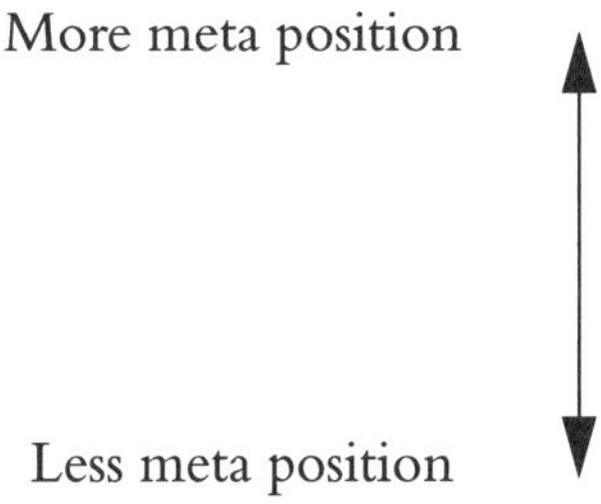

The second dimension, the focus on different realities, can also be understood as a spectrum. Before looking at this chart, Terrina wanted to remind us of a common scale that is based on more traditional methods of evaluating states of consciousness. Here, states are viewed in terms of their closeness to or distance from a *normal or accepted* reality of a given culture. On this scale, a person is closer to a defined *normal* or *abnormal range* of behavior.

Eagle revised this scale. He pointed out that what is regarded as "normal" for a given culture is based on a *consensual* reality.[2] This means that the definition of reality is based on what most people in that particular culture agree is real (not an absolute reality). Therefore, what is real or not and what is normal or abnormal are culturally determined. Eagle's spectrum, on the other hand, is based on personal experience, that is, whether a person's experiences are considered closer to a culture's consensual or consensus reality or closer to experiences that are not agreed upon *as* being *real* by that culture (nonconsensual or nonconsensus reality).

Consensus Reality ◄———————► Nonconsensus Reality

On the left side of this spectrum are the experiences people have (the events in their lives, the thoughts and beliefs that they speak about) that are considered consensual; the majority of people would agree that those things exist. People in such states are able to relate to you and have ordinary (consensually understandable) feedback in response to your interactions. At the other end of that spectrum are people in states in which their experiences are more dreamlike or indescribably mood-like. Here people talk about and focus on figures and fantasies that no one else sees or agrees are real. The further one gets toward the right side of the continuum, the less consensual feedback the person gives to your interactions.

Terrina said that as a mystic and outer-space individual she has to totally reverse her thinking to relate these concepts to Earth readers. "As far as I am concerned, everything that is called *nonconsensual* here is *consensual* for me because I live in outer space. That's my "Earth." I know that most of you in this class are upside down because your feet are in so-called Earthly *ordinary* consensual reality." She mused about all of this, but seeing our growing puzzlement, she would leave all of that for another discussion.

Terrina then added, "For the sake of simplicity, I have not included a third dimension, the time dimension. However, those who know a lot about how humans tick know that the amount of time you spend in a given state determines as much about your consensual or nonconsensual status as anything else. So, for example, everybody has momentary nonconsensual experiences, but those people who hang out there for long periods of time are more likely to pick up diagnoses such as 'psychotic' and 'schizophrenic.'"

Terrina then brought out a comprehensive diagram of states of consciousness that she and Eagle developed. In fact, just the night before, Eagle reappeared and met with Terrina for several hours to work on the overall diagram. Everyone wished that Eagle had stayed around long enough for the class, but he had urgent business to attend to in hyperspace and was unable to stay.

Terrina knew that everyone is terrified of graphs, but this one came from hyperspace and a voice told her graphs were good for consensual minds, which like practical applications. In the Diagram below, she shows the two dimensions just mentioned, as well as various states of consciousness that lie somewhere on this field.

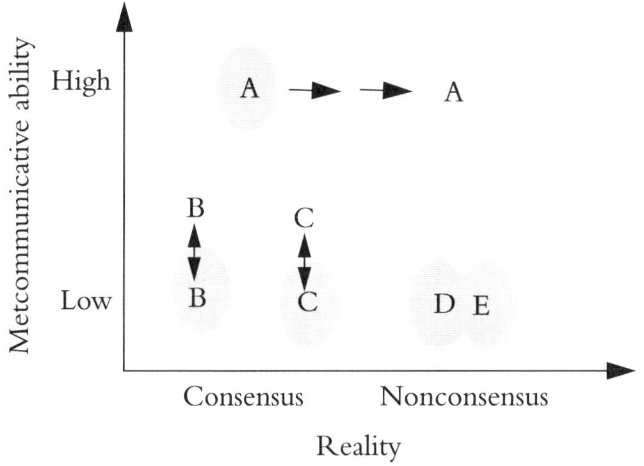

Terrina explained that each letter refers to a state of consciousness. She and Eagle placed balls around each letter to indicate that these states are not only static but also can move about somewhat on the graph, depending on the person's degree of metacommunication and distance from consensual reality. She now outlined these various states of consciousness on this map, focusing primarily on B and C because they are the ones that interest her in the moment and that are less known.

A = Meta Position

"A" refers to a state of consciousness in which the person has a high level of metacommunicative ability. Once again, Terrina reiterated, this refers to a state in which a person is able to reflect on his or her experiences, both primary and secondary. She can speak *about* her experiences and perceptions and have an overview. She will most likely be interested in, and able to follow, the general steps of unfolding mentioned in previous classes. She added that a person with a meta position can easily talk about consensual experiences. He or she can also be in an altered state, going through nonconsensual experiences, while still able to metacommunicate about those experiences.

Dona Carletta chimed in to recall one of Eagle's teachings. He has said that someone who is able to go into deeply altered states is like the shamans throughout time who are trained to go into altered states and maintain their awareness. This is also one of the major activities and trainings of process workers: to go into altered states while maintaining a meta position.

B = Consensual Reality

"B" refers to the consensus reality state of consciousness. A person in this state is *identified with* the consensual aspects of himself or herself. Everything that occurs in his or her life is related to that notion of what constitutes consensual reality. Such a person may have a meta position at times, a greater overview of his or her entire process, although it is less likely. Strong consensus reality states frequently do not include meta perspectives. It is easy for a therapist to become confused, having assumed that a client has this meta view because the person seems quite clear and analytical, but this is not always the case. You should not assume that the person you are talking with is speaking from a meta standpoint. He or she may be immersed in a consensual way of understanding his or her experiences and the world and may even *insist* on this understanding. Everything is filtered through this lens; this person will give feedback to your interactions that conform with consensual understanding.

Such a person usually wants your answers, advice, and interpretations from a consensual viewpoint and asks for your help with this. Such a person wants to know what her or his life experiences, dreams, or a body symptom mean in terms of consensus reality and is not interested in altering her or his state of consciousness.

Terrina reminded us of her favorite example from the class on extrapolation (Chapter 11): the woman with a cramp in her stomach. The woman described her stomach cramp with fists but was unable to unfold it further. She asked again and again, "What is it? What is it?" Eagle realized that she was in a consensual state of consciousness and wanted an answer about her symptom in consensual terms. Therefore, he entered into this mode and used a consensual reality method: *interpretation!* Interpretation allowed this woman to remain in her ordinary consciousness and understand what is happening from that standpoint. She did not have to alter her state of consciousness and explore her various parts. Hence he said, "You are a woman with a lot of strength and ability but you were never supported in it."

C = *Altered State*

"C" refers to what Terrina calls an *altered state of consciousness.*[3] She defines this as a state in which the person is temporarily identified with, or immersed in, one part of his or her process. When someone is in an altered state, there is a strong mood associated with the person's behavior and he or she is not metacommunicating about the experience. However, it might be possible to access the meta position if you ask the person to remember his or her metacommunication ability. (A person who is in an altered state and maintains a meta position would be located further upward on our chart.)

Although the person in a consensus reality state is also identified with one part of himself or herself, this altered state differs in a number of ways. First, as mentioned, there is usually a strong mood associated with the altered state, the content is less consensual, and this altered state demands different approaches (which Terrina will talk about shortly). Terrina described this type of altered state as follows. "Most human beings are in the middle of horrendous or beautiful stories, and much of the time experience themselves as *part* of this story. You are the protagonist, the victim, the child, or the hero. You become so identified with one aspect of this story that we don't realize that you do not have a greater overview or meta position. You are *identified* with one part of your process and see everything that happens through the eyes of that part. When you are in an altered state of consciousness, our actions might be overlaid with depression, elation, or fear. At the same time, your experiences are also further away from consensual reality. You may have experiences that others will not necessarily agree are completely real. Imagine a man who is depressed and feels like a failure, although he is the chief executive officer (CEO) of a large and profitable corporation. Others do not agree with his perception of himself. They try to convince him that he is a gifted person and that his perception of himself is incorrect. However, this does not change his mind. Hence, he is experiencing a somewhat nonconsensual mood or state of consciousness."

Terrina reminded us that people who come to therapy are frequently in this altered state of consciousness. "Why?" she asked. "People go to a therapist most often just because they are in the middle of a story or a mood with which they are unable to deal. They are identified with one aspect of the story and are hoping that the therapist will be able to give them a greater, outside perspective about what is happening. The problem arises, however, when the therapist assumes that the person has a neutral meta position and is able to *talk about* what is happening by standing outside of the drama of life. However, in the moment, this is not the case.

Terrina asked us about ourselves. "Recall the last time you were in a troubled mood. Remember calling up a friend to complain. Do you remember your tone of voice? Was it irritable, panicked, or desperate? When your friend tried to help, did you insist that nothing would help or sink further into misery or panic? Do you remember that it felt impossible to *hear* or *consider* what your friend was saying to you, even with the person's best intentions?"

Terrina said this was a moment when you were in an altered state of consciousness and that this state requires special methods, which she will speak about in the next class.

One way of grasping what is happening when someone is in an altered state of consciousness is to ask yourself, "Who's talking?"[4] For example, Terrina told us to imagine a woman in her forties whose head is lowered. Her eyes look up at you with brimming tears. In an upset and somewhat childlike tone, she says, "I just can't talk to my mother and tell her I'm hurt." You recommend that she try to approach her mother and she says, "I just can't!" Her head falls further forward, and she looks rather defeated. The important question here is, "Who's talking?" It is, most likely, a child who does not feel strong enough to interact with her mother. Without recognizing this shift, you can get very confused. You might think you are talking to an adult who you can give suggestions about how to deal with this conflict, but it is the child who will hear you and answer your questions. You will need to address this "child" using special approaches.

D= Extreme States

As we travel to the right on this continuum, letter "D" indicates an extreme state of consciousness. Here, the person has increasingly less access to the meta position, and the content of the person's experiences are quite far from consensual views of reality. In an extreme state the person does not *seem* to give feedback in the ordinary sense and is unable to *speak about* her or his overall experience. Terrina said that she stressed the word *seem* because Eagle has shown how feedback is actually occurring, but in a way that is different from what we expect from our outside perspective.

Terrina said that Eagle spoke explicitly about extreme states elsewhere, so she would not go into detail here.[5] Her main focus is on the consensus reality and altered states of consciousness because they are less known. She did say, however, that an extreme state is a state that is unusual for a given culture and which has occurred over an extended period of time. The person does not give ordinary feedback to outside input and is not meta communicating about her or his experiences. Therefore, you will need to use methods that step inside of the person's system and work with the person in the lexicon, so to speak, of the extreme state.

E = Comatose State

In a coma, the most extreme state of consciousness, a person does not talk to you, is not metacommunicating in the ordinary sense, is completely inside her or his experience, and is in need of someone to join her or him there. Special methods adapted to this particular state of consciousness are available elsewhere.[6]

To conclude the class, Terrina gave the following exercise. She said that tomorrow's class would focus on examples of, and special methods for working with, consensus reality and altered states of consciousness. Blue and green streams of light seemed to fly out of the top of her head as she recommended the following exercise.

Exercise
Identifying States of Consciousness

1. Think of a client who is difficult for you in some way.
2. Act out the client and recall the way in which he or she interacts with you.
3. Now try to identify the person's state of consciousness. What is your reasoning for this choice? What was the state of the person's meta position? Who was talking?

Notes

1. For more on this topic, see Arnold Mindell, *City Shadows* (New York: Routledge, 1988).
2. Mindell, *City Shadows*. For more on consensual and nonconsensual realities, see Arnold Mindell, *Dreaming While Awake* (Charlottesville, Virginia: Hampton Roads, 2000).
3. Charles Tart has a detailed and wonderful description of altered states and their relationship to consensual trance states in his book *Waking Up: Overcoming the Obstacles to Human Potential* (Boston: Shambhala, 1986).
4. Thanks to Julie Diamond for her help with this idea.
5. For more on extreme states and methods of working with people in this state of consciousness, see Mindell, *City Shadows*.
6. See Arnold Mindell, *Coma: The Dreambody Near Death* (Boulder: Shambhala Publications, 1989, and London: Penguin-Arkana, 1994. Currently available as an e-book at www.laotse.co); Amy Mindell, *Coma: A Healing Journey* (Portland, Oregon: Lao Tse Press, 1999).

Chapter Sixteen

Examples of Subtle States

Special methods are needed, to be "in sync" with, and adapt to, a person's state of consciousness.

To begin the next class, Terrina wanted to first give us a quiz on the various states of consciousness. Many groaned at the thought of another test but also felt challenged. Terrina said she would act out a number of different people and ask what state of consciousness each person is in. Terrina did warn us, as Dona Carletta had, that these examples are taken out of context and are simplistic, but they are fun to experiment with. Terrina must have become quite excited because the students suddenly saw a bunch of glittering lights spray out from the top of Terrina's head in a curving rainbow pattern. This shocked everyone but was also kind of exciting.

Terrina continued as if unaffected by this sudden display. She said that after the quiz, she would outline some of the special methods for interacting with people in the consensual and altered states of consciousness.

Quiz

Example One

> *Terrina first acted out a middle-aged woman who complains that she doesn't feel well. She complains in such a way, and with such a tone, that you begin to feel motherly toward her and are unable to focus directly on her sense of feeling unwell. What state of consciousness could this be?*

One student said it was an altered state of consciousness. Terrina agreed. She said that the person is in the middle of a story. You sense a particular mood in her tone and recognize that it is a *child* part of her that is speaking and that this child seems to be searching for a mother. She is not speaking from a metacommunicative position *about* her process but rather from the point of view of this child. Some people remembered a similar example Terrina had given the evening before.

Terrina showed that, as the therapist, you suddenly find yourself in the midst of a story that has not been directly spoken about but into which you are inadvertently drawn. You feel "dreamed up" to be mothering, in part because you have not noticed that there is a *child* who is asking for this. The experiences she is having are somewhat nonconsensual in the sense that (in consensual terms) she is a grown woman, not a child searching for her mother. She is in the middle of a *dreaming process* that is seeking completion.

Terrina asked, "What do you think would happen if you tried to talk to this person about not feeling well or if you tried to focus on what that unwell feeling is like?" Someone said that the woman would probably answer with a somewhat naive tone and say that she is not able to do what you are saying. "That's right!" Terrina exclaimed.

Example Two

> *Terrina then role-played a man in his twenties who says that he has a headache. When asked what the headache is like, the man replies, "What could the cause of this headache be? Could it be organic? What advice can you give me?"*

After some discussion, Terrina told us that this person is in a consensus reality (CR) state of consciousness. He is not interested in altering his consciousness and discovering more about his symptom but wants to remain in consensual reality and get straightforward advice. If your methods are geared toward this consensual framework, the person will probably feel seen and understood.

Example Three

> *Terrina next dramatized a teenager who comes into his therapist's office, slumps down, and says in a depressed tone, "I feel so bad today because I really blew my exam. I feel really stupid." Terrina encouraged people from the class to try to interact with this young man.*

Someone in the class said, "Oh, perhaps it wasn't as bad as you think." To this the client answered, "I was just incredibly stupid." Another person in the class said, "Maybe you were upset about something else that was going on? Or do you need more help with your schoolwork?" The client answered, "You mean you think I'm stupid too? I knew you didn't like me!" Terrina asked us to identify this teenager's state of consciousness.

One student said they thought this person is in an altered state of consciousness. The person who is talking feels that he is a failure; he is in the middle of a story in which another internal figure is putting him down and telling him that he is stupid. Terrina concurred.

Terrina wanted to conclude her discussion about states of consciousness by summing up several ways of approaching and working with people in *consensual* and *altered states* of consciousness. She reiterated that one of the reasons for studying states of consciousness is that interacting with and joining people in their particular states of consciousness can help them feel respected and related to. She asked the group to excuse her for being somewhat dry and didactic in the way in which she would now present various methods she was excited about, and she hoped we would understand that it is our feeling toward the people we work with and the unique nature of each situation that is of most importance and which must be adjusted to. There is no one "right" method.

Feedback from the client is the only true guideline for knowing whether or not you are on the right track. Negative feedback means that you should try something else or sit back and notice what happens spontaneously and let nature suggest the way. She also said it might take some time being with the person before you can determine his or her state of consciousness and have an idea as to what direction might be helpful. In any case, she outlined the following methods.

Consensual Reality Methods

Symbolic Interpretation

Symbolic interpretation (as mentioned in a previous class [see Chapter 10]) is one of the most common consensual modalities of therapeutic work. Think of a man who is in a CR state of consciousness and who always brings chocolates to his therapist. He is unable to focus on the experience of giving that chocolate. (The chocolate here is possibly symbolic of the man's sweet feelings.) Terrina suggested remaining in a consensual state and interpreting his behavior symbolically. You might thank him for the chocolates and say, "I'd like to know more about your feelings for me."

Terrina said that interpretation is close to another method called *talking to the primary process about the secondary one* (see Chapter 21). Here it is important to respect the person's primary process view of the world and language system, and to speak in a way that fits that language. For example, if someone's primary identity is linear and analytical, you will also need to speak in this way, no matter what you are trying to convey. Mirroring a person's primary mode of interacting with the world is one of the foundations of empathy.

Prescriptions, Behavioral Recommendations, and Advice

In a consensual reality mood, a person frequently asks a helper for advice and a prescription for behavioral change. In terms of the man in the example just given, you might suggest a program in which he begins to write down his feelings twice a day in a journal.

If someone wants to know more about his or her symptoms but does not want to alter his or her consciousness to find out more about it experientially, you can ask consensus-oriented questions such as, "When did the headache first occur? What was happening in your life at that time? At what time of day do you experience it? What medical approaches have you investigated?" You might also ask about dreams and associations and give an interpretation that helps to connect his or her symptom to the current life situation. Terrina commented that some therapeutic modalities are mainly geared toward intervening in a consensually oriented manner.

Gaining an Outside View

A helpful approach with people in CR states who are bothered by disturbing or upsetting secondary experiences is to gain distance from the experiences they are having. Someone may not want to alter his or her state of consciousness because of fear of being lost or overwhelmed by an experience in an unoccupied channel. For example, if someone is upset about a painful body symptom but is unable to focus on the feeling of the symptom because proprioception is an unoccupied channel, you might ask him or her to imagine *someone else* who has that symptom and describe what that person is experiencing. This approach makes use of their more familiar visual channel.

Another method mentioned previously for giving the client a sense of distance from her or his experience is for the therapist to act out the different parts of the process. The client can sit outside, so to speak, and direct the therapist as to how to act out the parts of her or his process and how to go further with it. Here, the client can remain in consensual reality while looking at and unfolding the process from a distance.

Indirect Methods

Terrina said that one of Eagle's methods which she liked best, and which we had already heard a bit about, is called "secret dreamwork." This has to do with doing dreamwork without ever working directly on a dream! Gossip is one of the best secret dreamwork methods. Simply begin to chat with the person about aspects of his or her dream in a gossipy way, so that it does not feel like you are putting too much focus on it. The gossip will lead you organically to the understanding that you need about that dream. Then give that information back to the client in a consensual, interpretive manner.

She mentioned the following example. A woman said she had a vague dream about a neighbor whom she does not like very much. In a very easygoing way, Terrina started to gossip with the woman about this neighbor. "Oh that neighbor," Terrina moaned, "she must be awful!" The woman chimed in and said, "Yes, exactly! She is just terrible. You should see the way she constantly talks about herself and just gloats about her house. It's disgusting!" "Oh," Terrina joined in, "that must be one of the most disturbing people. I don't know how you can stand living next door to her!" "Yes," replied the woman, "I'd like to give her a piece of my mind!" "Well," Terrina responded, "Why not do that?" The woman then looked shy and said, "Well, I wouldn't want to impose myself on anyone." "Oh, indeed," said Terrina and, returning to the discussion about the neighbor, she added, "but that neighbor, I bet she could go around and tell anyone what she wanted and wouldn't be shy about it!" "Oh yes," said the woman, "she wouldn't hesitate to say what she wanted!" "How would she do this?" asked Terrina. And, as the woman spontaneously began to act like the neighbor, she giggled and realized that this was something she herself wanted to be able to do but was shy about. At this point, Terrina began to speak to the woman in a more interpretive way about the two parts in her that are in conflict with one another: one part that is shy and does not impose herself on anyone and another part that is proud and outspoken about her own needs. Terrina and her client could then discuss ways in which this woman might appreciate both aspects of herself.

Patience Fosters Trust

One of the most useful consensual therapeutic tools is patience. Many people need time to get to know you before they are willing to venture into unfamiliar places. They need a friendly ear; they do not want to explore altered states of consciousness. Particularly, if some of their experiences have been scary or very painful, it may be too soon to get near these experiences. The person needs your patience, love, and ability to listen and understand. Patience fosters trust which is central to therapeutic work. Going slowly and not focusing on anything too difficult can be crucial for some people.

Surgical Interventions

When someone is afraid of his or her secondary experiences, another helpful method or metaskill is to approach the experience by asking the person to do something so rapidly that he or she hardly notices that it happened and can remain in consensual reality.

Think, for example, of someone who is utterly confused about his life and who doesn't know what direction to go in. This person also experiences shakiness in his legs. Therefore, the movement channel is unoccupied, but the client is too shy to actually get up and move. You can quickly dip into the movement channel by asking him to make a spontaneous motion with his hands for *two seconds* and then stop. She called this a "surgical" intervention because it happens so quickly that the person does not need to change his or her state of consciousness or feel that he or she is doing something peculiar. In short, the person's consensual reality is not disturbed.

Terrina said she frequently uses such methods when the client feels stuck and it would be helpful to find out a bit more information from the dreaming world about the person's situation. She might ask such a person to look at a wall and say the first thing that he or she imagines. Such fantasy experiences are meant to be very brief so that they do not disrupt the consensual atmosphere. Yet they help to bring up spontaneous, dreaming material rapidly. The information that emerges can then be interpreted and understood within the context of the person's overall life situation.

Altered State Methods

Terrina now discussed several approaches geared toward moments when people are in altered states of consciousness.

Read into Signals

Terrina said that a most helpful method in working with someone in an altered state of consciousness is to *read into* the person's signals. In an altered state of consciousness it is sometimes very hard to express what is happening. The person is immersed in an experience but is unable to metacommunicate about it. For example, if someone is silent and doesn't quite know what she or he is experiencing or trying to express, the therapist can try to *read into* the person's signals and then notice the person's feedback.

Imagine a client who is slumped over with his head in his hands. You might dream into these signals, imagine the larger ghost story, and say, on his behalf, "I don't feel supported, I am looking for support and not getting it. I'm going to go away until I find it." If he is also chewing on his lip, you might say, "I'm feeling weak but, somewhere, I am biting myself instead of biting you!" Sensitively go over edges for the person, and watch the person's feedback. He or she will correct or join you in some way.

Imagine a man walking into your office looking quite frozen with fear who briefly glances in your direction. He says hello and sits down when you request it, then looks down. If the person does not have *any feedback* in response to what you do, then he may be in an *extreme* state of consciousness. In this case, however, the person does have some feedback (he takes the chair, signaling his response to what you're saying); hence, he is in an *altered* state.

Terrina recalled such a client. She guessed the larger story surrounding the client's behavior as he walked into the room and said, "I'm happy you came. Don't talk to me yet. Don't talk unless you trust me. Notice what's happening to you inside." She said that she was attempting to join the person in his system and helped him unfold his experiences.

Complete the State by Switching Channels

A helpful approach, when someone is in an altered state of consciousness, is to complete the state. Imagine a woman who is very agitated and says she is feeling upset and disturbed physically but doesn't know why. When you try to talk to her about what is occurring in her body, she is unable to answer or does not know what is bothering her. She may be having an experience that is occurring in an unoccupied channel (in this case, proprioception) and, as a result, feels overwhelmed, afraid, or confused. Here it can be useful to help her complete or unfold the altered state she is in by switching channels. You might, for example, ask her to change channels and express her proprioceptive feelings through movement and sound. Through this process the larger message behind her experience is likely to emerge.

In another situation, a woman was feeling hopeless and had very little energy (proprioceptive channel), and the therapist began to feel hopeless as well. The therapist started to hum (auditory channel) a song that went with the feeling she was having and asked the client to think of a song that came to her mind. The music helped to unfold, deepen, and clarify the feelings they both were having.

Complete the State by Unfolding Posture and Movement

You can help complete a state and unfold the story by working with the person's movement or posture. Imagine a man who is very depressed and can hardly talk about his experience. You notice there are two parts: one that feels pushed down (depressed) and one that is pushing down on the person. You might recommend that the person push *you* down and say why he is doing that. If the client is unable to do that, you can ask him for permission to slightly push him downward. If he allows this, you should notice, and ask him to notice, the kinds of reactions that he has to your movements. Perhaps his muscles clench and slightly resist. Encourage him then to resist you even more. Then help this process unfold further by finding out who is pushing him down and what the struggle is about.

Here you are jumping into the system by taking over one part. You are helping to fill in the ghost role and complete the process by representing the energy that is putting down the person.

For example, Terrina worked with someone who nodded to her in a submissive way when he came in and said, "Excuse me, excuse me." She imagined the whole process in which there was someone with authority (a ghost figure) who was hovering over him and another who was stooped, trying to appease this figure. With the client's permission, Terrina acted out this authority figure to the client. She imagined a figure standing over the client who said, "Lower, lower, obey me!" The client agreed that this was the situation he was immersed in. Terrina then asked the client to switch roles and become the authority. The client was shy to do this at first, but then took on the role of this authority and began to act powerfully and in a commanding way. She said "You look great like that, wonderful. What a powerful man you are! I admire that." It turns out that this sense of authority was an important part of this man, who knew what to do and had a lot of good ideas. Yet this part of him was ordinarily disavowed.

Joining the Person

If someone is in an altered state and feels afraid of it, besides other methods already mentioned, another is to accompany the person into that state so that he or she does not feel so alone. Though this may be unusual for some therapists, and may not fit everyone's style, it can be very helpful to join the person, somewhat, in his or her altered state. For example, if a woman becomes anxious because she is feeling very "trancy" and unfocused, go partly into this state with her. Feel your way into this state as well and speak from that altered experience about the sense of tranciness. You might even hold her hand if the situation allows, and say you will be with her on her journey. Having someone else enter a state with you can be a great relief.

Also, it can be helpful to limit the amount of time to experience that state (as we saw with the CR state). Tell the person to experiment with that experience for only a minute and then come back to ordinary reality. This time parameter can provide a sense of security and safety.

Responding to a Person's "Part" Identity

Sometimes it is helpful to respond to the person in total consistency with the "part" with which he or she is unconsciously identified. Terrina used the previously mentioned example of a woman who calls you on the phone and interviews you as a possible therapist. You feel interrogated and on the spot. The woman says in a somewhat critical tone, "Is it worth it to come once to see you?" Terrina said that you might start to feel bad, have trouble thinking, and fall into an altered state yourself! Terrina recalled such a situation in which she herself was able to stay out of an altered state and realized that this woman was unconsciously identifying with a powerful part of herself. She said to the person on the phone, "With such a powerful director as you are, I know you'll show the way, but the problem is, you don't trust yourself enough. I'm sure you can use all your intelligence and speed to get into things and solve them." Terrina acknowledged that it is often difficult to grasp the structure so quickly, especially if you are emotionally affected. Frequently, it takes more time to understand and gain some distance from the process. However, she felt this approach was worthwhile mentioning.

Re-Establishing Meta Positions

Terrina told us to remember that an altered state is not as far away from the meta position as an extreme state of consciousness. Therefore, it may be possible to access the person's meta position. Terrina again drew from her bottomless well of examples. She told us to imagine a woman who is feeling gloomy about life. The therapist tries many ways and means of engaging her, but nothing seems to work; the woman is just plain miserable and unable to do anything. Terrina suggested that the client watch the therapist *act out* this depressed experience. The client might then be able to tell the therapist more about "your" situation, direct you, or even possibly give you advice as to what to do about it. As an alternative, you might use puppets to demonstrate the person's situation. This is similar to the method of "gaining an outside view" that was listed as one of the useful methods in working with the CR state of consciousness.

In another situation, Terrina recalled, this switching of roles happened organically. A therapist got very depressed in response to his client's seemingly impenetrable depression. This therapist followed his feelings and began to talk about what it was like for him to be depressed at that moment. He took over the client's state. The client then regained a meta position and began to convince the therapist that things were not that bad. The process unfolded from there.[1]

Appeal to the Meta Position

In some instances, you can appeal to the person's meta position. You can say, "I'd like to talk to that part of you that is outside of all of these difficulties for a moment. Do you think that would be possible?" Sometimes this works and the person gains access to the greater overview of the meta position. At that point, you can discuss the situation, or perhaps, as mentioned earlier, play it out for the person, and ask him or her for advice. For example, a man was upset about his life and felt unable to focus on anything. Terrina said, "I know that you are upset and I feel for you, but in order to help you, I need your full awareness and ability to put your attention on the kinds of experiences you are having. Will that be OK with you?"

Patience and Dreams

Again, if you have tried many ways and means and do not get positive feedback, it may be a moment to engage your trust and patience, knowing that the process will evolve and develop on its own time. Nature is wise and will do the work.

She reminded us of the woman she mentioned at the beginning of her first class (Chapter 15) who says she is depressed about her life, yet has secondary signals that indicate hopefulness: a glow in her eyes, expressiveness, and tends to encourage the therapist when the therapist is feeling uncertain. However, everything you do with her is colored by this depressed feeling. You can't seem to get around it. This woman dreamt that she went way down into the earth and then something lifted her up into the sky. In this case, Eagle realized the flow of the process and said, "You will feel down and spontaneously something, perhaps the grace of god, will lift you upward." The dream gave him a larger perspective of her process and reminded him that each person's process contains its own logic, its own pacing and flow. (See Chapter 17 for more on process-oriented dream interpretation.)

It was late in the evening, and Terrina glanced up at the sky. Everyone could tell that she was longing to get back to her own planet. She said that the last two classes had stimulated her to do a lot more research and that it was important for her to do that in solitude. She reminded us to consider these various states of consciousness when we are confused about our work with our clients. She thanked Dona Carletta for inviting her and without further ado, she flew off into the universe.

Notes

1. This is an aspect of "flipping," a method Arny developed for working with people in extreme states, see Arnold Mindell, *City Shadows* (New York: Routledge, 1988), 100.

Chapter Seventeen

Dream Maps

Dreams can be seen as maps that reveal the way in which a process progresses, momentary and long-term perspectives, and hints about pacing.

Dona Carletta introduced this class on dreams. She said that, although there are thousands of things we can learn about dreams and dreamwork, today she was anxious to focus on one aspect, which she calls *dream maps.* Although Dona Carletta was excited about this theme, she decided to invite another guest speaker to convey the details from his unique vantage point. His name was Rhino. Anticipating our reactions, she said, "No, Rhino is not his nickname. He is a real, live, talking rhinoceros!" She said that talking animals were not uncommon on her planet but that she knew earthlings might be somewhat startled. She said that Rhino was very good at explaining the way dreams are actual maps of the process. As an animal, Rhino was more open to the flow of nature than most humans. Though he moved slowly more often than not, he was extremely flexible and could change his direction and speed in the blink of a fish, or a tree, if necessary. Most people were surprised to learn that about Rhino—especially after meeting him.

Admittedly, it took Mary and all the others a bit of time to get used to the idea that their teacher this evening was a rhinoceros. They were aghast when he slowly waddled in and made his way to the front of the room!

When Rhino began to speak, they were even more shocked. He ignored their—oh, so unnecessary—reactions, checking them off to one of those strange human prejudices that animals can't speak and have less (actually, humans believe *far* less) consciousness. In any case, he said he had certain advantages over humans and had taken great pains to find ways of helping them understand the concept of dream maps. He told us he would do his best to explain the ideas and then return home for his daily bath. Dona Carletta nodded, understanding Rhino's needs. Rhino started out by outlining what were, to him, five important aspects of dreams as dream maps and then began his more detailed lecture.

1. **Dreams can help us know whether we are on track with someone.**
   Rhino said that if you don't know whether or not you are really on track with a client, a dream can confirm or deny the relevance of your current direction.
2. **Dreams give perspective.**
   Dreams can help us see the person's process in a greater context than we may have been aware of previously.
3. **Dreams show the flow of process.**
   Dreams can often help us see the person's momentary identity (primary process) and the experiences the person is moving toward (secondary experiences) in the future.
4. **Dreams give clues to the rhythm and pacing of the work.**
   Dreams can reveal the timing of a person's process and its natural pace of unfolding.
5. **Dreams give clues to new methods of working.**
   Dreams can bring new information about how a process

will evolve, thereby augmenting our work with our clients.

Recent Dreams and Childhood Dreams

Rhino said he first needed to talk briefly about the difference between recent dreams and childhood dreams. He knew that we had already learned a bit about this in our studies of the intake chart, but he wanted to add his perspective. "And yes," he said, anticipating questions from the group, "animals do dream!"

He said that childhood dreams we remember as adults are visual descriptions of *long-term* patterns, central lifelong processes. He shared Eagle's teachings that the difficult, scary, or awesome figures in our childhood dreams are actually allies that, if wrestled with, bring great power to our lives. Rhino reminded us that if a person does not remember a childhood dream, you can ask whether he or she has a childhood memory—the first thing he or she remembers from childhood. Recent dreams, on the other hand, are particularly reflective of the person's *current* life situation.

Dream Progressions

Rhino wanted to tell us more about dream progressions, that is, the flow of a dream or dream fragments from the beginning to the end. He said that when someone remembers an entire dream in which there is a situation that evolves as the dream unfolds (not just a dream fragment), frequently the beginning of the dream depicts the person's primary process and momentary life situation in symbolic, visual language. As the dream flows on, the later stages refer to further in the future and are more secondary. The middle of the dream shows the unique way in which the process is flowing between these points. If the person remembers a series of fragments of dreams, this may have a similar progression from the first fragment to the last. Sometimes, however, people do not remember the entire evolution of a dream because certain parts seem so significant and others are forgotten.

Rhino wanted to speak about the kind of dream people remember in its entirety and its evolution because these are the types of dreams he is fascinated with in the moment. He spoke of a therapist whose client is very creative but shy about it. This client, a man, identifies with being a gentle person who does not express himself well. The man also has skin rashes that he describes as "breaking out," but he is timid to discuss or express that energy in any conscious way. When the subject of his rashes comes up, he has a tendency to change course and ask how the *therapist* is feeling. Indeed, he is always kind, always attempting to adapt to what he thinks will please the therapist. In the meantime, the therapist is feeling a bit upset with her abilities because she has been unable to help this man gain access to his creative energy.

Guessing Dreams

Before going further, Rhino wanted to do something fun that he had observed Eagle do many times. He said, "If we go by the hypothesis that the beginning of many dreams is closer to the person's identity and the end of the dream reveals those process aspects that are more secondary, or further away from identity, what might this man dream?" Rhino asked us to break into small groups and experiment with *creating* a dream that this man might have.

This was one of Rhino's favorite learning methods, and everyone seemed to have a lot of fun doing it. In fact, Rhino discovered a byproduct of this exercise: Everyone became more enlivened and creative than they normally were!

In any case, Rhino reminded us that our ability to *create* a dream depended largely on our capacity to *transpose* the man's process structure into symbolic images and place these elements together in a dream or story sequence. People agreed that this man's primary process had to do with being gentle and adaptable and that his secondary process had to do with creative expression.

After much discussion and imaginative brainstorming, Rhino told everyone what this man actually dreamed. A very compassionate person came into a room of people and was very kind to everyone; after that, one person in the group got up and started to dance in an ecstatic way.

Dreams and Pacing

Rhino stressed that if you, like this person's therapist, are feeling that you are a failure, not really being of help to someone, look at the person's dream for clues. You can see the pattern of her or his process in the dream. This man's dream was comforting to the therapist because it revealed to her the course and pace of the process. That is, the dream showed that *first* there is a compassionate and loving person, *after* which the ecstatic energy arises. This is the *natural flow* of his process, meaning that the compassionate side of this man needs to arise and be affirmed first *and then* his creative, expressiveness will follow naturally.

Process-Oriented Dream Interpretation

Rhino now wanted us to focus on process-oriented dream interpretations. He explained that this type of interpretation simply describes, in ordinary terms, the flow of the process as it appears in the dream and relates this flow to the person's momentary situation and potential future development.

What would be a process-oriented dream interpretation of this man's dream? Rhino might say to the man, "First you will notice the compassionate side of yourself that cares for others arising. Enjoy that and appreciate it. Then your expressiveness will automatically emerge."

Rhino said that a helpful question to ask in relation to the dream is, "Where in the dream is the person currently? What spot in the dream reflects the person's momentary identity and current life situation?" Answering this will give you a clearer overview of "where the person is at" in the flow of his or her process and where things might be heading. In the preceding example, the man was at the point in the dream when the compassionate person entered the room.

It's All Here and Now

Rhino then presented a paradoxical concept. The dream reveals a flow over time and, simultaneously, the *entire* dream is happening in any given moment! Now what does that mean? Rhino said that you could see the whole dream happening if you look at the person's double signals. "Let's consider this man," Rhino said. "He appears very gentle and compassionate and, at the same time, you will notice signals of wildness or expressiveness, perhaps in his quick hand motions or a glint in his eyes, and certainly in his experience of his rashes. The whole process is contained in each moment. The way the process unfolds, however, is quite individual and can be seen in the dream. In this case, if the therapist appreciates his loving nature, this man may at another point be interested in unfolding his experience of his rashes or hand motions."

More Pacing Examples

Rhino wanted to mention another favorite example about pacing and timing in connection with dream-like information. The example was about a little boy who was brought by his parents to a therapist because they said he was "antisocial." He preferred to be alone and did not make friends with others. The parents were worried about the child' s development and his ability to relate to other children. The boy drew a picture (which is analogous to a dream) of a caterpillar in a forest. When the therapist asked him about this picture, the boy told the following story: "Once upon a time there was a forest with one caterpillar. One day the caterpillar turned into a butterfly and it began to fly with many other butterflies."

Rhino told us his process-oriented dream interpretation of this child's picture-story. He said that the child is in a primitive stage (caterpillar) and will naturally grow up, mature, so to speak, and develop friends (other butterflies). He told the parents that they needn't worry; the child would eventually develop social skills and relate well to other children.

In another situation, a young adult who just got out of school was about to start an apprenticeship. He felt tired of being in structured settings and wanted to drop the job and assume a freer and more creative lifestyle. When he described this situation to his therapist, the therapist didn't know what the right direction would be for him; should he drop the apprenticeship, or not? What did he dream? He dreamt that there was a very unusual child in the neighborhood but that it was not yet time for him to become friends with this child. In this case, the dream showed that although the young man wants to *befriend* his more unusual or creative self, it is not yet time—though this alternative will develop in the future. For the time being, he needs to adapt to the ordinary world of work and apprenticeships, knowing that, later, he will realize his creative nature more fully.

Guessing about the Person Based on the Dream

Rhino reminded us that we could also guess details about a person's life (extrapolation) just from hearing the person's dream. He said that this was a great way to learn about dreams and their relationship to the person's overall process: Present a dream and guess the person's age, the meaning of the dream symbols, the process structure, the types of addictions, body symptoms, and relationships the person might have.

He reminded us of a previous class in which we heard about a woman who was depressed and dreamt she was lying on a couch and was going to take the scissors to stab herself. There we were challenged to guess this woman's age and translate her symbolic dream material into everyday terms.

The Wisdom of Process

One of the biggest lessons from all of this, Rhino said, is that the dream shows the wisdom of the process, of nature. In the example of this depressed woman just mentioned, we ordinarily think that it is awful to feel so bad, and we want to help her get out of that situation as quickly as possible. Most of us would do everything we could to help this woman fight her inner critic so that she would feel better about herself. However, the dream progression shows that it is by unfolding the experience *within* her depression that she will find a way to cut out that inner critic and that then something renewing will follow.

Some people said that this was a very hard thing to accept and that it goes against their impulses. Rhino understood this very well and said that he is sometimes like that too. But, he added, if we cannot alter what is happening even with the best intentions, he said, dreams will always give us a deeper glimpse into the path of nature—in this case, into the wisdom and understanding of the woman's unfolding journey.

A student protested, "But if the dream is just 'happening,' what use is the therapist?" Rhino thought this was a wonderful question. He said that, in essence, the therapist is an *awareness facilitator* who helps the person gain an overview of, bring more awareness and adjust to, this natural flow. Rhino said he thought that was plenty to do.

Nature's Path

Rhino knew that this type of thinking requires a *beginner's mind*—a mind or heart that is focused on the flow of events rather than on attaining a particular goal, even when that goal is healing. He said that more would be discussed about this in the class on "Who's Your Boss?" (See Chapter 25.) He then looked at us with a serious, deep look in his eyes and said, "Tell me, what are your goals for people? What are you *really* trying to do? Are you there to determine what is best for someone, or to follow nature? Are you trying to determine what nature should be doing, or are you a follower of the Tao?" There was quiet throughout the room as people pondered their most basic beliefs.

As an animal, Rhino was more interested in nature than in the desires and ideas of people. And he knew that others had their own beliefs and goals. Yet he quoted Eagle saying that he never heard a dream that any human or animal was able to get around. He recalled a woman who had a near-death experience. She discovered only when very close to death what life was really about for her and why she wanted to live. At that dramatic moment, she found her true reasons for living, and this discovery called up in her a great warrior who wanted to make big changes in her life. Rhino said, "One would think that there would be an easier way to get to this point. And for some, there is. However, this woman's process had its own course, though that course goes against much of what our minds and hearts feel *should* occur." He reminded us that process is much stronger than any of us; its path and timing will reveal themselves, but only if we use a beginner's mind.

Rhino continued to say that many people get confused about dreams that have unexpected sequences in them. He told a dream of a woman in which there are nasty business people after her in the beginning of the dream. The woman runs away from them and jumps into a river. Ordinarily, we would think that these mean figures symbolize secondary processes that she needs to integrate. However, since they occur at the beginning of the dream, they may very well be indications of her primary process. Rhino warned, however, that we should not make a rule of this; we must check it out with our clients. In this case, it turned out that these nasty figures are close to her identity; she has a very negative view of herself and forces herself to fit into ordinary, everyday situations that are quite uncomfortable for her. We see from the dream that the more secondary process for her is *the river.* The river represents her ability to let go, to drop out of consensus reality, and follow her dreaming experiences.

Dream Elements as Links in a Chain

Rhino threw in one more tidbit about dream sequences. He said that the ending of a dream might help the person relate to earlier parts of the dream. For example, he reminded us one more time of the woman who was depressed and grabbed the scissors. The final state of "death," of complete detachment, might just be the attitude or metaskill she needs, to deal with her inner negativity. She may be able to look at her inner critics in a detached way and even offer them tea and a friendly chat!

Therefore, a dream can be contemplated not only as a map of linear events and processes but also as a map of circular routes in which each part is embedded in, and related to, the other parts. One figure or aspect of a dream may bring just the metaskill that is needed to deal with another dream aspect. In other words, all of the parts of our dreams are like links in a chain that are bound to one another in a mysterious pattern. Just how that pattern will express itself and how we will use those parts to deal with one another is a creative project.[1]

Rhino's Summation

Before finishing, Rhino wanted to sum up some of his main points about dreams:

1. *The dream is a progression or flow.*
   Frequently, the beginning of a dream in which there is an evolution or story is closer to the person's primary process, and what occurs later reflects secondary processes.
2. *The person is at a point in that flow.*
   You can tell where the person is *just now* in the dream by listening to him or her, watching his or her behavior, and connecting this information to the dream activity.
3. *The whole dream is happening here and now.*
   The entire dream is happening right now in the person's signals and overall process.
4. *You guess about dreams and behavior through symbolic thinking.*
   You can attempt to guess what a person dreams by listening to and observing his or her story and behavior and then translating that information into symbolic images. Conversely, you can guess what a person might be like from hearing one of his or her dreams and translating those symbolic images into everyday behavior and activities.
5. *Dream images are like links in a chain.*
   The images in a dream are like links in a chain connected and interacting with one another. Sometimes the experiences that occur at the end of the dream provide the metaskill for how to work with various other parts of the dream.

Rhino suddenly looked a bit agitated and said that he was overdue for his bath and his nap. Before leaving, though, he wanted to give us an exercise that he highly recommended.

Everyone had become quite fond of him and sadly said goodbye. They then tried the following exercise with a partner.

Exercise
Dream Maps

1. One person, the "client," tells a short piece of a dream. The helper asks for a couple of associations to the dream figures or parts, knowing to wait until the client offers an *emotional* association, not just a definition. The helper should make a few notes about the dream and associations on paper. Now put the dream aside.
2. Next, the "client" talks about herself, her life, and her problems. After a few minutes, the helper should discover something secondary in the client's language or behavior—something incomplete, mysterious, unsaid. Now the helper encourages the person to amplify and unfold this secondary experience.
3. The helper should notice when the edge arises. Explore the edge, try to go over it, ask about the person's belief system that makes it difficult to go over that edge. Respect the person's feedback. Notice where the person is in the moment, in respect to the new emerging process.
4. After fifteen minutes the helper should try to connect what happened in the work with the dream progression. The following questions can guide the helper:
   a. Where is the person *just now* within that dream map?
   b. Does the dream bring any new information about the direction or flow of the process?
   c. What direction were you, the helper, going in, and is that direction similar to the one in the dream map?
   d. Attempt a process-oriented dream interpretation, such as, "You were [there], now you are [here], later you may experience [this and that]."

Notes

1. For much more on dreams and dreamwork, see Arnold Mindell, *Dreambody* (Portland, Oregon: Lao Tse Press, 1998); *The Dreammaker's Apprentice* (Charlottesville, Virginia: Hampton Roads, 2001).

Chapter Eighteen

Dreaming Up

Your feelings can be a crucial key to understanding the process.

Dona Carletta returned to her teaching post again. She said that one of the most important tools a therapist has while working with others is her or his own feelings. The therapist can understand these feelings and reactions in such a way that the knowledge benefits the client. As mentioned in the class on the Big Flirt (see Chapter 8), many therapists bring their cases for supervision because they have strong feelings that arise in their work with clients, and these feelings have obscured their ability to understand what is happening and what to do.

In this class Dona Carletta wanted to look specifically at feelings that arise *while* working with someone and that then diminish after the person has left. Eagle calls these feelings "dreamed-up" reactions.[1] This means that the feelings you have are responses to the momentary unconscious signals of the other person. Dona Carletta said that the concept of dreaming up is part of a process-oriented paradigm that differs from the traditional way of viewing individuals as separate and distinct from one another. The process work paradigm sees both people as interconnected through their dreaming processes, their edges, and subtle signal exchanges. When the client emits certain unconscious signals, the therapist's body experiences and reacts to them; the therapist changes. And vice versa. This is what is called dreaming up.

Dona Carletta recalled one of Eagle's simple examples of dreaming up.[2] A woman is primarily very nice and accommodating but double signals by shaking her head no to Eagle's recommendations. Even though he did not see this signal consciously, Eagle started to feel disturbed and unconsciously began to stiffen in reaction to this woman's double signal. At this point, both of them began to double signal to one another without realizing it. In fact, Dona Carletta added, this is typical of many confusing relationship interactions!

Dona Carletta said that, of course, dreamed-up reactions could occur in *either* client *or* therapist in response to one another. She giggled and said, "For example, if the client brings four bouquets of flowers to the therapist and the therapist dreamed that nobody loved her, the client is most likely dreamed up by the therapist's unconscious need for love!" Dona Carletta quoted one of her colleagues who said that the dreaming up process "... is a two-way street. It is conditioned by the complex interaction of the client's and the therapist's edges."[3] Her colleague goes on to say, however, that in the therapeutic setting it is the therapist's responsibility to carry the awareness of the dreaming-up process.

Therefore, Dona Carletta wanted to stress the therapist's awareness of his or her dreamed-up feelings and the way in which he or she can make these feelings useful for his or her client. In tomorrow's class, she said, she would focus on the therapist's subtle feelings and describe a helpful meditation practice to use while working. She also reiterated that if the therapist's feelings persist, it is very likely that the therapist has *also* touched upon something in her or his own psychology and this is a signal for the need for inner work. She assured us that in a later class she would focus more deeply on the therapist's personal psychology.

Dona Carletta remembered Eagle saying that one of the dangers of the dreamed-up dynamic is that the therapist gets possessed by one part of the process and, from that perspective, insists that her or his viewpoint is right. She or he might stop noticing anything else that is occurring, and in a sense, slip into an unconscious altered state of consciousness! Because of this phenomenon, a lot of time goes by when the therapist is in a trance state.

She added that many therapists find themselves dreamed up to support the person's *secondary* process. They then try to get the person to *grow* in a particular direction instead of using their awareness to support the *whole* process. Dona Carletta reminded us that if we realize we are sliding into a dreamed-up state, or begin to feel confused, we can always look at the intake chart or seek a supervisor's advice, or both, to gain a greater overview of how these feelings fit into the overall process. She said that an important key is learning how to bring our dreamed-up feelings into the client-therapist situation in a conscious and useful way.

Dreaming Up and Double Signals

Dona Carletta stated that one of the safest methods for working with dreamed-up reactions is to look for those reactions in the client's signals. For example, in the earlier scenario, Eagle could go back and notice the woman shaking her head no. Dona Carletta described another situation from a case supervision in which the client sat hunched over and complained that he felt afraid and alone. The therapist said that, after a while, he often begins to feel especially supportive toward this man. Dona Carletta asked this therapist to act out this scene. Dona Carletta continued, "If you replayed what happened and looked carefully at the man's signals," Dona Carletta observed, "you would have noticed that there were a couple of moments when the man sat up very straight in his chair. He then returned to his hunched position." The therapist did not register this momentary signal but instead began to feel like supporting this man. "In other words," Dona Carletta said, "the supportive process that was still in the ethers of the man's dreaming, materialized, so to speak, in the (unconscious) supportive behavior of the therapist. The therapist was picking up this "sitting up straight" inner part of the man (a secondary process) that supported him, but with which he was not yet in contact." Dona Carletta said one possible method of dealing with this is to go back to the client's double signal and ask him to explore what it is like to sit in that upright way.

Dreaming Up, Ghosts, and Roles

"As you can see," Dona Carletta remarked, "the therapist is often dreamed up as one of the 'ghosts' in a person's process." In other words, the therapist becomes a channel for a particular ghost that is not yet represented. She told us about one of her sessions with a teenager who told her emphatically that he wanted to break out of the restrictions his parents place on him. Although Dona Carletta is ordinarily quite radical, she was surprised to find herself suddenly feeling very conservative! She said that if you were to listen to this young man carefully, you would notice that his parents are *secondary figures* who are restricting him. They are like ghosts in the momentary atmosphere he is yelling at. Dona Carletta suddenly found herself becoming these *conservative ghosts!*

Dona Carletta said she also discovered her conservative reactions in the figures of the young man's dream in which a *schoolteacher* was disciplining someone. She also found the roots of her feelings in the teenager's signals. She noticed that while he spoke about breaking out of restrictions he had a slightly guilty expression on his face. This expression implies that there is an inner (or possibly outer) figure that is angry with him for this behavior and makes him feel guilty about it.

Dona Carletta cautioned again that if we do not realize we have entered a dreamed-up state, we might fall into thinking that our viewpoint is *the* correct one. In this case, we might become the authority and insist that this young man stop what he is doing. "An alternative," she continued, "is to become aware of our dreamed-up reactions and see them as one part of a larger field or story." In this situation, she asked the teen if he had guilty feelings about what he was doing and the teenager replied that he did. Dona Carletta explained that she decided to make positions or roles in the room for the various figures, in this case, the authoritarian and rebellious sides. She and the client went in and out of, and interacted from, these positions until the teenager felt he had come to a satisfactory resolution between these parts.

Dona Carletta said, "In general, when you begin to have strong feelings when you are with a client, it is very helpful to ask yourself, 'What role am I possibly occupying in this person's process and in the interaction between us?' and 'How does this role relate to the person's ordinary identity?' One possibility, then, is to make *roles* for these various parts of the process."

Metacommunicating about Roles

Dona Carletta explained that after noticing the feelings we are having and the ghost role they may represent, and noticing the role the client seems to be identified with, a useful method is *metacommunicating* about these roles. "For example, if I'm having feelings of taking care of a client and these feelings seem a bit exaggerated, I might ask the client, 'Did you notice how motherly I am? I hope it's having a good effect. Is this something that you need? Are you feeling like an unloved person who needs loving care?'"

Dona Carletta said you can also imagine the larger ghost story that includes both roles. "For example," she continued, "imagine that you feel that someone is acting inflated and irritating. You feel that the person should be more humble. One way to deal with your response is to create a ghost story. One possible story would have a person who has never been supported enough and someone else who wants to bring that person down. You might say to the client, 'Are you acting uppity because you were never supported?' You are identifying both roles and placing them in the context of a story." Dona Carletta paused for a moment, recalling her own reactions to Huffy during an earlier class

Dona Carletta mentioned another situation. "Imagine a client who goes inside of herself and refuses to talk. The therapist, who is normally quite patient and caring, feels irritated. The therapist might imagine the role he is in as someone who doesn't like that the person retreats and wants her to come out. The therapist might say, "Are you going inside because you have been forced to come out all the time?"

Indirect Metacommunication

There are many times when it is not appropriate for us to express our feelings to clients. In that case, Dona Carletta said we can notice what we are feeling and metacommunicate that information by asking the person if he or she ever feels that way.

"Imagine that you are working with a client," said Dona Carletta, "and he says that his boss criticizes him a lot. You notice that you have a strong negative reaction to this boss, but the person doesn't seem to react at all. You might simply say, 'Am I having a reaction because you aren't?' Again, it is helpful to ask yourself again and again, 'What role am I occupying in the process?' If you frequently feel tired when you are with a particular client, you might ask the person whether he ever finds himself spacing out and feeling exhausted. If you, as the therapist, feel worthless and intimidated when you are with a particular client, you might ask the client if she ever feels insecure."

Using a Shamanic Style

Dona Carletta said that many of us have shamanistic moments now and then, when we need to drop out and follow our feelings, intuitions, and visions while we are working. In these moments, our process asks us *not* to notice signals or try to figure out the structure of what is happening. If used wisely, this method can bring important information and be of great benefit to the client. Some people go to therapists just because they are seeking this intuitive, shamanistic approach.

In this case, *consciously allowing yourself to drop out* can make space for dreamed-up reactions to arise and thereby bring up information of which you were previously unaware. Dona Carletta said that this is one of her main methods though she understood that this was unusual for many. She mentioned one of her clients, a woman. Both the client and she felt very blocked and were unable to do anything in the session. Dona Carletta felt bad for the woman but a bit upset with her as well, although she did not know why. With her client's permission, she relaxed, dropped her conscious mind and its goals, and let her imagination guide her.

Dona Carletta had a rather unusual vision. She saw an intense looking figure approaching the woman and giving the woman what looked like a quick "zen chop" to the back of her head. While this was not especially shocking for Dona Carletta, who knew she could be a really wild creature, she thought that it would shock the woman if she said it to her. But her client insisted that Dona Carletta tell her what she saw.

The woman said, "Why would that figure do that to me?" Dona Carletta allowed her dreaming nature to go further into that figure and said, "That figure wants to say, 'It's enough! Drop your personal history!'" Surprisingly, the woman began to laugh uncontrollably. She said that this was a relief to hear and was exactly the message she needed! She was anxious to drop her identity. She was bored and wanted desperately to open up to something new in her life.

"By the way," Dona Carletta added, "I forgot to mention that, had I watched the signals of this woman, I would have noticed that 'chopping' signal she gave when she unconsciously slapped her thigh in a staccato-like manner a couple of times while speaking."

Dona Carletta acknowledged that we might feel shy or afraid to bring in our inner experiences in this way, that it may not be a style for everyone, or every situation! This all depends very much on the particular context, the person we are with, our mood, the overall scene, the timing, the relationship with your client and his or her process, and the therapeutic school from which we come. She also said that some therapists who would like to use such states of consciousness might not have a full awareness that allows them to simultaneously retain an overview, to notice feedback, and to process the ensuing situation. Instead, these therapists may get lost in the altered state and never be found again! In such a case, more training in altered state awareness is crucial!

In any case, she reminded us that we can start anywhere on the river and come to the same place. What direction we actually take to get there is a matter of magic and the moment. She ended by suggesting the following exercise.

Exercise
Your Feelings and Dreaming Up

1. Think about a situation in which you had a strong reaction or feeling about a client but didn't know how to make that feeling useful. Describe to yourself the client's behavior and your ordinary behavior with her or him.
2. Think about what aspect of the client's process you may have been experiencing and which of the methods just described might be applicable and helpful.
3. Imagine using this method with your client.
4. Finally, ask yourself if your 'dreamed up' reactions or feelings could in some way be related to your personal process as well.

Notes

1. For an in-depth look at dreaming up, see Arnold Mindell, *The Dreambody in Relationships* (Portland, Oregon: Lao Tse Press, 2002); Joe Goodbread, *Radical Intercourse* (Portland, Oregon: Lao Tse Press, 1997).
2. Mindell, *The Dreambody in Relationships*, 34.
3. Goodbread, *Radical Intercourse*, 122.

Chapter Nineteen

Discomfort and Meditation

Your sense of discomfort can be the beginning of an important awareness process.

Now that we had studied a bit about dreaming up, Dona Carletta wanted to briefly focus on the therapist's ability to notice her or his *very subtle* feeling changes while in the midst of interacting with a client. Unlike the Big Flirt, which is a strong, overall feeling-sense of a person, these feelings are minute, subtle, and momentary; they pass quickly but also may contain the keys to the deeper process that is trying to unfold. Yet, this can so easily escape our attention.

Eagle has always said that our work with people is a continual awareness meditation. It is a space in which we have the opportunity to bring our attention to subtle feeling changes inside of ourselves and our clients and, through this focus of attention, discover very meaningful and central aspects of the process. He describes these subtle feelings as "sentient tendencies," as experiences that flit by before they even begin to unfold and express themselves in an overt way.[1] He frequently offers his fail-safe advice: "If you don't know what to do, follow your awareness."

Dona Carletta said that it is easy to get out of touch with ourselves while we are working and to not notice these subtle feelings. Some of us have learned to blot out our feelings while interacting with others. Some have even learned to ignore subtle feelings as a way of life. It is common for a therapist to be so focused outside, on the client and the content of what is occurring, that he or she loses contact with what is transpiring within. Subtle feelings are ignored or simply assumed to be extraneous to what is occurring with the client. She added that perhaps it would help for us to feel that we are like sensitive instruments that notice minute signals even if we are not aware of these signals consciously.

"Imagine someone telling a sad story very quickly," Dona Carletta said. "As you listen to the story, there is a moment when you begin to feel slightly depressed. If you were able to stay centered in yourself, you might recall the *exact moment* in that story when you began to feel depressed. To retrieve that moment, one option is to ask the person to go back to that particular place in the story and to explore what was happening for him or her at that moment. It is possible that you, the therapist, unconsciously noticed the person skipping over his or her deep feelings at that point. By refocusing on that moment, the client may be able to deepen his or her experience.

Dona Carletta stressed that it can also be a big edge to focus on our feelings because some people we work with set up systems in which it is forbidden to notice or express feelings. It can take a heroic effort to focus on feelings in that case.

Dona Carletta reminded us that not all client situations (or therapeutic modalities) allow us to explore and express our feelings, and that preference must be respected as well. There are times when it is not appropriate to focus overtly on feelings with a given client. In those moments, she said, we can do this entire process internally, or we can wait and investigate our feelings at a later time. Either way, it is useful to maintain the perspective that our feelings are part of the larger field between our clients and ourselves. She then reminded us that these methods, as well as all others presented in the various classes, are not meant as programs but are part of a flowing palette of tools that can be called upon and adapted depending upon the unique client-therapist situation.

Discomfort

An important feeling to notice and to focus on while interacting with someone is a slight sense of shyness, uptightness, or discomfort. "For example," Dona Carletta said, "you might suddenly feel discomfort in response to what someone has done but not know why you feel this way. Your feeling may occur so quickly that you do not even realize what has happened. You might think to yourself, *Oh, it wasn't such a big deal when she looked at me that way. I must be overreacting.* With that frame of mind, it is hard to hold that moment and give that feeling space and time for exploration. If you mention this feeling to your client and he or she insists that it has nothing to do with him or her, then it may be an aspect of your personal psychology that you need to explore at another time." One central source of discomfort is a double signal. Dona Carletta reminded us that double signals occur outside of the person's primary identity and therefore express themselves in incomplete motions, sounds, or postures that are not understandable at first. The incongruence inherent in double signals can cause a slight sense of discomfort.

"For example," Dona Carletta continued, "imagine that someone who is ordinarily quite friendly is momentarily cold toward you. This shift is confusing and makes you feel temporarily uncomfortable. However, you may not consciously register what has occurred. You feel a slight sense of discomfort but do not know why. If you let this moment pass without self-reflection, you may begin to feel disoriented.

"If you recall what the person did that made you feel uncomfortable but do not find out more about it, you may find yourself beginning to wonder whether the client does not like you or you did something to hurt her or him or, alternatively, find yourself turning against the person or labeling her or his behavior. Later, you might start to think that person is too cold or too insensitive.

You will forget that the thing that made you uncomfortable—the double signal—is just the beginning of a process that is trying to unfold. The ensuing process may be very different from the way in which you experienced the original signal. You will forget that you need to get to the very root of that signal to find out what it is actually expressing.

"If, however, you have a meditative type of awareness and catch the moment when discomfort occurs, you might think to yourself, *Hmm, discomfort is happening. Let's give this feeling a little space, a beginner's mind, in which to explore the moment when I became uneasy.*"

Awareness Process

Dona Carletta stressed that the metaskill or the *way* in which we focus on our feelings of discomfort is very important. A great deal of sensitivity is required. Otherwise, pointing out a double signal will make the person feel put down or embarrassed. We are all extremely vulnerable around our double signals precisely because they are unconscious to us. Therefore, this must be done with care.

Dona Carletta suggested, "Imagine a client who is ordinarily a bit distant and suddenly comes close to you. In that moment, you notice a sense of discomfort." She suggested that one possible way of exploring this is to follow your meditative awareness and say to the client, "'I need a moment to focus on my own feelings. Is that OK with you?' If the client agrees, you might continue, 'This is nice and intimate. But it goes quickly and I have inner reactions that I need to focus on.' After that, if the situation allows, follow your inner awareness to recall exactly what happened and what signals made you feel the discomfort, saying, 'What made me a bit uncomfortable was a motion you made, this one … Perhaps it was trying to convey something I didn't understand.'" She then explained that you can guess more deeply into the signal such as, "'Maybe I haven't seen or appreciated you enough.'"

Dona Carletta continued to elaborate, saying, "If your guess is not right, you might invite the client to go back to that spot and to meditate on her or his own experience, to get to the root of what she or he was trying to express. You might make a frame for exploring that moment by saying something like, 'Oh, I felt something at that point. Perhaps you could go back and meditate on what happened. Let's just go slowly and follow our awareness and try to find out what is happening at that moment.' If it is a movement process, ask the person if it would all right to explore what is happening in slow motion and process the subtle feelings that arise in connection with it. Or if the person is shy, you might ask him or her to imagine what he or she would do if the process went further. Then try to get to the essence of what he or she is expressing."

Dona Carletta outlined some of the steps in this awareness process. They are not meant as a linear procedure, but for the sake of clarity, she outlined them in a step-by-step sequence. She reminded us that the metaskill here is sensitivity toward the client and compassionate attention to your own awareness process.

1. **Notice an uncomfortable moment and trust your feelings.**
   Notice when something happens that makes you feel some discomfort such as feeling shy, ill at ease, frozen, or vulnerable. Notice your tendency to doubt your experience, to feel that you are "just uptight," "projecting my stuff," or "off the point." Notice how you ignore your experiences because you cannot connect them to what is happening or cannot understand them right away. You will need a sense of compassion to hold your attention to these subtle moments.
2. **Make space for your experience and use your awareness.**
   Make space and begin to focus on those subtle feelings. Notice exactly what you are feeling. Go backwards in time and recall what was happening when you began to feel discomfort. What were the person's signals at that point? Recall each movement, the speed, the looks, the gestures, the sounds of the other person during that

interaction. Ask yourself, "What was it that made me feel uncomfortable?"

3. **Get to the root or essence of that signal.**
When you have found the signal or interaction that made you uncomfortable, the next step is to go deeper. Ask yourself, "What is the root of that signal, what is its very essence?" Would it be a deep desire for appreciation or contact? A sense of pride? A spiritual sense of compassion? A longing for freedom? Do this process internally and if appropriate share your insights in a sensitive way with your client if the situation permits. (*If the client feels that your understanding of that experience is not correct, or if he or she is uncomfortable hearing your insights, make a frame and invite her to go back to that mysterious point. Encourage him or her to meditate upon that moment and try to get in touch with the essence of what he or she was trying to express.*)
4. **Notice feedback.**
If the client insists that this is all your psychology, then acknowledge that this must be part of your own process and explore this experience at another time when you are by yourself. Otherwise, unfold the process further by exploring the essence of that experience and helping the client realize that essence in his or her life.

Dona Carletta concluded the class by presenting the following training exercise that would help us focus on our own awareness process. She said that if there were only one thing that we learn from these classes, this would be the most important.

Exercise
Discomfort and Meditation (in pairs)

1. One person is the "client," one the "helper." The client should begin to talk about problems or issues. The "helper" should begin to work with the client in any way that she or he likes.

2. As the two work together, the helper should notice any slight feelings of discomfort, uneasiness, or sensitivity that she or he has.
3. The helper asks the client for permission to make a little space to explore her or his feelings of discomfort. The helper meditates and reports on what she or he is feeling.
4. The helper goes back over what happened at the point when she or he became uncomfortable, trying to recall each thing that occurred, what signals made her or him feel shy or uncomfortable, and guesses at their essence. The helper then offers this to the client in a compassionate way.
5. If the client disagrees with the helper's perception, or would like to investigate her or his own signals, the helper then asks the client to go back to that moment and meditate on the essence of what he or she was trying to express. Together, helper and client unfold this aspect of the process by getting to its essence and discussing how this essence might be useful to the client's life as a whole.

Notes

1. For a full discussion of sentient tendencies, see Arnold Mindell, *Dreaming While Awake* (Charlottesville, Virginia: Hampton Roads, 2000).

Chapter Twenty

Inner Strength and Wisdom

A person's unconscious inner strength can subtly direct what is happening without the therapist knowing it.

When Dona Carletta arrived for class this evening, she said that she was going to speak about a typical therapeutic situation that often confuses or upsets therapists: the moment when a client is growing into her or his own power, inner authority, and wisdom but is not yet identified with it. This strength is not yet at the person's conscious disposal and therefore sometimes appears secondarily in the person's double signals of resistance in the form of subtle negativity toward, or criticism of, the therapist. Many of us recognized this situation either in our work with others or in ourselves!

Dona Carletta continued, saying that, in these situations, many therapists feel upset by the person's unintended resistance. The therapist may take it so personally that she or he feels hurt, put down, or irritated by what is happening and loses access to her or his meta position. Because this is a type of situation that is frequently brought for supervision, Dona Carletta wanted to place special focus on it, even though some of the information she would discuss in this class had been spoken about in previous classes.

She reminded us that being of service to the client is of utmost importance. In this instance it may mean helping the person gain access to this inner knowingness or authority and make it useful for his or her life, but *how* to do this is food for this evening's studies. She added that, although for simplicity's sake she will use the terms "power," "strength," and "authority" throughout the class, they are somewhat limiting descriptions for deep inner processes that, when unfolded, might be experienced as a feeling of centeredness, a sense of confidence, an ability to defend oneself, relating to oneself instead of others, the capacity to follow one's own dreaming, or at the level of the essence, the experience of being an immovable heavy rock that is "just so."

The Client's Directive Power

A most typical situation, Dona Carletta continued, is as follows. "Imagine a woman who says she is tired and at a loss for what to do next to resolve her problems. She says that she's sure the therapist will know what to do. The "therapist who knows what to do" is secondary for her. The woman smiles when the therapist makes suggestions, but she doesn't seem to follow any of them. In fact, if you watched her closely, you would also notice that she subtly shakes her head no to everything the therapist suggests."

Dona Carletta warned us that we, as therapists, might begin to get irritated and simply label the client resistant. Or, if we do not see her double signals, we might think, because she is smiling, that she is happy to follow anything we say. However, though she appears compliant, another process is *happening simultaneously.*

Dona Carletta then told us that this woman complains that she has a tendency to withdraw in relationships, and that this tendency does not make her happy. Dona Carletta said, "At this point, a greater overview would be most helpful. This woman identifies herself as being tired and not 'knowing' what to do. Her secondary process has to do with directing what happens and 'knowing' what to do. Perhaps she was never allowed to follow herself and always had to follow an authority figure such as a parent. This is expressed through negative feedback to the therapist's suggestions. With this overview of her process, we might suspect that she withdraws from others to first find *her own* direction and to believe in who she is. At times this need to follow herself might be expressed by canceling appointments with her therapist. Dona Carletta also added that sometimes a client will seem to be in a trance state when you interact with him or her. This may also be an indication of a past abusive situation that makes it difficult to follow or protect oneself. For some it may have even been dangerous to follow one's own impulses, needs and preferences. In all cases, it is very important to go slowly and carefully, following the person's signals and feedback as to how to proceed."

Background Processes in Body Signals

Dona Carletta spoke about one of her clients who does not face her directly but who is turned slightly to the side. Intuitively, one day, she asked the client for advice about a problem she (Dona Carletta) was trying to figure out. The client really liked doing that. As he was helping Dona Carletta, the man turned directly toward her. Dona Carletta then assumed that, while turning to the side could be expressive of many different types of experiences, in this case, the client's signals were an expression of an inner authority or wisdom of which he is not aware yet. Helping Dona Carletta with her problem gave this man a conscious sense of this authority. He could experience his own wisdom instead of always being in the "client" role, the person who has troubles and needs someone else's help. Here, Dona Carletta brought out the background process without having to focus on it directly.

It's Happening Already

"Now, I would like to present a real mind twister!" Dona Carletta happily announced. She told us about a situation in which the client and therapist discovered that the client had a great deal of strength and inner-directiveness being communicated in his double signals. The client said he was a bit shy but agreed to try to unfold and experience a bit more of that inner strength.

The therapist tried all sorts of ways to help him gain access to that power. She asked him, for example, to feel that power in his body and walk around the room with that feeling. Each time, the man started to follow the therapist's suggestions but then quickly stopped. This happened again and again, and the therapist became quite frustrated and even a bit pushy!

Dona Carletta started jumping up and down with excitement, though no one knew why. "How is his strength manifesting?" she asked. Before anyone could answer she blurted out, "The strength or resistance to following the therapist *is already happening*, every time he stops! In other words, while *trying to be strong*, he *is strong*. One process is imbedded in the other. Did you get that?" Dona Carletta asked. Some nodded their heads.

She continued to explain, "Not following the therapist's direction, in this case, is his unconscious way of knowing and directing the situation. He is showing that, ultimately, he has to be the leader and determine when the right moment is to do something and when not. She continued to say that if the therapist fails to notice this particular way of expressing strength, she might continue with her program to help this man *be powerful* without seeing that it is *already happening*. The therapist could bring the man's attention to the way in which he does not follow her suggestions and could compliment him on the ability to follow himself.

One student asked Dona Carletta whether this wasn't just a form of resistance that needed to be overcome, for progress to occur in the therapy. Dona Carletta replied that that was a traditional way of looking at this man's behavior. "However," Dona Carletta continued, "in this situation, when the therapist noticed and appreciated the way the man was saying no to her, the man became aware of his inner strength and ability to determine what *he* wanted. Indeed, he needed more conscious access to this *resistant* behavior.

The man later told his therapist that his strength often came out as resistance in relationships and, indeed, he seemed to sabotage many of his friendships in this way. Ultimately, he was able to use this strength and inner knowing more beneficially in those relationships and in his life as a whole.

Dona Carletta once again emphasized that of most importance in this example is the therapist's ability to remain awake while focusing on a particular method. She said that it is easy to become fixated on a "good" idea to such a point that we do not notice the subtle interchanges that are happening simultaneously. She said that the method of dealing with discomfort mentioned in the previous class could help in this case. She also reminded us of the analogy of the river. While following one current, notice any other that is occurring at the same time.

Dona Carletta just could not help herself at this point and said that she had to toss in another example that was somewhat off the main theme of the evening, but it just jumped in her mind. She allowed herself to veer off her intended course as a way of modeling the most important aspect of her teaching as a whole: to follow and change according to the flow of events, rather than staying firmly with your intended direction. Her example had to do with the idea, *it's happening already.* "Here's a funny situation," she said. "Imagine that a therapist has discovered that her client needs more access to his spontaneity. The therapist tries to help the client 'be spontaneous.'" Everyone in the group laughed, recognizing this paradoxical bind! Dona Carletta giggled and continued, "While the therapist is trying to *get the client to be spontaneous,* the client scratches his nose or suddenly has to get something out of his jacket. The therapist waits patiently and then continues and says to the client, 'OK, let something spontaneous happen!'" Dona Carletta chuckled and said, "How many times have we missed the fact that the thing we are trying to *make happen* is *already happening*? The spontaneity has already occurred but did not fit into the therapist's program!" Most of us nodded our heads vigorously, recognizing how many times we have been in such situations.

Dona Carletta's Personal Experience

Dona Carletta paused for a moment as her thoughts returned to the theme of the evening. She said that the entire discussion of inner power reminded her of a time in her life when an inner, negative critic bothered her. This critic demanded perfection from her and constantly told her she was not good enough. Many people in the group were shocked that she had had an inner critic! She said that, yes, she had been severely plagued by this critic, particularly in the early part of her life. During those days she was quite depressed, although you would never know it today.

In any case, during that time, she asked her therapist for assistance. However, no matter how well meaning her therapist was, or what methods her therapist used, it did not seem to help. Dona Carletta remembered saying to her therapist over and over again that nothing seemed to work. She said she was just too depressed and was convinced that she was a lost cause and that nothing would ever change. The therapist also began to get depressed.

After some time, the therapist began to discern the secondary current in this interchange. She noticed Dona Carletta's *insistence* on *not changing* and *being a lost cause.* The therapist realized that this was a way of actually fighting the inner critic's demands that she be perfect and perform well! In her (unconscious) refusal to change or "get better" was a part of Dona Carletta that was able to stand against that critic's demands and instead follow herself.

Dona Carletta told us that from an early age she had been taught not to fight back when criticized. Therefore, the whole process had gone internal, and the "fight" appeared in a kind of subtle, less useful way for her. Because this resistance was not at her conscious disposal, she experienced it more as a detrimental, inhibiting factor in her life rather than as a personal resource from which she benefited.

The therapist pointed out how strong Dona Carletta really was, because no one could get her to move out of her misery! Dona Carletta began to realize this and slowly gained access to her own wisdom and magical abilities. The interesting thing is, when she was able to consciously use this source of inner wisdom and power, the critic seemed to disappear. In fact, another way to look at it is that Dona Carletta had integrated the energy of the critic and was using it today in her teaching.

Dona Carletta said that even the most horrible figures often contain the seeds of energies and creativity that we can use in better ways in our lives. However, each of us is at a different place in respect to such negative inner forces. Sometimes it's important to understand how someone is feeling in respect to this critic, sometimes the person needs to fight this inner critic, and at other times he or she may be integrating the critic's energy—or any of a multitude of other possibilities.[1]

Moment-to-Moment Awareness

Being attuned to subtle moment-to-moment interchanges between oneself and the client can be very helpful in discovering the idiosyncratic ways in which a person's strength may be expressing itself while the focus is on another process. Dona Carletta mentioned an example that Eagle once described, which was similar to a situation mentioned in a previous class. "Think of a man who projects his own inner authority and wisdom onto the therapist. Ordinarily, this man feels afraid of people and is unable to make decisions. Now listen to this verbatim transcript," she said.

Client: (Standing slightly hunched over at the door to the office, looking rather timid, says to the therapist) *Can I come in?*

Eagle: Yes, *of course.*

Client: (They both enter the room and sit down.) *Do you think this whole mess will get better in two or three months? I feel it might, but what do you think?*

Eagle: (Realizing that this man's secondary process is the "authority" he sees in the therapist, replies) *I think you know. You're a smart man and you are probably a bit timid about it.*

Eagle realized that there was a negative father hovering over this man (a ghost) that made him feel inferior. Eagle thought the power of that negative father might be something the man would be able to access for himself. The dialogue continued as follows:

Eagle: *I'd like you to do something for me. Would you get up and try to be an authority figure?*

Client: *I can't.*

Eagle: *Go ahead and try it. It may even shorten therapy.*

Client: *I can't.*

If you remain aware, Eagle noted, you notice that the client is saying that he *can't* be authoritarian, but at the same time, he is already being his own authority by saying no to Eagle's recommendations.

Eagle: *I'm asking you to do something and you're not doing it! You're going against me. What a powerful man you are!*

Eagle recognized the man's resistance as an expression of his own inner wisdom and commended him on it. The man seemed surprised and delighted to have discovered this ability. More in-depth work then focused on helping him gain access to his inner knowledge and his ability to make incisive decisions about situations in his life.

Movement Work

"If you are unable to approach someone's secondary strength directly," Dona Carletta said, "it can be helpful to use the *transposition* method of changing channels (discussed in Chapter 13). In this instance it is most important to explain to the person what you are going to do—to frame your method—before proceeding further.

"Think of a woman who seems to go blank and unconsciously resists each of the therapist's suggestions. If you encourage this woman to direct what is happening, she will most likely refuse. So what are your alternatives?

Dona Carletta said that, in such cases, sometimes a channel change to movement (if the situation allows touch) can help so that the person can experience her strength physically. Dona Carletta described such a situation in which she said to her client,

"Excuse me for a moment, but if it's OK with you, and when you are ready, I'd like to get a bit closer to you and slightly pull on one of your fingers. If you don't want me to do that, just say so. Will that be OK with you?" The client agreed and Dona Carletta then continued, "I'll show you first what I'm going to do. I'll pull slightly on one of your fingers. All you have to do is follow your own impulses and make any movements that you like." The client said she would like to try.

When Dona Carletta pulled slightly on the person's finger, the woman began to pull back subtly. Her pulling back was very minimal, but Dona Carletta noticed it and encouraged the woman to follow that impulse and pull back and use her strength as much as she liked. A kind of tug of war ensued in which the woman realized how strong she was and how she wanted to determine what was happening. She was able to get in contact with her inner strength.

Noticing Power through Your Feelings

"Your feelings can be a great indicator of the client's power," Dona Carletta continued. "Imagine that every time you see a client, you are afraid of her. When a supervisor asks you what you are afraid of, you are not sure. You simply feel a powerful radiation from the person that makes you feel uncomfortable and uneasy. As a result, you feel paralyzed and unable to do much of anything when you are with that client."

In such situations, you can study your feelings to understand the process. Ask yourself, 'What makes me feel so afraid? What, in my fantasy would make me so fearful?" As an alternative, you might say to the person, "You have such a powerful radiation. I'm imagining there is a great strength in you that would like to express itself." Another possibility is to show the client the power you imagine in her or him, as if it were a role in the field, and ask the person whether he or she senses that power in her or himself. It is quite possible that the person feels dominated by such power. In that case, you might process the interaction between these two roles.

Negativity, Judgment, and Criticism of the Therapist

Dona Carletta now bought up an area that made a lot of people nervous. It had to do with the moment when a client has a lot of secondary wisdom and power and it appears as criticism or negativity toward the therapist. Dona Carletta said that at such moments the therapist frequently feels hurt and takes all of the criticisms personally. Many people moaned in recognition. "And," Dona Carletta added quickly, "it can be very important to study what you are doing and find out what you can do better!" She said that we would investigate more about this theme in an upcoming class entitled "Trance-ference."

She continued, "If a client can criticize you *and* help you change, this could be a very important experience for her or him, particularly if she or he was never allowed to interact in such a way with an authority figure. Most of us were not encouraged to confront or challenge authority figures in our lives. In fact, we may have been put down or punished for even trying. So, it is a big thing to discuss the way things are going with your awareness facilitator. In such a situation, supporting the client to be critical of you can be a relieving and awakening process for that person.

"Let's imagine that you say to your client, 'Please go ahead and say something negative to me.' The client smiles but hesitates. You might answer, 'It seems you need support in your negativity. It's scary to talk negatively to a therapist, an authority figure. I want to support you in it. I can even take your role.' Then you might go over to the client's side and speak for him until he is able to pick up that role himself."

Sliding into a Ditch

"In any case, when the client's criticism emanates from a secondary experience of authority and power, he or she needs your help to gain access to this power. However, you might be so 'knocked out' and upset by this criticism that you lose access to your abilities. You may feel suddenly defensive, hopeless, like a failure. Your own inner critic may start yapping while you slowly slide into a ditch!" Dona Carletta consoled us by saying it's really human to react in this way and that it's unrealistic to expect to remain unaffected simply because we are "professionals."

One of the students, Tom, said that this situation was particularly hard for him. He was so overwhelmed by his own inner critic that he always "went unconscious" in these situations, either feeling bad about himself or starting to fear or dislike the client. Dona Carletta said that one of the best remedies for insecurity is detachment. "But," she added, "who has it in such moments?" She said that the therapist's own inner work is always important here and that we would hear more about that inner work in upcoming classes (see Part V on the therapist's psychology).

Dona Carletta told us to consider a situation similar to one discussed in a previous class. Imagine a person saying to a therapist "Is it worth it to come to you? Can you solve all my problems in one hour?" The therapist, in response, feels quite intimidated and "on the spot." Dona Carletta asked us what we would surmise about the person's process structure from this brief glimpse. One student said that this person has an inner critic and is very intelligent but the intelligence is most likely secondary for him; that is the reason why the therapist was so strongly affected by it—it was a flirt!

Dona Carletta said that was right. She told of one such situation with one of her clients in which she attempted to see the larger process surrounding the signals. She said to the client, "With such a powerful director within you, you can easily show the way. But I imagine you don't trust yourself enough. I'm sure you can use all your intelligence and speed to consider your situation and come up with several options." The client said that he doubted he had the intelligence to solve his problems. Dona Carletta replied, "Oh, I guess you were never supported to believe in your full intelligence and potential."

"Of course," Dona Carletta assured us, "when you are in the midst of things, it is hard to have such an overview. That's when supervision can help. Staying centered in your awareness during intense situations such as these, as well as in any moment-to-moment interaction, is the way to avoid falling into one unconscious role or part of the process. The client then has to rebel against you, and you end up in a struggle without much awareness. While this may be important or inevitable in some instances, it usually does not help the client to become aware of what is happening or to gain access to her or his inner strength."

Reacting

Dona Carletta had more to say. "Sometimes a client will continue with her or his criticism of you to a point that you feel you have no alternative but to react. You experience yourself as the 'one being hurt' and the client seems to be in the role, albeit unconsciously, of the 'hurter.' In some situations, if you react *just a bit,* while still supporting the person as a whole, it can be helpful.

Dona Carletta told us about one of her supervision examples in which a therapist reported that his client was quite mean to him. Dona Carletta suggested that the therapist act out this client. When Dona Carletta interacted with the client, she imagined the larger situation surrounding the client's behavior and said, "Ooh, that hurts. You must do that to protect yourself, but it's painful on the other side. Is this how you treat yourself inside? Was someone hurtful to you in your life?" Here, Dona Carletta tries to understand the client's behavior, imagines that this client also suffers from the same kind of downing behavior inside himself and that he has experienced such hurtful behavior at some point in his life. She then suggested going further by processing the "hurter" and the one who is "hurt."

In this situation, Dona Carletta said she was reacting but simultaneously remembering her good feeling for the person and seeing the larger context in which his behavior was occuring; she remembered the person's entirety rather than just this one part or role.

In other situations, it is not appropriate or helpful to react outwardly. In such instances, one possibility is to imagine the essence behind the person's signals. In one of Dona Carletta's cases, she imagined that the client was aching to be able to talk about deep feelings she was having, but that discussing her deep emotions had been forbidden in her family. Dona Carletta said to the woman, "Instead of being hurtful, tell me all the strong feelings behind what you are expressing in your criticism of me."

Finally Dona Carletta threw in the idea that there are moments when the situation between client and therapist turns toward relationship work and the client is hoping you will be a "real" person with whom he or she can interact. Dona Carletta said that she would address this topic in the class on therapeutic relationship work (see Chapter 26). She ended this class with the following exercise.

Exercise
Discovering Inner Strength and Wisdom (in pairs)

1. One person imagines being someone whose power is secondary. This person expresses resistance in the background either through (1) body signals, movement, saying no to all interventions, resisting all help, or (2) adapting in the foreground but subtly directing what is happening in the background.
2. The other person works with you by experimenting with any of the methods mentioned earlier, such as:
   a. *It's happening already.* Notice the power inherent in the client's behavior in the moment.
   b. *Movement work.* Change channels and use movement to bring the background process to the foreground.
   c. *Use your feelings to imagine the background process.* Notice what you are feeling and imagine a powerful "ghost" that might be creating that feeling. Ask the client whether that ghost is something he or she can use in life or feels victimized by.
   d. *Encourage the client to be critical of you.* Ask the client to tell you how you can change.

Notes

1. See Sonja Straub's helpful paper on the inner critic, "Stalking Your Inner Critic: A Process-Oriented Approach to Self-Criticism." (Unpublished thesis, Research Society for Process Oriented Psychology, Zürich, 1990).

Chapter Twenty-One

How Processes Go Hand in Hand

Focus on the whole river; one current or process can be used for the benefit of the other.

This evening Dona Carletta started her discussion immediately and with great intent. She said that she wanted us to know the importance of being receptive to a person's *whole process* rather than favoring one aspect over another. Process work focuses on the flow of this whole process and the interrelationship between the parts. Appreciating the entire process is important because it makes the client feel you really understand him or her as a whole person. She added that while the primary and secondary processes often appear antagonistic, one of them might actually benefit the other. In this class she would address this reciprocal relationship.

Dona Carletta admitted that she was feeling a bit tired of giving examples and explanations. She wished she had a better way of presenting the information but she felt it was exciting and important information to think about and store somewhere in our bodies and memory banks, so she went over her edge and continued.

Using the Primary Process for the Benefit of the Secondary Process

Dona Carletta said that a most useful approach when working with people is to *talk to the primary process about the secondary;* in essence, this is a method of appealing to the wisdom of a person's primary process (ordinary identity and beliefs) and enlisting its help in gaining access to the person's secondary process. She said that this method is an empathic one because it supports and appreciates both primary and secondary processes. And, she added, this is an aspect of the natural style of many therapists.

She mentioned one of her colleague, Rhino's, favorite examples. A farmer came to see Rhino. This man identified himself as a "rough" and "down-to-earth" person. The man's secondary process had to do with sensitivity and feeling. In this case, it was important to use what Dona Carletta liked to call the *clothing* or the *metaskill* of his primary process to appeal to his secondary process. This means that Rhino's suggestions would have a rough and down-to-earth feeling quality about them. Rhino said to him in a somewhat gruff yet good natured and humorous way, "Hey, come on. Be more feeling or I'll give you a knock over the head!" "If you do not relate in this type of way," Dona Carletta warned, "such a client wouldn't even notice what you're talking about, and he certainly wouldn't respect you!"

The person's primary process is the ground upon which his or her beliefs are built. Without relating to this basic earth portion, the person probably won't believe you and certainly will not feel understood. Dona Carletta said that she had also learned, through working with diverse groups of people in diverse cultures and planets, that people won't feel open to you if you don't relate to their primary style of communication. Of course, she added, this requires that you have access to numerous states in yourself.

"Think of a woman who is very analytical and intellectual," Dona Carletta said. "This woman has a lot of feelings but is very shy about them. To *talk to the primary process about the secondary process*, you can first explain what you are going to do in an intellectual way; appeal first to her intelligence about why it might be important to discuss feelings. The woman will feel joined in her primary process and will have an intellectual basis from which to continue."

On the other hand, Dona Carletta warned, it's possible to become immersed in the client's primary process and never come out again! "Imagine working with a couple who are very kind," Dona Carletta said. "They have created a joint primary process—an atmosphere, so to speak—wherein it is difficult to bring up anything new or conflicted. It is possible that you will feel consumed by that primary process to the point where you will not be able to intervene at all!

"Eagle says that the big work in therapy is opening up the cramp of the primary process to admit the dreaming world. It takes a lot of sensitivity to respect the primary process while bringing in new secondary experiences.

Dona Carletta continued with her examples. "Now, think of someone who is primarily very exact and scientific and whose secondary process is very wild and impulsive. How could you use his primary metaskill of exactness and scientific acuity for the benefit of, and to explore, the secondary one? One possibility is to recommend to this man that he *think out a logical sequence of events* to help him gain access to the category that houses wild feelings.

"Think about someone who is primarily tough and suffers from a heavy addiction problem. With one such client I said, 'Do you think you are *tough enough* to overcome your addiction?'"

Dona Carletta mentioned that we could also apply this concept to movement processes. She had us imagine someone who is primarily rigid and exact in his thinking and complains that he occasionally has jittery body movements. "In addition to asking him about his medical condition and symptoms," Dona Carletta said, "and to investigate those movements, you can use his exactness as your metaskill. You might say, 'Let's use *exact awareness* on those jittery movements.'

"In another case, a woman's primary process was quite contained and controlled; she had a tendency to trip and fall down (secondarily). Dona Carletta recommended creating a safe position from which to experiment with this falling process. One possibility is to have the woman sit on a chair and experiment with lifting her arm and letting it drop down, as if it were falling.

Using the Metaskill of the Secondary Process for the Benefit of the Primary Process

Dona Carletta said that, in some cases, it is most beneficial to use the attitude or quality of the *secondary process for the benefit of the primary process.* She hoped this would not get too confusing.

Imagine someone who identifies with having a lot of unfinished tasks and who is unable to get anything accomplished. The woman also says that *events in her life are happening very quickly.* Dona Carletta used the secondary process of rapidity for the benefit of the primary one saying, "Let's get the unfinished tasks settled in the next two minutes!" The woman was shocked, then relieved, because she usually drew out her difficulties for months on end, never getting them solved. She needed access to that speed to get right into her difficulties and clear them up rapidly.

Dona Carletta added one more example. "Imagine a woman who is upset about a relationship problem and who dreams about a very compassionate figure who can heal. This figure is secondary. You can help her use that compassionate and healing metaskill as a way of dealing with herself and the relationship problems that are upsetting her."

Rule of Thought

After studying how to best use one process in service of the other, Dona Carletta came up with a useful rule of thought. She said that it may be too complicated to remember while you are working but was fun to think about:

> *When the identified "problem" is in the primary process—*
> *use the metaskill of the secondary process.*
>
> *When the identified "problem" is in the secondary process—*
> *use the metaskill of the primary process*

She reminded us of the farmer with whom Rhino worked. The problem was that he did not have access to his feelings; they were secondary. Rhino used the man's primary rough style to help him gain access to his feelings. Dona Carletta encouraged us to apply this rule of thought to the earlier examples. She then gave us the following inner work exercise.

Exercise
Using the Metaskill of One Process for the Other

1. Think about a client with whom you are having difficulty.
2. Determine what the client's primary process is; determine the secondary process. Remember, to identify what is secondary, recall the kind of things that *happen to* this client.
3. Determine whether the problem is located in the primary or the secondary process.
4. If the problem is in the secondary process, imagine using the metaskill of the primary process to gain access to the secondary process. And vice versa.

Paradoxical Methods: Prescribing the Primary Process

Before finishing, Dona Carletta wanted to present a few more ways to use the quality of one process for the benefit of the other. The first is a kind of paradoxical intervention in which the therapist prescribes the primary process.[1] This approach is a way of appreciating the primary process and setting up circumstances such that the person wants to focus on his or her secondary process.

Dona Carletta gave the example of someone who is afraid to talk about certain (secondary) topics. We might show appreciation for this fear by saying, "Let's drink tea. Maybe then we'll talk, or maybe not. Why not wait until next year?" The client then might be relieved or might insist that we discuss these issues.

Dona Carletta spoke of a person who ordinarily follows others and secondarily has her own inner direction (as discussed in Chapter 20). In a good-hearted and compassionate manner, the therapist might use a movement approach to prescribe the primary process. The therapist might recommend that the person do a number of movement activities such as moving forward, moving backward, standing up straight, etc. Initially, the client will try to follow what the therapist says but sooner or later will become fed up with being told what to do and will begin to follow herself or himself. The therapist must, of course, do such things with a compassionate metaskill.

Supporting the Whole Flow

Dona Carletta said that there is a tricky type of dynamic wherein the person continually vacillates back and forth between one process and the other. For example, a man began to express a spontaneous side of himself that he described as "nonconforming." However, after doing this for a few moments, he suddenly became afraid and upset about his behavior. Dona Carletta observed that this fluctuation between the two processes happened a number of times. She took this pattern seriously and proceeded to prescribe it: she recommended to the man that he first do one process *and then* the other. He should be wild and then apologize; be conforming and then spontaneous. She chose this method because it follows the exact flow of the client's process and conveys appreciation of the entire flow (both back *and* forth) rather than one part. The whole process is valued rather than one *or* the other experience.

In another situation, a person who was primarily rational became upset after experiencing deep emotions during a session. To respect both processes, the therapist described these two parts to the client—one that is rational and the other that is emotional—and asked the client how to deal with the conflict.

Appreciating the Whole

Dona Carletta had discussed another angle from which we can appreciate the whole by focusing on a previously mentioned topic: having a strong reaction to something a client is saying or doing and a tendency to make the person feel bad for his or her behavior. Here is a helpful example from Dona Carletta's therapy practice.

A man continually spoke about wanting to go back to see an old friend whom he said was very abusive to him but whom he hoped would be kind to him. Yet, every time he went to see this person, the friend was very cruel to him. Dona Carletta felt that he should stop wanting to go back and see this person and break out of his destructive pattern. "The challenge is, how do you bring this feeling into the conversation without making the man feel bad about his hopes and dreams?" Dona Carletta asked. Most people were silent as they pondered this dilemma. Dona Carletta answered her own question by saying that she asked this man more about his hopes and dreams, knowing that these are very important to him. Then she found a way to support the overall process—including the man's feelings and her own reactions—by saying, "I want you to have that dream, and I hope you do get it. But is it realistic with that particular person?" The man was then able to explore all of the various sides of this emotional issue.

Dona Carletta concluded the class for the day and said that tomorrow we would focus on moment-to-moment awareness and fluidity.

Notes

1. Milton Erickson is well known for prescribing the primary process as a paradoxical intervention. See Milton Erickson, *The Nature of Hypnosis and Suggestion,* Vol. 1 of the *The Collected Papers of Milton H. Erickson on Hypnosis.* (edited by Ernest L. Rossi. New York: Irvington, 1980).

Chapter Twenty-Two

Moment-to-Moment Awareness

Remaining steady in the midst of the flow is one of the therapist's most important abilities.

By this time, Mary had begun her own research. As she walked with Dona Carletta to class that day, she said she had been exploring the theme of *fluidity.* Mary said that she had noticed the importance of fluidity while studying case control sessions. For example, she was fascinated when, during case supervision, the therapist acted like the client and either Dona Carletta or Eagle interacted with that "client." Mary noticed Dona Carletta and Eagle's ability to adapt to and flow with the unfolding process, rather than holding fast to any particular concepts or ideas. In those moments, Mary felt the essence of process work, although it was very hard to put into words. It had to do with following the moment-to-moment unfolding of events.

Mary observed the way in which Dona Carletta would begin to focus on one direction with a client and then suddenly change in response to the client's feedback. She saw how Eagle realized that a second process would arise subtly in the interaction between him and the client. Both of them were acutely aware of the tiny, moment-to-moment changes in the communication between therapist and client, including behavioral signals, voice tone, pauses, postures, use of language, and subtle feelings. There was an underlying wave that danced and murmured and echoed throughout the interaction. Mary recalled some of the things she had learned about process as the flow of the river and how the interaction with people is something like a meditation practice. She remembered that being attuned to the client's feedback and signals was one of the ways to get in touch with this moment-to-moment flow.

Mary, on the other hand, felt more rigid than ever. She said she often felt uptight when working and was unable to notice the minute changes that were occurring between her and her client. She had a tendency to grasp hold of names and labels rather than immerse herself in the flow. As she spoke, the exuberance with which she had described her observations of Eagle and Dona Carletta began to ebb, and now she looked as though she were tied up in knots and feeling a bit hopeless.

As Dona Carletta listened to this last part of Mary's narrative, she noticed a sense of discomfort in herself. She focused on this feeling and then told Mary that something about what Mary was saying felt uncomfortable to her. She went back in her mind to some of the negative statements Mary had said about herself. Dona Carletta suspected that it was Mary's inner critic that was speaking, rather than an inquisitive part of her that was interested in learning. Mary said this was true and spoke about her tendency to be negative toward herself.

Dona Carletta said that there would be plenty of time to focus on Mary's critic, but she wanted Mary to remember that she actually had a very fluid nature. She reminded Mary of the many times in her life when she had followed her inner feelings and had turned around and made big changes in her life. Dona Carletta also said that Mary was a very sensitive woman who was acutely aware of feedback. Therefore, she had a natural gift for following the changes and flow of process. And, she added, Mary was basically a 'movement and flow-oriented' person; after all, she had an extensive training in dance some years ago. Mary felt flattered and tried to open up to this loving feedback.

Movement and Fluidity

As they approached the classroom, Mary recalled some of her movement training and suddenly had an idea about how to help the students experience this sense of fluidity in a kinesthetic way. She told her idea to Dona Carletta, who thought it was a wonderful way to have an inner experience of the flow before focusing on cognitive information.

Dona Carletta began the class saying, "Before going further intellectually with a very key concept of our work, let's try to grasp the basic principle by doing an exercise that Mary will present." Mary said that in her experience, many of us get so caught up in the content of what is happening with our clients that we lose contact with the flow of the river. Since this was the theme of the day, she hoped that this exercise would give each of us an experience of this flow in our bodies. Afterwards, we could remember that inner body feeling and apply it to our work with others.

Mary said that the exercise must be done in pairs, that it is a kind of movement meditation, a variation on two T'ai Chi exercises called push hands and sticking hands.[1] She said that T'ai Chi teaches us that it is important to be in harmony with the movement of the universe and to be flexible and soft. The main idea is to do as little as possible to accomplish all things. If you have an opponent, become one with her or him, sense what that opponent will do before he or she does it. The exercise challenges us to use our body awareness to notice the subtle shifts and changes that occur while moving with our partner and learn to flow with those changes.

Exercise
Sensing Subtle Changes in Movement

1. One person is "A," the other "B."
2. Face one another with wrists touching. Place one foot forward and the other back. Move hands and arms and bodies in circular fashion, maintaining contact at the wrists, rocking forward and backward on your feet as you move.
3. After a minute or so, "A" begins to move the arm in any way he or she wants and "B" tries to stay in contact the whole time.
4. After a few minutes, switch so that "B" is the leader and "A" tries to stay in contact.
5. Discuss this experience with one another. What did you notice? What did you learn?

After ten minutes of silent movement, everyone gathered to share their experiences. Some people said that they almost anticipated where their partner was going to move before he or she moved. Others found it difficult to sense the subtle feedback and changes. Some said this was a good way of training an inner body wisdom that moves and adapts without thinking. Most noted that it was important to maintain an inner steady center that was quiet and able to shift and change as needed.

Mary said that this sense of flow was what fascinated her the most about the therapist-client interactions. Mary hoped that we would now be able to transfer this body feeling toward such interactions.

Moment-to-Moment Awareness

Dona Carletta then said that the fluidity of following a moment-to-moment interaction with someone is like a beautiful dance, and that it requires two complementary metaskills: one is the ability to change direction as subtle cues emerge; the second is the ability to remain still, steady, and aware in the midst of the many micro-changes.

As an example, Dona Carletta talked about a case supervision session in which a man spoke about one of his clients, a teenager who has been in a lot of trouble at school and has a kind of rough demeanor. This young woman has been put down a lot but has beautiful dreams that indicate that she has a lot of inner riches and wisdom. She is brought to therapy by her parents but doesn't want to be there. Following is a short segment of the interaction as it unfolded between Eagle and the teenager, as played by the therapist:

Eagle: How you doing?

Teen: OK, but my parents bug me. They're always on me to do stuff.

Eagle: For what now?

Teen: Homework. It's boring, I don't want to do it.

Eagle: Why not?

Teen: I just don't, OK?

Eagle: What?

Teen: I just don't, OK?

Noticing the challenging tone in the teenager's voice, Eagle continues:

Eagle: Let me think about it. You sound pretty tough.

Teen: I can be pretty tough.

Here Eagle joins him in his tough behavior and asks him if he heard him correctly.

Eagle: I felt that. It was like you said, "Fuck off, mister." Did I interpret that correctly?

Teen: (sarcastically) You're a bright guy!

Eagle: Thank you. Right. Let's see if I'm smart enough to know what to do next.

Teen: I'm watching, too!

Here Eagle notices that the teen is, indeed, evaluating him to see if he is smart enough, which tells Eagle that this "brightness" and the ability to know what to do may be secondary for her. So at this point, Eagle turns the table.

Eagle: What would you advise me to do? Because I believe in the things you know.

Teen: Phew, I'm on the spot here, I don't know!

At this point, the therapist spontaneously stepped out of his role and said that he felt that this type of interaction would be very helpful with that young woman. This was a way to help the teen feel valued as someone who has a lot of wisdom. Normally, she is looked at as a loser and a troublemaker. However, as Eagle showed, the therapist could give her a sense of her own intelligence and wisdom.

Dona Carletta said that each of us has our own way of flowing with the moment-to-moment changes of the river. She said she had some difficulty describing this way of fluidly working. Some of the students gave the following descriptions. One said that it felt like there is a multiplicity of things happening and the therapist is appreciating this multiplicity, not being forced to pick one. Another said that the therapist stays "close to herself" and has the feeling that nothing needs to happen. It is simply an awareness project. Another said that he would call this "pacing"—the therapist drops his or her paradigm and simply follows the pace of the client and places his or her attention on minute details. One other student said that there is no distance between the therapist and client; there is an intimate connection at this level of flow, where both are joined and focused.

Dona Carletta's Client

Mary asked Dona Carletta whether she could talk about her observations of Dona Carletta working with a woman during a seminar; Mary had taken careful notes. Dona Carletta agreed. The client was depressed about herself and her relationships. She didn't know how to deal with things and was feeling hurt by her friends.

The woman said she was very introverted and didn't know how to get along with people. Here is a piece of that dialogue:

Woman: I feel sad and upset about those relationships.

Dona Carletta: Would you like to tell those people how you are feeling?

Woman: Oh, I don't know. It feels so hard and I am so hurt.

At this point, Dona Carletta decided to let herself move into her shamanic inner realms and fantasize about what was happening.

Dona Carletta: I'm imagining a woman who goes deeply inside herself and expresses herself from there. She is not simply relating to others in an extraverted way.

Woman: Sounds nice.

Dona Carletta: May I go inside and try to do this myself?

Woman: Oh, yes.

Dona Carletta: (closes her eyes and describes what she sees in her imagination) I have the imagination of a child running over to you and you holding that child as the mother.

Woman: That would be nice. I like the sense of mothering, and I need it. Gee, I realize I have been pressuring myself so much. Maybe I'm trying to pressure myself into doing something in my relationships.

Dona Carletta: What would the mother in you say to that?

Woman: She would say I don't have to do anything. That would be a relief! That mother is very sweet to me.

Dona Carletta: Why don't you try to be that mother to yourself. The mother in you will know what to do all the time.

Woman: (in a low tone) Oh, yeah.

Dona Carletta noticed that the client did not give good feedback to her suggestion. Why? In this moment, even though it is a loving suggestion, the woman experiences Dona Carletta as "pushing her" to do something.

Dona Carletta: I notice I made a suggestion that I thought was good for you, but was I motherly enough? Did it feel warm and pressure-less?"

Woman: Well, not really.

Dona Carletta: Good that you notice this. Whatever you do, check out if it feels loving enough. That is all you need to do. Nothing else.

Perfection

Dona Carletta discussed one more example from Eagle's supervision. A therapist spoke about a woman who complains that she can't stand her neighbors' yard because it is so perfect and neat. Her neighbors are also always gloating about how perfect and wonderful their family is. The neighbors criticize the woman and tell her that she should have a neater yard, but the woman doesn't want to do this. This woman has a low self-image and a tendency to take drugs.

Eagle: It must feel terrible to be criticized by your neighbors.

Woman: I don't mind, I just ignore it and take drugs.

Eagle: How does that feel the next day?

Woman: Not so nice, but that's OK.

Eagle notices that there are two parts to her process: one that is interested in orderliness, and another that takes drugs and is "not orderly."

Eagle: I bet there's a perfect and orderly part of you that is upset with your taking drugs so much.

Woman: Well, I feel a bit out of sorts but it's not so bad.

Eagle now realized that he was trying to separate the parts and help her realize that she has an orderly part (which is secondary) that might want to clean up her drug habit, but from her feedback, this may be too early.

Eagle: Perhaps I'm separating things too early. Maybe there's a part that isn't happy with the way you are, and another part that wants support for how you are. Both things are true.

Woman: I do feel you support me a lot in my life; you're the only one.

At this point, Eagle notices that she picks up on the idea of support and the feeling between her and the therapist. He begins to flow with this change.

Eagle: That is so touching, I can't think anymore. My mind is empty. It's amazing to hear that. Letting that in is almost more than I can imagine.

Woman: I always feel better after our discussions.

Eagle: I feel that love from you. I didn't know you had such a big heart; well, I did. You're a very feeling person and I felt it. I could spend *hours* with that feeling. But I wont' take up your time.

Here, Eagle is holding on very closely to her feelings. He is orderly in the sense of not skipping over them but focusing exactly on them. He is showing the woman that she can be orderly with her awareness and check out each feeling that she is having and cherish it. She can explore her feelings bit by bit without skipping over them. Hence, she could have a "clean yard" inside when it comes to her feelings. By doing this, she will begin to treasure herself and value who she is.

Although it is not possible to focus directly on her "perfection and orderliness," he is able to do it in an indirect way in relationship to these feelings. Dona Carletta reminded us of our earlier studies of subtle transpositions. Here, Eagle uses transposition and places the emphasis on her ability to notice and appreciate her feelings.

Many people struggled to comprehend this example and were touched by it, but worried that they would not be able to notice such things in the moment. "Ah," Dona Carletta responded. "I know what you mean. It is not always possible to be aware of all of this in the moment, but it is exciting to study and think about.

And as I mentioned earlier, this is not a program as to how to behave; each of you will have your own way of doing things. The examples I have brought merely point in the direction of fluidity."

At the Edge

She also said that this whole discussion doesn't really have to be so complicated. In general, to get in touch with your moment-to-moment awareness at any time, you can simply state what is happening. Doing so can be especially helpful when you are working at the edge with someone. If the person goes over the edge slightly but then snaps back to her primary process, it can be helpful to simply say, "What I notice is that you went into an unfamiliar place for a moment, and now have returned to your ordinary identity. That seems to be where we are at in the moment." You bring awareness to the whole process that is occurring and then the person can sense what he or she would like to do with that awareness.

She also said that there are certain types of relationship entanglements that occur between the therapist and client in which it is impossible to *do* anything concrete. The only possibility seems to be for the therapist to use her or his ability to metacommunicate about what is happening from moment to moment, stating "this is happening and now that is happening." Dona Carletta said we would learn more about this in one of the classes on therapeutic relationship work (Chapter 26). And with that, she ended the class.

Notes

1. See Howard Reid and Michael Croucher, *The Fighting Arts* (New York: Simon and Schuster, 1983), 107- 110.

Chapter Twenty-Three

Atmospheres and Frameworks

It is important to develop a special atmosphere and framework within which to work.

Boxey, an artist, therapist, and friend of Dona Carletta's, took over the next class. She wore a painter's cap, and there were numerous paint brushes tucked into her belt. Her clothes were full of splatters of paint. She said she would only stay for a brief visit as she was in the middle of making one of her landscape paintings. She began by reminding us that the best idea in the world may not work if you have the wrong metaskills. "Similarly," she added, "a good idea or intention will not be helpful if it is not accompanied by the right atmosphere or framework." This was her theme for the evening.

Boxey used the metaphor of painting. She said that when she paints a still life, she puts a lot of emphasis on the environment surrounding the particular objects. "Of utmost importance to me is the special atmosphere and feeling in which I embed the objects that I draw; the surroundings and atmosphere create the special mood and feeling of the subject I am painting. Likewise, it can be very important to create a special atmosphere or framework in which you do your work with your clients." She added, "Although this theme has wound its way into many of the previous classes, I feel it is appropriate to place a special focus on it today. So let's explore some of these therapeutic atmospheres and frameworks."

She told us that sometimes we are not aware of how influential the subtle things that we do or the special atmosphere we create can be. She told about a woman she worked with over the course of many years. Boxey thought she was doing good work with this woman over that period of time. However, when the therapy ended, the woman told her that the most important thing she did during those years was once when Boxey held her hand. Sometimes we don't even know how the subtle things we do or the atmosphere we create affects the person with whom we are working.

Atmosphere: Who is Working?

Boxey told us to think about how important a special atmosphere would be in the following example, which is similar to one we had heard previously. "Think of someone who is feeling depressed," she said. "This woman feels that she *should* work on herself and correct her problems." (Boxey reminded us of our studies about states of consciousness and the concept of "who's talking.") "In this case," she continued, "it is the woman's negative critic who is speaking and saying she should get her act together. The woman attempts to focus on her problems, but unconsciously she sees everything through the eyes of the critic and hence is quite punitive toward herself—and more depressed."

"Now," Boxey said, "if you begin to work with her on her difficulties, you may inadvertently be seen as another critic who is trying to get her to change. You have fallen into the system, which is doomed to fail! In this case, it is most helpful to find another starting point, to develop another kind of atmosphere before focusing on any of her issues. If I were there," Boxey said, "I would create a more loving and warm atmosphere first. Perhaps

I would ask her about nice things that have happened in her life. Only after a kind-hearted and more generous atmosphere is developed would I begin to help her focus on her issues."

Boxey noted that this topic might remind us of our studies of states of consciousness. This is a special method that is sometimes useful when people are in altered states of consciousness. She recalled the example of someone who is in a panic. The person overwhelms the therapist with numerous issues but is so panicked he can hardly concentrate. "What do you think will happen if you start to work on these issues?" Boxey asked. Someone replied that it would be difficult because the sense of panic would consume anything that you try to do.

"That's right," Boxey said. "And you will find yourself trying to satisfy the one who is panicked. You are locked into that system. In this instance, it is helpful to take a step back, to create an atmosphere, if possible, that allows the person to have some distance from which to process his experiences." She said that in one such instance, she recommended saying, "You have problems, but let's have a cup of tea. We won't solve them this way." If the client says he or she doesn't need a cup of tea, he might say, "But I need it for a moment."

Boxey said that creating such a framework has a lot to do with our metaskills, our feeling ability to create a generous environment in which to work. She reminded us that most people go to therapists or seek out friends in the hope that this person will have an outside and detached—but loving—viewpoint toward their difficulties.

Framing the Secondary Process

Now Boxey wanted to talk about frameworks, that is, creating a frame in which events can happen. She liked the idea of frameworks because they reminded her of framing pictures and also of her name. She said that a frame can be crucial when something secondary spontaneously arises during a session. For example, if the client gets up to move and stumbles while walking, this is a special moment that requires a frame. This frame helps to hold onto, make a space for, and appreciate what has occurred. If something shocking or uncomfortable happens, you might make a frame and ask the person to explore what happened in slow motion and notice the subtle feelings that arise in connection with it.

Or, as we have learned previously, if the person is shy or afraid to explore this experience, we might suggest setting up a frame in which the person is asked to experiment with that new behavior for only two minutes. Or we might make another frame in which we act out this new behavior while the person looks on and advises us.

Framing Relationship Conflicts

When a conflict arises with the therapist, creating a frame can be quite important. Boxey said that she knew we would focus on this more in a future class on therapeutic relationship work (Chapter 26), but she just had to "put in her two cents" now.

"In one case," Boxy told us, "a therapist spoke about a situation in which a client had a conflict with the therapist." Boxey recalled Dona Carletta recommending to the therapist in this situation to say to the client who was upset with her, 'This sounds like a conflict and if it's OK, we'll address it when you're ready.' If the person agrees and the situation allows such an interaction, and you have checked this out a number of times to be certain, you might say, 'When you're ready, let's begin to interact with one another and I'll do my best to help you with your side and your defense. Is that OK with you?' Here you are creating a framework and boundary within which the person can feel safe and in control while dealing with a conflict with you. You can stop many times, refer to this framework, and ask your client if things are going OK for her or him. And, you are encouraging the person to notice consciously how he or she can defend himself or herself.

"Think of a client who feels that everything you do is wrong. This person has left many other therapists. The client experiences you as an invasive person. How might you approach this? One possibility is to metacommunicate about it: Frame what is happening, such as, 'I think you may not want to work with me soon. Shall we think about that now?' Here you are beginning to metacommunicate about what is happening, creating a frame for this experience, and making it possible to approach this conflict consciously. Perhaps this woman is shy about her negativity and is acting this way because she has been very hurt in the past. If she is agreeable, you can approach the conflict and help her interact with you about her disgruntlement—but only after a clear framework is set up.

Relationship Work and Channel Changing

Frameworks can be crucial when trust issues emerge. Boxey spoke about one of Dona Carletta's supervision sessions. A client was not sure he could trust his therapist. Dona Carletta suggested that the therapist say, "Check me out and see if you can really trust me." In this particular instance, the client replied that he doesn't want anyone in his space.

Dona Carletta said that, if and when it is right at some point to explore this man's need to keep people out of his space, it would be important to set up a safe framework. One possibility is for the therapist to say, "If it's OK with you, I'd like to explore your need for space. That seems very important to me." If the client agrees, she suggested continuing to develop the framework by saying, "In a moment, if it's all right, I'd like to come just a bit and very slowly into your space. As I come closer, please notice what happens to you. I promise I'll leave whenever you say it doesn't feel safe." If the client is OK with this suggestion, she added, "How many minutes should we do this? What would be right for you?"

In the relationship situation just described, you are giving the person full leadership of and direction over the situation. You are setting up a difficult situation that he is already involved in, helping him to go into the situation consciously, follow his feelings, and direct what happens. Boxey reminded us that there are numerous ways to frame and work with situations such as those mentioned thus far. Our personal style and the momentary situation with our client determine the pathway.

To close, Boxey added a few framing methods that we have already discussed in other classes.

Talking to primary process about secondary: Here we have learned that we can set up a framework that is related to, or appeals to, the person's primary process. For example, if a person is very analytical and has a lot of body symptoms, we might talk first to his analytical mind about what we would like to do.

Dream maps: The overall pattern of a dream may give a larger perspective or frame in which to explore someone's process.

Ghost stories: If we find ourselves slipping into a dreamed-up state, we can notice what role we are in, what role the client is in, and then step out and create a frame in which the two roles are represented.

Boxey drew one of her paintbrushes out of her belt and waved it in the air as if painting an exclamation point—supposedly signifying the end of her discussion. She then encouraged us to try the following exercise.

Exercise
Developing a Framework/Atmosphere (in pairs)

1. Both people decide on an imaginary situation in which framing would be helpful, such as:
    a. A moment when someone becomes shy about something secondary that has arisen.
    b. A moment when someone is panicked and asking for help in an agitated way.
    c. A moment when a relationship conflict with the therapist occurs.
2. Act out this scenario together (one person is the helper, one the client).
3. The helper should experiment with setting up a framework and atmosphere as described earlier.
4. Continue to process the situation together.
5. Discuss the results.

Chapter Twenty-Four

Magical Patterns and Creativity

Magic and creativity are important and frequently overlooked aspects of therapy.

Starleeka was a master magician and wore one of those big witch hats when she flew around. She had a way of turning up in the most unpredictable moments and had been doing so for quite a number of years. No one knew where she came from or where she lived. They only knew that, for her, all life was utterly magical. She devoted herself to studying and performing tricks, pranks, and miraculous wonders. She descended on the group this evening at the time class was to begin and said she wanted to delve into the area of magic. Apparently Dona Carletta knew she was coming, for she was not there that evening.

Starleeka was in a really good mood (she usually is!) and said she was tired of the focus always being placed on difficulties and pain. She wanted to bring in some "sparkles," although she knew that this was not politically correct when dealing with the realm of therapy. Nevertheless, she reminded us that focusing on secondary experiences is always a numinous, unpredictable, and magical thing, whether we are exploring a double signal, a ghost, or something that catches the person's attention for a split second.

Where's the Numinous?

Starleeka said she noticed that many therapists have a tendency to ignore or forget magical or amazing moments that happen with their clients, in favor of stressing the difficulties that occur. Yet, these awesome moments frequently provide the solutions to those very difficulties.

For example, a therapist said that his client was stuck. After a long description of the difficulties the therapist quickly mentioned, almost as an aside, that the client has an uncanny way of pulling out of a rut at the last moment. Sometimes near the end of a session, he said, the client (who is a singer) talks about a song whose words and feeling tone contains just the information that was needed to solve her problems. After some discussion, Eagle told the therapist that he did not have to worry about this woman; in the last second, she will spontaneously discover a creative solution to her problems.

Starleeka spoke of a magical discovery that Eagle had formulated in this regard: identifying an amazing, comforting, miraculous, or loving moment that has happened in the person's life and applying the quality of that moment to the person's problems. For example, one woman told her therapist that her boss was hard on her the preceding day. She said she had tried to present new ideas to her boss but was so nervous that she stumbled over her words. The boss reprimanded her, and the woman ended up feeling very badly. When the therapist asked her whether there was anything at all that happened that day that made her feel well, she recalled feeling cozy and warm in the morning when she was waking up. The therapist asked her to recall this feeling for a moment, and the woman said that it gave her a sense of inner support and warmth. The therapist then asked her whether she could imagine what it would be like to have that cozy feeling while speaking to her boss. After taking time to imagine this, the woman sensed that this would allow her to proceed more slowly and confidently with her presentation.

A Funny Incident

Starleeka wanted to tell us about a funny incident that happened in one of her classes while exploring this theme. She had told the people in that class that she wanted to find out about a comforting or loving thing that had happened to them recently and how that incident might be of use to them in a more general way in their lives.

She was about to present an inner work exercise and started to say, "Think about the difficulties that you …" However, before she could finish her sentence, something unexpected had occurred. Just before everyone started focusing inwardly, a few got up to get their jackets because they were a bit cold. Another person reached into her bag and got out a muffin that she had been waiting to eat and took a quick bite. Another person, who had brought her cat to class, put the cat on her lap and started stroking it.

Starleeka broke out laughing so hard she couldn't continue the exercise! No one knew what she was so tickled about. It took her a few minutes to recover and tell everyone what happened. She said, "The exercise is done!" Everyone was bewildered. Starleeka had screeched, "The spontaneous, comforting, and loving element already occurred!"

Everyone in that class looked around in deepening bewilderment. No one knew what she was talking about. Starleeka clarified, "I was going to give you an exercise to find out what comforting thing had happened to you recently. And what happened?" Suddenly people looked as though they had been caught with their hands in the cookie jar! They realized the *comforting things* they had *already* done, just as the exercise was beginning. They started to laugh, too!

Starleeka pointed out to them that because of their focus on the upcoming "exercise"—probably suggesting the need for concentration and effort—everyone was going to ignore these spontaneous, comforting occurrences and simply continue working.

Starleeka said that this was her point, exactly! Most of us disavow or forget these experiences and feel we must get on to the "real" work when the so-called real work would be far less necessary (if necessary at all) if we made more use of our comforting, magical moments.

She then said to that class, "Let's go further and try to value those spontaneous things that arose. Each of you, ask yourself what each spontaneous act was trying to bring you. What was the deep essence, the basic quality, of the experience?" People tried to get deeper into the experience of "getting a muffin," "stroking a cat," and "putting on warm clothes." Some said that these experiences were methods of becoming cozier and warmer, of treating oneself lovingly and finally a deep sense of "being at home." The students pondered how these feelings might help them with their personal difficulties, and they noticed how easily they could ignore the *comforting* moments.

Now, in today's class, Starleeka decided to lead us through the following inner work exercise which she had adapted from one of Eagle's.

Exercise
Focusing on Comfortable or Awesome Moments

1. Think about a problem that is bothering you. Write it down.
2. Think about yesterday or a day last week. Where did you go? What did you do? With whom did you interact?
3. Now ask yourself whether there was something that made you feel well, comfortable, happy that day (if it wasn't mentioned before). Perhaps it was something awesome and wonderful that you haven't mentioned yet. Perhaps it was something very small that you would normally overlook.
4. What was that experience like? What is its essence, its basic quality?
5. Consider that you might need more access to this essential quality. Look at the problem you wrote down, and

consider how this essence might help you resolve it somehow.

Doing Things Unconsciously

Now Starleeka wanted to talk more about other types of magical moments, this time about the value of being unconscious! Although it usually seems best for the person to become aware of, and consciously follow, his or her process, this is not always the case. She said some processes indicate that being *unconscious* or using some other magical solution is best.

Think of a young woman who was upset about many things in her life. During her conversation with Starleeka, she casually mentioned a children's story about a puppet that is troubled. The puppet walks over to a meadow and sits on the ground. When the puppet gets up again, it is healed. When Starleeka asked her how that happened, the young woman said that she didn't know; it was just magic. The puppet simply felt better.

Starleeka looked at this story as she would a dream sequence. She said to the young woman, "Don't worry, you can focus on your problems or not. A healing will happen automatically, naturally, even without your trying or without your awareness. You don't need to do it consciously. It will happen spontaneously." The young woman was delighted. She had believed that she had to work *hard* at her problems, and that approach was depressing her. She was relieved to know that a magical solution would naturally occur.

Starleeka spoke about another magical moment that occurred in one of her seminars. She asked whether anyone wanted to work on something in the middle of the group. She looked around and saw a woman's hand rise in the air quickly. Starleeka asked this woman if she would like to come to the center. The woman looked surprised and said yes. When she came to the middle of the group, she said she was very embarrassed. She had not intended to raise her hand; it seemed as though her hand went up spontaneously! Starleeka understood the meaning of this experience and told the woman that her process had to do with following things that happen *spontaneously.* She did not have to *do* them but could watch them occur. The woman was delighted. She experimented with *not doing anything* and simply enjoying following the spontaneous occurrences that happened to her.

Here is another example. A therapist described a man who is very conscientious in his inner work on himself; he tries to study and analyze everything that happens to him. The client also tends to sleep a lot, though he is bothered by this and would like to get up earlier. He told his therapist that being asleep was a nice feeling because he could be passive and not do anything. The therapist complained to Starleeka that he felt there was something missing in their work together.

Starleeka understood this man's experience of sleep as a secondary pattern that is trying to unfold. She recommended that the therapist apply the essence of "sleep" to their therapeutic work. She advised that the therapist tell the man that he does not have to be directly involved in achieving conscious psychological change. Instead, he should feel free to sit back, tell stories, and daydream without feeling he has to integrate any of it into his everyday life. Starleeka also recommended that the therapist join the client and daydream with him as well.

Finding the Magician

Sometimes the process suggests that the therapist be a magician! Starleeka really liked this idea, since that was her identity. However, many of us were skeptical and felt she had gone too far, swaying things to her own worldview.

Starleeka just laughed at our skepticism and asked us to consider a woman in her forties who came to one of Eagle's seminars. As they were working with one another in the middle of the group, the woman said that she felt as though there were walls enclosing her and she didn't like it. She looked toward Eagle and said in a childlike voice "Take these walls away!" Eagle said, "How are we going to take the walls away?" The woman replied, again in a childlike tone, "They should just go away!" Eagle jumped into this story and said, "Well, let's call in the special magician to make them go away!"

Starleeka pointed out how this illustrates some of the things that we have been studying. First, this woman is in an altered state. In the moment she does not have a meta position. Instead, we are speaking to the "child" who is upset by the "walls." The woman's magical statement beckons a magical intervention. Eagle jumps into this "story" with her and begins to search for the great magician.

He looked around, trying to locate the wizard somewhere in the air, and said, "Why aren't you answering us, wizard? Aren't you going to answer us and take these walls away?" The woman replied, "But, you have to tell the story about it first," and started to cry, again like a child. At that point, Eagle took into account the idea of a story and her crying and said from the child role, "But if I tell the story, I'll cry." At that, the woman flipped out of the child position and spontaneously stepped into the role of the wizard. She became the magician and said she was going to do magical things to make those walls go away. The story unfolded further in a creative and meaningful way.

Following Your Dreaming

Starleeka reminded us that each of us has our own personal style of working. She loves to go into her own dreaming to gain information. She knew that Dona Carletta had spoken about this to us earlier. She was aware that this was not always an acceptable route, but she wanted to mention it because it placed the focus on the therapist's creativity in general.

Starleeka mentioned a client who was having difficulties in her relationships. Starleeka intuitively felt that working on the problem directly would be disastrous. Instead, she focused on her inner process and had a spontaneous vision of this woman wrapped in a blanket and looking very inward. The woman looked like a wise, beautiful, and earthy person. When Starleeka described this to her client, the woman said that she "felt seen," and that she needed support for that part of herself. She was relieved that Starleeka had not tried to get her to focus on her inner critic or her relationship problems directly. She said that she had been feeling quite unsupported and afraid to approach any of her problems. She needed the experience and feeling of this wise woman inside herself before approaching her difficulties.

The Therapist's Creativity

Starleeka said that it is crucial for therapists to have some access to their creativity. Eagle has mentioned that if we are not connected to our own dreaming, we will get tired and bored and might want to switch professions.

Starleeka flew around a few times briskly in the air. The buzzing sound that came from this was a bit disconcerting. Once she landed, she looked fiercely into the eyes of the students and said, "OK, friends, how creative do *you* feel when you are working? If you are trying to help others open up to the creativity in their lives, you will need access to the magician inside yourself as well!"

"Actually," she continued, "let's forget about therapy for the moment. During the day, do you find yourself waxing poetic? Do you feel intellectually creative? Artistic? Musical? Do you break out into dance? Do you ever let go of your ordinary intentions and allow yourself to dream? Do you do any of these things in therapy, or do you always remain in one reality?"

She said that having access to our own dreaming nature is very important for our well-being. She remembers Eagle frequently saying that the therapist's ability to create a dreaming atmosphere can help the client dream as well. "If we are asking that our clients develop many sides of themselves and their creative abilities, then how about ours?" Starleeka suddenly looked a bit nervous and quickly reminded us that our first responsibility is to the client, and that it is important to always keep our periscope (meta position) above water and make sure that whatever happens is useful to the client.

It was time for Starleeka to travel home. She left us with this exercise on creativity and then flew away.

Exercise
The Therapist's Creativity (in pairs)

1. One person is the "client," the other is the "therapist."
2. After a few minutes, the therapist gives himself or herself permission momentarily to let go, be creative, be an artist, singer, or poet, and dream into the situation in any way that is appealing.
3. The therapist keeps his or her periscope (meta position) up at the same time, watches the feedback of the client, and unfolds what occurs in any way that is useful for the client.

Chapter Twenty-Five

Who's Your Boss?

The ultimate guide is the flow of events, not the therapist's conscious goals.

At the beginning of the next class, Dona Carletta was not to be found. There was, however, a strange rustling sound that came from the back of the room. As people turned around to see what the source of the sound was, they saw a person shrouded in odd clothes slowly coming forward. Some of the older students recognized him and exclaimed, "Hobo is here!" A great sigh went through the group. Many had heard about Hobo, although he hadn't been seen in many years. In his absence, he had become something of a cult figure.

The story goes that, although he had become a very talented and desired therapist, he dropped out of sight a number of years ago and was not heard from again. No one really knew what happened to him. Apparently he had hidden himself in the back of the room the evening before and had become so inspired by Starleeka's discussion of the creativity and dreaming of the therapist that he felt compelled to come forward.

If you asked him what he had been doing these past years, he would probably say that he was searching for a pathway to dreaming. He knew that it was only the dreaming process that would make him feel at home in this world. He was a deeply spiritual person, and for all the successes he has had in his life, they were all meaningless as long as they were not connected to the deeper flow of process or the Tao.

Apparently, as a child, Hobo had been creative and fanciful. However, since he was raised in a very traditional family, he was frequently told to concentrate on his studies and stop his wandering mind. This confused him so deeply that he lapsed into despair for many years without really knowing what was bothering him. He began to have strange dreamlike experiences and to have trouble distinguishing between night and day, dreaming and waking life. He concluded that the rest of life would be a hopeless affair.

Dona Carletta was fond of telling us what happened when she met Hobo. One day, during one of his despairing years, Dona Carletta found him aimlessly roaming the universe. She brought him back to her star where she listened to him and helped him see that he was really a shaman who had been born into a traditional family—like so many people. This was the first time he had heard the word *shaman;* it was deeply relieving to him to learn that people all over the universe had had experiences such as his, which broke down the barriers between night and day. Dona Carletta told him that, with such a gift, he would one day be able to help others follow their dreaming as well. Hobo then studied process work. He was delighted to find that the basis of process work *is* dreaming and that it incorporated artistic modalities. He felt he had finally come home.

Hobo had always been a very compassionate person with an intuitive ability that allowed him to sense deeply into another's experiences. He was quite popular and very loved and admired by clients, students, and colleagues alike. He was an unpredictable teacher and frequently surprised his students by singing a song or standing on his head.

However, as time passed, he became disillusioned with his work. Although he had learned to follow and revere the dreaming process, he found himself inadvertently sinking back into the tendency to solve problems, apply "techniques," and try to heal people. He developed all sorts of consensual goals that he was unable to attain, began to feel inadequate, and was always exhausted at the end of the day.

Without fully realizing what had happened, he decided to leave his practice and started to wander the universe. Some might say that he had a mild chronic depression. If he couldn't have that spark of dreaming and a belief in the wisdom of nature in his therapy practice, he decided his only alternative was to drop out. Perhaps he would become a roaming musician and thereby find his way back to the dreaming process. Yet, he was also aware that, ultimately, it didn't really matter *what* he was doing. The question was not whether to be a "therapist" or an "artist" or a "businessman" but whether he could relearn how to maintain a constant connection to the flow of process in each moment. One could say that he was going through a midlife crisis—the search for a deeper, spiritual life—though no one was sure how old he was at that time.

For a while during his roaming period, Hobo did become a musician and tried to pour his agony and hopes into song. He named one of his musical characters "Bird of Paradise." The job of this bird was to take those of us who are locked into ordinary life and transport us to other dimensions. We hoped that Hobo, or that bird, would bring a renewal of our dreams as well. Now, as Hobo slowly walked forward from the back of the room, he sang in the melancholy voice of the bird:

"So fly away to paradise
Think of the beauty to come
Spread out your wings and let them glide
To the ends of time."

Where Is Nature Going?

There was a great pause after Hobo stopped singing. We had been transported to another time and space. He had brought up the central feelings that were in all of our hearts and minds. We wondered whether we were Taoists who followed the flow of events or therapists who had programs and goals. Did we consider ourselves the masters of our lives or was nature our guide? A spiritual crisis befell us. What were we really doing working with people? What *is* our job and who is the boss?

Hobo began to speak as if he were having an intimate conversation with himself. He said that our work touches the very essence of human life itself. "Is it up to us to 'change' people or up to nature to direct the course of things? How much can we 'do'? If someone is suffering and we can't fix that, is it right? Can I let it be? How much is my responsibility? If I have tried everything I know, is that all I can do?"

Hobo stressed that he had learned—and forgotten—that ultimately, the biggest question to ask oneself is, "Where is the process flowing? What is trying to happen or unfold?" He added, "And is this path the same as or different from where *I* want to go?" He said that we could learn this by considering the many cases in which the direction events seem to be unfolding is so utterly different from, and at times even contrary to, the therapist's values and ideals. Hobo stressed, in his unstressed kind of way, that opening up to process, in general, is very important, but especially, opening up to those aspects that go against what we expect is very important. He mentioned that we had considered some of these thoughts in our previous class on dream maps.

Hobo was clearly enjoying his return to the classroom. Happily he retrieved from his memory bank some examples. He spoke about a person with a long-term mild depression, someone who just bears life and is not really interested in anything, someone who feels life has no meaning. He paused for a moment, seemingly meditating on the depression that he himself has had. "All of us want to help someone out of a depression. And we should try. But I recall a very interesting discussion in which Eagle said that, in many cases of mild chronic depression, it can be meaningful to go down into the depression, to relax and drop all intentions, and find out what is trying to unfold. In some cases, *going down* is a way of giving up aspects of this life, of our identities, and getting in touch with what is really meaningful to us.

He spoke of one woman who was plagued by a mild chronic depression in which life was OK but it "just went on" and she had lost her interest or excitement in things. It seemed that nothing helped her feel better. When she did go down into her depression and gave up hope, she suddenly experienced a spiritual uplifting and a sense of connection with god.

Hobo then mentioned another example of a man who doesn't react when someone attacks him. The person seems passive and unable or unwilling to defend himself. Many people in the class assumed that this man needs help to feel his own strength and learn to speak up for himself. Hobo said that this is exactly what the therapist tried to do. However, after many attempts, the man did not seem able to do this. Time and time again, he gave negative feedback to this suggestion.

"What did the man dream?" Hobo asked. "He dreamed that he was walking down the street and approached a number of people. Suddenly a magical figure came by and then disappeared." Hobo continued, "Here we can understand this dream sequence as showing that the man has an ability to drop out of ordinary reality and bring up his dreaming capacity. If you followed this dream sequence, you might act out such a relationship situation and as it unfolded, recommend that the man momentarily drop out of relating and follow his spontaneous visions and impulses. His dreaming process would find its own magical solutions to the relationship difficulties, solutions we could never have imagined from our ordinary frame of reference. If you do not find this path of nature, you might spend all of your time trying to get this man to defend himself and miss the depths that are guiding him."

Hobo said that many therapists, particularly in the beginning, think that it is their fault if the client isn't "growing," that they have done something wrong or haven't been smart enough. And, of course, we should always learn more and do the best that we are able to do. And, as mentioned before, if we get consistent negative feedback, we might be on the wrong track.

Hobo recalled a moving example of following nature's path that had to do with a woman who was dying. The woman's secondary process involved having an immense amount of love. The therapist was frustrated because he could not help this woman consciously get to that point in herself and the woman's time was running out. Eagle told the therapist that this woman would get there when she was near death. Eagle said, "Love her where she is. Nature will bring her to that spot before she dies. He recommended saying something to the woman like, 'Don't worry, you'll develop that near death. I won't press you. I love you just as you are.'" This is a compassionate heart—loving and appreciating this person for who she is at that very moment, her own nature, timing, and pathway.

Hobo reiterated something we had learned: that the role of the therapist is to be an *awareness facilitator,* someone who notices what is happening, helps the client with his or her awareness, and follows nature as best he or she can.

Detachment and Patience

Hobo spoke of two important metaskills here: detachment and patience. How do you develop these metaskills? Time and experience may teach these automatically. Hobo said that, although he became disillusioned a number of years ago, he noticed that with age and experience and the chance to do long-term work with people, these metaskills do develop over time.

He also said that *failing* is one of the best and most painful teachers. After failing and finally giving up, detachment often comes. Also, sometimes we learn detachment from people who are in extreme states and who do not necessarily *change* in the *ordinary* sense; they teach us that we are not the directors of life. Others teach us patience. Hobo reminded us "life unfolds with or without us." Many were touched by Hobo's words. Before leaving, he gave the group the following exercise.

Exercise
Following the Path of Nature (in pairs)

1. Begin working with a partner. The "therapist" first tries to do what he or she thinks should be done to help the "client" change in the direction deemed "growthful" by the therapist.
2. After ten minutes, the therapist becomes an *awareness facilitator* who simply notices and comments on what is happening, trying to have a sense of detachment, noticing the direction nature is going and following it as well as is possible, adjusting to negative feedback by opening up to the direction nature is presenting.
3. After another 15 minutes partners discuss the effect these two styles had on both of them, taking time to articulate the differences between the two styles from both the therapist's and the client's perspective.

Part Four

Dealing with Relationship Situations

Chapter Twenty-Six

Therapeutic Relationship Work

When you enter into a relationship process with a client, you must retain an outside awareness of, and appreciation for, all the parts of the field, as well as remembering that your responsibility is always to the client.

Dona Carletta returned to class. She said that one of the most common situations that therapists bring to supervision is a relationship issue emerging between the client and therapist. Frequently the therapist feels so emotionally immersed in the situation that she or he is unable to gain an overview and does not know how to proceed. Dona Carletta decided to use this class to speak generally about aspects of this topic and to go further into specifics tomorrow evening.

First, she reminded us of the guidelines we have already learned. She said, "Remember that, if you have strong feelings when you are with a client, you may be responding to being *dreamt up* as a *part* of the person's process. It is helpful, at that point, to consider your feelings as one *role* in the field. If there is something that attracts or disturbs you about a person (the Big Flirt), it might be an aspect to which he or she needs more conscious access. Strong feelings that persist after you have left the client may indicate a need for you to do your own inner work.

"In addition," she continued, "typically a moment comes when a client *insists* that you drop your therapeutic role and interact as a *real* person. He or she is asking you to step into the relationship channel as an authentic person." Dona Carletta acknowledged that this issue is a challenging and widely debated one. "In some therapeutic modalities it is important to never express your real feelings as a therapist. Therefore, the way in which each therapist deals with such a situation depends on his or her school of therapy, what is important and useful for the client, and also the therapist's individual style."

Dona Carletta stressed that entering into the relationship channel is tremendously challenging for therapists. "In fact," she said, "many therapists may first have to remember what it's like to be real! A lot of therapists are so used to staying *outside* of situations that they have forgotten how to be natural!" The therapist becomes so wound up in her or his professional persona that he or she is no longer a genuine person. Dona Carletta said that relationship work may even bring the therapist to personal growing edges, and he or she will need to learn to deal with this challenging clash between personal psychology and therapeutic work.

Not Entering the Relationship Channel

There are many reasons for therapists to stay *out* of the relationship channel with clients. One is the need for a projection screen upon which the client works on his or her issues, which requires maintaining clear boundaries and roles (see Chapter 28 for more on dual role awareness). Dona Carletta wanted to add a number of other reasons she has observed over her years studying therapists' work:

Losing awareness. In general, the client relies on the therapist to act as the awareness facilitator; anything that compromises that role is a potential danger to a client. Relationship situations in which the therapist is involved can rattle the therapist and muddle her or his awareness. He or she may lose the ability to, first and foremost, serve the client's needs.

For example," Dona Carletta said, "a therapist may feel so strongly about a particular aspect of the relationship interaction that he or she becomes utterly one-sided and insists on its correctness. She or he may then fall into an altered state and lose track of the client's process. At that point, the therapist loses her or his overview, no longer notices the client's signals, and is unable to help the client further with the relationship interaction. The therapist, in this moment, might potentially abuse her or his position of rank. Dona Carletta said that the topic of rank would be discussed in greater detail in another class (see Chapter 28).

In one such situation, a therapist felt that his client was too harsh and needed to be more open and accepting of others. When the therapist said this to the client, the person's head fell forward and she became quiet for a long time. The therapist was so firm in his belief that he did not notice this feedback, nor did he help the client express what she was feeling. It turned out that, actually, this client was ordinarily *extremely* open to others and unable to consciously defend herself. Hence, the *harshness* that the therapist reacted to was the client's unconscious attempt to stand for herself. In this situation, she was especially afraid to speak for herself because of the therapist's authority and power. In addition, the therapist was especially strong in his reactions because of his *own* edges concerning defending himself. Therefore, he lost perspective and became unconsciously entangled in the relationship situation.

Too little training. If the therapist has not had enough training in how to remain centered and aware and use her skills during relationship work, he or she might become inadvertently hurtful to the client.

The focus is not relationship work. Sometimes therapists feel that the focus is on the relationship channel between client and therapist, but actually it is not. In such cases, the client may say that he or she wants that type of interaction but gives other signals to the contrary.

In one such situation, a client said that he wanted to be friends with the therapist and wanted the therapist to be more personal. The therapist entered into this and began to speak about herself. In a supervision session, Dona Carletta asked the therapist to show what happened at that moment with the client. When the therapist acted out this situation, it appeared that, as she began to talk about herself, the client looked down and seemed uninterested in what she had to say. In fact, it turns out that the client did not really want to relate personally to the therapist; she (the client) just needed to feel free enough to say that she wanted to be friends.

In another situation, a client accused the therapist of being mean to her. The therapist took this personally and began to enter into the relationship situation. However, the client gave negative feedback every time the therapist attempted to speak personally about what was occurring. It turns out that the client did not actually want the therapist to be a *real* person but was in the midst of struggling with an inner negative critic and needed help with that interaction.

Missing prior signals. If the therapist has not noticed early indications of a difficult relationship process in the subtle signal exchange between client and therapist, the situation may escalate to the point that the therapist becomes upset and erupts with extra strong feelings. The client, then, may be unable to deal with this and feel hurt by what the therapist does.

For example, Dona Carletta told us to imagine a client who is subtly but consistently negative toward the therapist. For a long time, the therapist does not quite consciously notice this negativity. Then, down the road, something happens that really upsets the therapist and, at this point, because the therapist was disturbed earlier—but unaware of it—he gets very upset with the client and loses his meta position. The client feels very bad when this happens and is unable to defend himself against the therapist. Dona Carletta said that the therapist's reactions could have been minimized if he had noticed the client's subtle negative signals earlier.

Entering the Relationship Channel

Dona Carletta now addressed the other side of this issue. She said that we might try many methods to stay out of the relationship situation but the client may still insist that you interact as a real person. While still respecting each therapist's style of working, Dona Carletta felt that it was important to consider why it might be significant for a client to interact with a therapist as a "real" person. "What could the potential significance of this relationship situation be for the client? Why might it be important to enter into the relationship channel?" Some of the responses from students in the class were as follows:

Interaction with the therapist's unique personality. The client is coming to the therapist as a real person with specific traits. He or she may need to experience the therapist as an individual with particular traits and characteristics, and possibly as a model of behavior that he or she is growing into.

Interaction with a "real" person. Many people have never had the opportunity in the past to interact with someone in a deep and meaningful way, either positively or negatively. A client may hope that it would be possible to finally do so with a caring and aware therapist who can help with this interaction process.

For example," Dona Carletta said, "imagine a man who has never had a chance to interact in a real way with someone in an authority position. The client has this opportunity with you." You will need to step into this interaction in an authentic way while simultaneously helping the person interact with, and react to, you in a satisfying way. This is a great chance for the client to experiment with someone he or she trusts with such an interaction." She reminded us that process work views relationship as one of the many channels through which we experience and learn about ourselves.

Relationship channel myth. The focus on individual psychology can be limiting and may obviate the importance of developing not only as an individual but also in relationship to others. This can be particularly significant for a person who has a larger task in the world. A client's persistent focus on the relationship channel with the therapist and others can indicate that the person's myth involves a task connected with social interactions, community life, something on a global scale.

"Also," Dona Carletta stressed, "we do not live in a vacuum. Our personal psychology is intimately linked with the world around us. Placing our focus solely on individual work can negate the importance of the social context and our interconnectedness with the larger world that we live in."[1]

Challenges to the Therapist

Dona Carletta told us that when a therapist enters the relationship channel with the client, she or he will be challenged to enter into a potentially disorienting emotional arena while remaining conscious and aware. During moments when the client dislikes her or him, the therapist will be challenged to maintain some detachment and clarity and also to be aware of any inner criticism that may ensue. She or he may also have to learn to fail, to give up, and admit that she or he is not up to certain situations. The therapist may have to deal with the kinds of feelings that arise when the client expresses love or admiration or when the client wants to be friends. It is hoped that the therapist will grow, as well, from the situation, and possibly gain a greater sense of detachment. Ultimately, she or he will need to learn to carefully follow the moment-to-moment relationship interactions and signals.

Dona Carletta added that, over time in long-term therapy situations, the focus turns more and more toward interactions between therapist and client. Hence, the therapist is called more and more into the situation as a real person and is challenged to maintain her or his therapeutic abilities while in the midst of relationship interactions.

Framing

Dona Carletta talked about how there is always the danger of falling *unconsciously* into a relationship situation with a client. An important skill to remember is "framing" as introduced by Boxey in a previous class. Framing the situation creates a defined and safe space within which to explore the interaction. It also helps the therapist and the client gain more awareness of what is happening.

Dona Carletta told us to imagine that a client wants to bring up a relationship issue with the therapist. "How might the therapist frame this situation?" she asked. Someone said, "It seems that we are entering into a relationship situation together. Does this feel right for you?" Dona Carletta was pleased with that answer.

She recalled a situation in which she recommended the following to a therapist. The therapist was disturbed by something a client was doing in relationship to her. She advised, if circumstances allowed, that the therapist say something like, "I think what you are doing is important, but I'm left with an uncomfortable feeling. I don't know if this is all me or partly you or if it's coming out of the sky, but I wonder if we might address it at some point." In all cases, she stressed that it is crucial to watch the client's signals and feedback to be sure that it is right to enter into the relationship channel.

Dona Carletta said that the underlying principle here is that the therapist and the client have a contract to work together on the client's issues. If the therapist is going to change that contract and enter into a relationship situation, then the client's agreement is essential.

Maintaining a Periscope

Dona Carletta said that entering into the relationship channel requires a crucial skill that Eagle calls *keeping our periscope up.* In other words, the therapist goes deep into the water while part stays above the surface, maintaining his or her awareness.

"For example, imagine that a conflict with a client arises," she said. "If you do bring your feelings into the interaction, do not forget to notice the signals of the client. Let's say that the person looks down. Check out whether it is right for her or him to be in relationship to you at all. If it is, you might say, 'I see you looking down. Was I too much, too hard?' If the person has a difficult time expressing herself or himself, imagine into what he or she is feeling and speak for her or him, taking the person's side and telling her or him to correct you if you are interpreting the signals incorrectly. In essence, help that person represent his or her side in relationship to you."

Supporting the Whole Process

Dona Carletta wanted to stress one more crucial point that stands out from her long studies of case control situations and which has been touched upon previously. She sincerely stated that it is something she is just beginning to really grasp.

She noticed that in relationship situations with clients, we frequently become polarized and stand strongly for one side or another of the process, thinking that our position is the *right* one. She emphasized her own learning: Anything we experience when we interact with clients is a *part* of the picture and not the *whole truth*. The side that we are experiencing is not right or wrong, but *one* of the parts that is emerging. Our job is to support the *whole*, not one part or another. Again, the ultimate goal is to follow nature, to notice what arises, and to put the weight on unfolding the *entire* process rather than on any one particular part. Dona Carletta added that this is really a fundamental as well as an advanced skill, something that requires much practice and awareness training.

To end the class, Dona Carletta presented an exercise that requires framing and maintaining our periscopes. Everyone tried this exercise with a partner for 30 minutes and then took a break for the evening.

Exercise
Relationship Work and Maintaining a Periscope (in pairs)

1. One person makes up a situation in which he or she is the client who wants to the therapist to be real or who wants to enter the relationship channel in some other way. The other person acts as the therapist. Begin to act out this scene together.
2. The "therapist" tries to use the framing methods mentioned earlier to ask the "client" if he or she would like to enter into the relationship channel. The client reacts to this recommendation.
3. The therapist uses her or his periscope to notice the person's feedback and signals. If the person gives negative feedback, the therapist can then try using any other methods that do not involve the relationship channel such as the Big Flirt or dreaming-up methods in which the therapist brings in her or his feelings as a role.
4. If the client is agreeable, the therapist stays awake and helps her or him interact in the relationship channel. The therapist can experiment by moving between expressing some of her or his feelings and helping the client follow her or his signals and reactions. If the person is unable to express his or her side, the therapist can support and speak for the client's side. All the while, the therapist keeps up her or his periscope, making sure to put the weight on the whole *process* and not on one *part*.
5. After 20 minutes, discuss what happened and your learning with one another.

Notes

1. See Amy Mindell, "Discovering the World in the Individual: The World Channel in Psychotherapy," *Journal of Humanistic Psychology* 36 (1996), where I go into this in more depth, particularly in regard to the world channel.

Chapter Twenty-Seven

Trance-Ference

Clarity about boundaries, feelings, and power as well as a sense of detachment and the ability to follow moment-to-moment interactions are crucial skills for dealing with relationship work.

Dona Carletta continued the discussion about therapeutic relationship work. She began this evening's class by saying that transference situations are among the most common, and probably one of the most widely written about, issues in psychotherapy. Traditionally, the term *transference* refers to a client's projection of positive or negative feelings about a parental figure onto the therapist. *Countertransference* refers to the therapist's *counter*-reactive feelings about the client. Countertransference in process work means that the therapist is either dreamed up as an aspect of the client's process or has feelings that arise about the client that are related to the therapist's personal psychology, or both. In a process-oriented view, the labels of *transference* and *countertransference* are states in flux. Dona Carletta chuckled and said she liked to refer to this phenomenon as "trance-ference" because when you project something onto another person, it is as though you are in a trance, unconscious of what is occurring.

Dona Carletta acknowledged that this topic is much too extensive to cover comprehensively in one short class, but that she would discuss a few beginning ideas that will help with this "trance-ference" experience.

Positive Feelings

One of the central reasons for a client to go to a particular therapist is his or her positive feelings about that person. The client is attracted to particular characteristics in the therapist, and if things go well, the person will eventually integrate or find these qualities in him or herself.

Carrying the Client's Positive Feelings for You

She said that people will want to project Mother Earth or Father Spirit onto us as a therapist and that it's a loving act to carry this projection for a short period of time. However, it is common for a therapist to feel embarrassed about these projections and not "up to" the image that the person imagines him or her to be. Such therapists may say that the client is not seeing him or her clearly. Therefore, it can be hard to carry such a positive transference. On the other hand, another pitfall can occur. If the therapist is the kind of person that *needs* to be loved, she or he may bathe in the client's appreciation and lose awareness completely! One such therapist was so happy about a client's love for her that she never saw the client's subtle, but continual, negative feedback to her interventions!

In any case, she said that if we do not take up a positive projection to begin with, the person will begin to dislike us. However, at some point, it is crucial to help the person finally get to know and integrate that projected characteristic inside himself or herself.

Dona Carletta mentioned the following example. A man is depressed and has many problems that he thinks he will never resolve. He never had any kind of parental support, and he believes he is unable to change in this lifetime. He sees his male therapist as a warm, older man. He is hoping the therapist will act fatherly toward him. He tells the therapist that he is everything the man could hope for. Dona Carletta recommended that the therapist say to this man, "What is the *everything* you are seeing? Tell me the details of how great I am." Once these details are explicit and the therapist has picked up the projection for a while, Dona Carletta suggested that the therapist eventually help the man take this "warm, older man" inside himself. For example, the therapist might ask, "How can you take me with you? Feel where I am *inside of you.* Am I in your heart, in your head? Act like me now and see how much of me feels right for you to carry."

Learning to Relate and Have Real Contact

Dona Carletta said that sometimes a client has strong positive feelings toward us as a way of learning to relate to, and express, loving feelings for another person. "Think of a very shy and lonely woman who has very positive feelings for you and is shy about them," Dona Carletta said. "Ordinarily, this woman has a tendency to avoid her feelings." Dona Carletta said that she had had a client like that. She said to this woman, "How much do you like me? " The client changed the subject, and Dona Carletta noticed that this was an edge. She held that *edgy* moment and said, "Perhaps we can go back and you can tell me what you feel even if it's difficult." The woman finally said that she has never been able to love anyone.

Dona Carletta continued: "Because the person is so interested in you, it can be helpful, at this edge, to talk about yourself if the situation and your style allow. Talk about how you have been where the client is, how difficult it has been for you at times to express your feelings for someone else. The client may feel quite understood and will have a model of someone who was able to grow over that edge."

Moment-to-Moment Awareness and Staying Centered in the Flow

As mentioned in the previous class, some of the most difficult moments for a therapist to handle occur when the client would like to transform the relationship into friendship or an intimate connection and does not want to pay anymore. Dona Carletta said that this can throw us off balance and make it difficult to retain our abilities.

"It is important to be clear about your boundaries and feelings," she commented, "all the while not putting the person down for his or her feelings. At the same time, it is important to stay open to the person's reactions to you. In one situation, she suggested that a therapist say, 'No, I'm not interested in that but I admire you for being able to express your feelings.' This is a compassionate way of being clear while not making the person feel bad for having such feelings.

"If the person insists on focusing on the relationship," Dona Carletta continued, "make sure you frame the situation, as mentioned in the previous class, saying something like, 'It looks like we're in a relationship interaction, a real person with another person. Is that OK? Will that be all right for you?' Then check out the feedback a number of times before going forward."

Dona Carletta recalled a certain situation in which a person felt that the therapist must be in love with her or her life would be ruined. This is one of the most difficult situations that a therapist can face. Dona Carletta said that such situations put the therapist on edge and his or her ordinary intelligence doesn't seem to help. In such situations, a helpful approach is to use our moment-to-moment awareness (as spoken about in Chapter 22). Stay centered as much as possible while metacommunicating about each interchange that occurs.

Think of someone who would like the therapist to be her partner, not her therapist. Eagle briefly demonstrated the use of moment-to-moment awareness in one such situation during one of his classes.

Eagle: I think you are a very nice person and I like seeing you here for sessions, but I'm not interested in an outside relationship.

Client: I'm hurt by that.

Eagle: I see that that hurts your feelings. I'm very sorry about that.

The client then pauses for a long time.

Eagle: *(commenting on her signals)* I like that you take your time. It's an important aspect of you.

The client gets up and, in a testing sort of way, takes Eagle's notebook off his desk.

Eagle: What you did shows me you don't agree with me and that you'd like to debate it further.

The client then paused and said the following.

Client: Thank you for recognizing my power. That's actually what I had hoped for in wishing to have more contact with you.

Negative Feelings

It can be very difficult for the therapist when a client has negative feelings toward her or him. The therapist might begin to feel so bad about herself that she forgets all that she's learned, goes unconscious, loses her meta position, and may get depressed or angry. If, on top of all that, she has a strong inner critic, its yapping may throw her into a tremendous inner turmoil. Some therapists have responded that these situations are so difficult for them that it does not seem possible to get through them. During one of his discussions with Dona Carletta, Eagle was reassuring about this. He told her that therapists should not feel they are up to handling every situation; they should have a heart for their limitations. He stressed that it may even be important at a certain point to say that you are not up to dealing with a particular situation. "We are only given what we are able to do. We are only this, and that is beautiful," he often says.

Dona Carletta told us that the moment when a client has negative feelings toward the therapist could be a very important moment in therapy. She mentioned a few reasons for the negativity that stood out in her mind. The most obvious reason is that the personality or style of the therapist and that of the client do not go well together. The negativity may also be a way to draw in the therapist so that the person can work out old relationship problems or difficulties with authority figures in a trusting environment. Negative feelings toward the therapist may be an attempt to level the roles so that the therapist does not have so much power above the client. It may be an attempt to make the therapist fail, go down, and reveal his or her human limitations. In turn, this may help the client feel like a wise and powerful person, not simply a "client" in need.

Detachment and Moment-to-Moment Awareness

Dona Carletta said that, when dealing with situations in which the client has negative feelings toward the therapist, it is especially helpful for the therapist to gain some sense of detachment, although this may be very difficult to do. It requires a type of personal development in which you have gained some distance from your own position and identity. Dona Carletta said a bit of detachment can give us the sense that what is happening is meaningful. It also enables you to be both inside of the process and outside it, helping the client, at the same time. Sometimes it is helpful to enter the relationship situation while maintaining a sense of "the person's eternity."

Dona Carletta told us about one of her clients who had already seen many therapists. This man said that none of these therapists had been good enough for him. He didn't seem to like Dona Carletta either. He came into Dona Carletta's office, sat down, and did not talk much. She imagined his "not talking" as potentially caused by a trauma from someone like his father or partly attributable to fear, or as a combination of these. Dona Carletta attempted to interact with the man from a detached and open point of view, while following the moment-to-moment flow of events.

The client comes in, looks distrustful, sits down quietly, and looks down.

Dona Carletta: I'm happy you came. Don't talk to me yet. Don't talk unless you trust me. Don't even look at me. Just notice what's happening to you inside.

Client: I don't like your way.

Dona Carletta: What don't you like about it? You are courageous to dislike me! I'm the authority and you're disobeying me. I think that's so important.

Here Dona Carletta said that she notices this man's behavior and affirms it. She is imagining the larger ghost story and encourages the man to disobey her authority. It is possible that he has not been able to do this consciously in his life.

Dona Carletta: Go ahead and be as critical as you feel. I must be a terrible therapist, worse than others, you can see right through me. You notice I don't know what to do with you.

Client: You shouldn't say you're not confident.

Dona Carletta: You'd probably be better in my job.

Dona Carletta explained that she is standing for her own power as the therapist in this situation while praising the man for his ability to disagree with her. She is helping the man become conscious of, and have access to, *his own* authority. She recalled Eagle teaching that most people have never had an authority figure who stood in her or his power *consciously,* while bowing down and appreciating the other person's strength as well. He also said that if you are not sure whether you are using your own power consciously enough, you might ask the person if he or she needs more support to stand against you.

Framing and Metacommunicating

Dona Carletta then spoke about a supervision example similar to one mentioned in the previous class on Hidden Strength. She encouraged us to review that chapter for more on dealing with negativity. She spoke of a client who constantly criticized his therapist but, in this particular situation, was not ready to have a personal interaction about it. The therapist felt quite hurt and asked Dona Carletta how he, the therapist, might focus on this difficulty without losing his own awareness and without hurting the client. Dona Carletta recommended using framing (Chapter 23) to see the larger picture and saying something like, "That hurts a bit, but I imagine it was meant to protect you." Here, she clarified, she is creating a new frame, a new container, in which to view and understand what is happening. Simultaneously, she imagines further into the meaningfulness behind the client's behavior. In this particular situation, it turned out that the therapist and the client subsequently had a fruitful discussion about how the client needs to protect himself. The client is often too exposed and is easily hurt, so he unconsciously lashes out first, as protection. Eventually, the focus was placed upon the client's growing awareness of his sensitivity and his ability to protect himself while interacting with the therapist.

At this point, Dona Carletta told us to recall a situation in which a client liked or disliked us. She then told us to experiment with imagining using any of the various methods just mentioned.

Countertransference Feelings

Dona Carletta said that we have already spoken about a therapist's strong feelings about a client, in the discussions about dreaming up and the Big Flirt. It may also be that the feelings a therapist has about a client are related to the therapist's personal psychology and that this is a signal for inner work. Here Dona Carletta was mainly interested in how to process countertransference situations in the moment when the therapist's feelings become part of a larger relationship situation with the client. "Again," Dona Carletta reiterated, "if you step into the relationship channel with your client and at the same time have strong feelings about that client, a great deal of awareness is required." She wanted to give a couple of brief examples. She hoped that the following examples would provide a beginning point for our learning.

Falling into the System

"There is a basic concept that Eagle has spoken about many times," Dona Carletta said. "After working with hundreds of therapists over the years, he noticed that if someone continually accuses you of being a certain way, and even if you do not initially feel this way, there is a good chance you will end up feeling this way some time in the future. For example, say a client accuses you of being like his or her negative parent. Although most of us would do everything we can to *not* fall into this negative parental role, it will most likely happen unconsciously at some point. You will act like, and begin to feel like, that negative parent in respect to the client."

"Why would this happen?" Dona Carletta asked. "One reason is so that the person can finally have a direct confrontation with the figure that was so negative to them. Think of a therapist who is quite kind-hearted toward a particular client, yet the client accuses the therapist of being tough, just like his father was. After time, the therapist becomes upset with this person and acts like a disciplinarian toward him. No matter how much inner work this therapist does, he can't seem to help but feel that this client should stop being so lazy and "get his act together."

"Now," Dona Carletta continued, "let's say that the client insists that you enter into this relationship conflict. You have checked it out many times and finally feel that this interaction is important—or, at least, inevitable. At this point, after you have tried everything else, you have no choice but to climb into the system, remain awake, and remember that your first responsibility is to your client.

Dona Carletta reminded us about the importance of creating a framework for the relationship situation, and to metacommunicate about what is happening. The therapist might say, "It looks like we're in a conflict, and when you're ready I'd like to step into the side that says you need to get your act together, and help you interact with me. Will that be OK with you?" Make sure this is all right with the client before proceeding.

In one such circumstance, having stepped into the relationship situation, the therapist said to the client, "I think you are sloppy and undisciplined and I want you to get your act together." The client slumped down a bit and the therapist spoke for him, saying, "That is too hard on me, I'm really a good person and have my own way of doing things." The client liked this and sat up straight. The therapist continued on the side of the disciplinarian and said, "Yes, but there are things you need to do and you're not doing them!" The client then said that he has always been tough on himself and that what he really needed was time to dream and allow new ideas to emerge. The way he harangued himself was driving him crazy, and he also felt so sad about living in a "useless" state. He began to cry. The therapist started to feel very empathetic toward the client and no longer felt so strongly in the disciplinary position.

The various sides of the issue subsided as the client and therapist had a deep discussion about these two polarities inside this man and how they have been at a stalemate: the conflict has blocked the man from going forward with his life. "In this case," Dona Carletta pointed out, "it was helpful for the therapist to frame the relationship situation and consciously step into the side of the disciplinarian because it manifested and clarified the deeper structure behind what the man was experiencing. The man then had a chance to deal with this role with more awareness. However, this can only occur if the therapist remains sensitive to the client's signals as well."

Becoming a Parent

Dona Carletta mentioned another typical situation in therapy. "Imagine someone who doesn't love himself very much and the therapist is beginning to feel very parental toward him. However, the therapist becomes overly attached to this feeling and is continually worrying about, and trying to help, this particular client. He, the therapist, is attached to taking care of and saving this person. The therapist begins to act like the mother or father the person never had and feels responsible for the client's well being. If the person is not doing well, the therapist feels guilty. If the client is doing well, the therapist is elated! (See Chapter 30 for more on the therapist's mood.)

At some point, however, the client begins to feel indebted to the therapist and eventually begins to rebel against him. With this shift in sentiment, the therapist begins to grieve the loss of the person, feeling hurt and betrayed that the client has not seen and valued how generous he has been.

What is an alternative? Dona Carletta said that a more useful scenario would be that the therapist recognizes this motherly or fatherly drive toward the client and, at some point, asks the client whether it feels good to be parented and, ultimately, whether he needs to find that mother or father inside himself, assuming that the feelings the therapist has are also part of the client's inner feelings and process.

At that point, Dona Carletta looked as though she suddenly remembered an appointment that she needed to rush off to. She said that she would leave the discussion at that, although she knows this is just the tip of the iceberg of a much greater study. She encouraged everyone to have a good evening and ended the class without giving us an exercise.

Chapter Twenty-Eight

Notes on Ethics and Awareness

Knowledge of basic standards and increased awareness go hand in hand when addressing ethical issues in therapy.

Tonight's class was on ethics and awareness. Dona Carletta started out by saying that any discussion of ethics is part of an ongoing dialogue that is intimately tied to the evolution of the field of therapy. As we learn more and more about ethics, our decisions and standards are continually updated and transformed. Hence, anything that can be said about ethics is true only for this moment in time and will evolve as we all grow in our education and research into such an important topic. She also added that the way we deal with situations in which ethical questions arise depends very much on our school of therapy, standards in our communities, and training.

She stated that ethical guidelines are a crucial protection for clients. Rules and standards make us conscious of therapists' potential misuse of power. Remaining solely with rules, however, may inhibit therapists from increasing their *awareness abilities* when "ethical" moments arise in therapy. Because of the need to stay close to the rules, therapists might miss valuable opportunities for their clients' learning and growth.

This thorny topic was Dona Carletta's focus. This evening she wanted to approach the subject of ethics from a practical point of view. In addition to standards and rules, she wanted to think about the questions, "What new learning can we gain from studying ethical situations that arise in therapy? How can we increase our abilities to be more aware and useful to our clients when ethical situations arise?" Dona Carletta wanted to challenge us to increase our awareness about subtle signals and processes that may emerge in such situations.

She said that the methods she will describe are meant to enhance and augment the therapist's current methods of dealing with such situations. She added that rules and standards are especially crucial when therapists have not had enough awareness training in dealing with ethical moments.

She said she is well aware of the fact that the class this evening is an introduction and that the topic demands a more in-depth and extensive study by everyone involved in this field. She said she would mention a few of the many important ethical areas that she feels need to be considered.

Boundary Issues

One of the most contentious and highly debated ethical issues in therapy, she said, concerns boundaries. How much of a boundary should a therapist hold with a client? How well defined should the roles be? Instead of debating the various positions on this issue, Dona Carletta wanted to put her focus on our awareness training.

"Imagine that a client wants to drop all boundaries and be physically closer with you." She said that this may surprise us but, "In process-oriented terms, if a person talks a lot about *boundaries*, this means that the 'boundary' *is happening in the moment;* the boundary is a secondary process that is appearing in some manner in the person's secondary signals!" She reminded us that anything that is spoken about is somehow happening simultaneously in the present. Dona Carletta was aware that this might be a new and unusual concept for many to consider. She said that another way to understand this is that this *boundary* is like a ghost that is arising in some form in the momentary field between the therapist and client.

For example, one such person seemed quite open with his therapist about what he wanted. However, carefully observing his signals revealed that when he spoke about getting closer, he had a very slight shoulder motion backwards. When unfolded, this movement revealed that he really feels more reserved and shy than he was expressing. His 'boundary maker' is secondary and needs to be appreciated. In fact, this man said that he has a tendency to push himself way over his own boundaries too quickly and does not appreciate his hesitations.

Another way in which the 'boundary' may arise, Dona Carletta said, is via the therapist's feelings and signals. The therapist might feel consciously open to a client but have a slight hesitation in her or his voice or gesture suggesting something other than an open response. Dona Carletta told us that going slowly and staying aware of these minimal signals, which can be crucial to the process as a whole, is of utmost importance.

When strong feeling interactions occur that test a therapist's boundaries, it can be very important to understand the deep process behind a person's expressions. Dona Carletta reminded us of the example about the man who was flirting with his therapist, from the class on the Big Flirt (see Chapter 8). As mentioned earlier, flirting itself can be indicative of a life-and-death issue. The fact that this person feels love could be an enormous blessing for him or her; perhaps it is his or her *only* link to life. Hence, putting your attention solely on the creation of strong boundaries as a therapist could sidestep this important process altogether. Dona Carletta added that any sensitive therapist would sense a deeper process behind what a person is expressing and find out more about it.

In one such supervision session, Eagle commented about the complex nature of a therapist's responses to such situations. He said it is important to "be clear about your own boundaries and limitations *and at the same time* have *no boundaries* in the sense of caring for and being open to this human being. Be clear about who you are but not restrictive of the person's love and deep process." This statement touched many in the class. Many people pondered the beauty and the challenge of simultaneously being so open and deeply caring toward the wholeness of another person while being clear about one's own limitations. Holding and living this paradox was something they strived for. Dona Carletta paused when she heard people's thoughts. She felt that we could focus on this one topic for an entire evening. Yet, she had much more to say and decided to move on.

She spoke about another example similar to one mentioned during a previous class. "Imagine a man who wants to be friends with his therapist. The therapist might say that such a shift in roles is not permissible, thereby establishing a clear boundary." She said that in this situation, however, a real friendship was not the point. It turned out that the client did not have any friends. He was very shy in relationships and didn't know how to be close with someone. His attempt to come out in a definitive way and say, "I want to be friends with you, not just a client" was an attempt to put the focus on this painful area of his life and, he hoped, get help from the therapist about it.

Third Parties

Dona Carletta continued. She said that whenever a third party is spoken about in therapy, it is a ghost role in the moment between client and therapist. "This occurs," she said, "at any time when someone is spoken about who is not there at the time. This third party might also arise when ethical or legal proceedings are insinuated or discussed either in connection with what the therapist is doing or when the client speaks about such proceedings connected with others. Regardless of whether actual ethical or legal action occurs, the 'courts' or 'lawyers' or 'judges' are also ghosts *in the moment*. If the momentary situation and the client allows, you can bring in these 'judges' as one role in the field and process the interaction with this position." Dona Carletta said that, in one such situation, a client who was quite shy said that he was going to court because he was unfairly treated at his work place. In addition to discussing this outer situation, Dona Carletta asked this man if he would like to step into the role of the "courts" and speak from this position. When the man did this, he became one of the lawyers who could defend his case. As he began to speak, he started to feel his own sense of power and beliefs, to which he had not previously had access. He realized that he needed this sense of confidence more generally in his life. Together, he and Dona Carletta further processed the interaction between part of him that feels inferior and his sense of confidence.

Red Light, Green Light

When situations arise in therapy in which the client speaks of a type of behavior that he or she is engaged in that is hurtful or abusive, the therapist may have to call the authorities or tell the client to stop such behavior. This is very important.

"At the same time," Dona Carletta said, "when these things are in place, it is also important to continue to use your full awareness." She added, "It is difficult to retain an open mind and consider that what a person is doing might have *some* significance we are not yet able to see from the outside. The person's behavior may be so upsetting to us that we simply need to say stop to that behavior. In any and all cases, you must follow ethical guidelines and your feelings. If you are in a position to remain a bit open, one helpful thought," Dona Carletta said, "is 'Stop and then go; red light, green light.' First and foremost, stop the abusive behavior. If the situation allows, then, find out the potential meaning behind it and how the person might also grow and change without having to be so abusive or hurtful."

For example, imagine a father who says that he does not like his child. The child cries and is emotional all the time and the father says he would like to get rid of this child. Dona Carletta said, "The most important thing is to protect that child. If you fear for the child's safety you will need to stop the abusive behavior and tell the man clearly that you don't agree with his behavior. In serious cases, legal action may need to be taken."

Dona Carletta continued, "We can also ask ourselves whether there could be an aspect of his process that we might remain open to." She continued to describe what happened in this situation. After further investigation, the therapist realized that this man also has a *child* part of himself who was never taken care of and who is still looking for love. The *child* was a third party in their conversation. Realizing this, the therapist approached him with a more loving attitude and helped him with his own sense of self-love. When this happened, the man's hatred of his child dissolved. It turned out that this man was, actually, a very feeling person but his nature had never been appreciated.

If we missed this aspect of his process we would potentially push it to the side, increase his sense of not being loved, and perhaps inadvertently exacerbate the problem. Dona Carletta said that, in extreme situations, no one really wants to deal with such people and therefore they usually are put away and may not be dealt with again. Once that happens, there is little chance for them to find someone who is compassionate enough to see the larger process that is trying to occur.

Dona Carletta said it could also be helpful to try to see the larger story around why someone would be so negative or hurtful. Perhaps the person was never seen or understood. Perhaps he or she was continually put down by parents or by an educational system. While there is no excuse for hurting someone else, and strong measures must frequently be taken, we should also be careful not to discard aspects of the process that are potentially meaningful for that individual.

Body Contact Awareness

The subject of touch is another area that is quite complex and requires a great deal of study. Once again, Dona Carletta placed her focus on our awareness training. She was interested in the way in which greater awareness could increase our ability to discover and unfold processes imbedded within issues surrounding touch in such a way as to be beneficial to the client. However, Dona Carletta said, if the particular situation allows touch, doing anything touch-oriented requires in-depth training so that the therapist remains awake during body contact and is able to notice feedback and minute signals. She spoke about the following example.

A client said that he never had any body contact and needed to explore that area. The therapist was not sure this was a good idea, but the client persisted in his request. The therapist didn't know what to do and brought this case for supervision. After much discussion, Eagle advised the therapist to set up a *frame* in which to explore touch. He suggested that the therapist and client slowly move their hands toward one another in slow motion and that the therapist notice any of her own and the client's slight signals that occur during the process.

The therapist decided to try this with another student in the class. The therapist and student moved their hands very slowly toward one another. Eagle encouraged the therapist to use her moment-to-moment awareness and notice any slight signals arising in herself or the student. The therapist noticed at one point that the student moved three of his fingers off to the left, ever so slightly away from the therapist's on-coming hand. The therapist mentioned this, and the student focused on this signal. The student said that, actually, he was feeling a bit shy. The therapist encouraged the student to explore this sense of shyness. The man said he felt very introverted and needed time to go inside of himself before coming out and relating. The student was surprised that the bodywork so quickly brought to the surface his inner process around relationships. The therapist spoke about his need to heighten his awareness abilities when working on contact issues.

In light of this discussion, Dona Carletta gave us the following exercise to try for ten minutes in pairs before continuing with the class.

Exercise
Subtle Movement Signals in Relationships

1. Partners sit across from one another and explore contact by slowly moving their hands toward one another.
2. Both people should notice the subtlest signals in themselves, such as slight movements, sounds, breaths, twitches, and so forth, and comment about them.
3. Amplify and unfold these signals and describe what is happening in words.

4. Each person should follow whatever process emerges, compassionately unfolding his or her signals in relationship to the partner.

Sexual Feelings

Another ethical dilemma can occur when sexual feelings arise between client and therapist. Dona Carletta said that this is a highly complex area that requires an in-depth discussion. As a beginning, she reminded us of one method that we had discussed in a previous class about getting to the essence of such feelings.

Dona Carletta told us to think of a situation in which a therapist is attracted to a client and feels quite upset about that feeling. "In addition to following the ethical rules around such an issue," Dona Carletta said, "a helpful skill is to find out what it is exactly that attracts you about the client. Once you know that, get to the essence of that signal; find its root. What is the basic tendency behind that signal? Once you find that essence, you can ask the client about this part of him or herself and unfold that characteristic further. This is also an aspect of the therapist that he or she will need to focus on in his or her inner work as well.

"For example, one therapist was upset because she felt attracted to a client and asked a supervisor what to do. The supervisor asked him exactly what it was about the client that attracted her. She said it was the client's smile. The supervisor asked the therapist what the essence of that smile was. The therapist meditated for a while and said that this smile seemed to convey a sense of absolute openness and a kind of innocence or beginner's mind. The therapist then recognized that she needed more of this feeling in her own life. The supervisor also recommended to her that she ask the client whether these were qualities that the client was shy about as well and that should be explored. When the therapist did this, the client responded that he recognized these qualities deep inside himself but was shy to live them more fully. They then focused on unfolding this experience of openness and beginner's mind and the edge to this experience, in this case, an edge that both the therapist and client shared."

Dual or Multiple Relationships

Dona Carletta said, "Many of the issues just mentioned can be described in terms of dual or multiple relationships—a very contentious issue in the therapy field connected with various ethics and rules." She continued, "We are used to thinking that the roles of therapist and client are clearly defined in the therapeutic setting. However, in the course of therapy, other roles may simultaneously arise and be submerged underneath the defined client-therapist roles. For example, a client may suddenly want to be a friend, not only a client. The roles of parent and child may surface and subtly influence the therapist-client roles. This overlapping of roles frequently influences and disturbs the work in an unconscious manner."

Dona Carletta said that dual or multiple relationships are not specific to the client-therapist situation. In any given relationship we find this momentary overlapping of roles. For example, in a couple, there may be moments when one person becomes a teacher and the other the student. In a family situation, the children sometimes want to, or actually become, the elders in the family, while the parents find themselves in, or hope to be able to temporarily become, a child again. She said that in the client-therapist situation the task of the therapist is to bring awareness to these multiple roles and to make them useful.

Dona Carletta told us that in therapy, ethical standards protect the client because, as anyone who has experienced such multiple relationships knows, it is easy to lose awareness in such situations and in so doing, potentially injure the client. She continued, "In addition to these measures, there is a great deal we can learn about the subtle interactions that occur when multiple relationship situations arise between client and therapist. Multiple relationships require a great deal of awareness to follow the exact signals and experiences that emerge.

Dona Carletta first wanted to take a look at some of the many dual or multiple relationship situations that can arise in therapy. One well-known situation includes those moments when personal relationships (as opposed to therapist-client relationships) become an issue. Sometimes the therapist begins to feel more like a *teacher* who wants to educate a *student*. At other times, the client becomes a teacher to the therapist!

Rank

Beyond these more obvious types of multiple relationships are those that arise in therapy (and in life in general) that are not as frequently addressed, yet which underlie, and are crucial influential forces in, the relationship. One of these has to do with *rank*.[1] The therapist obviously has more rank in relationship to the client because the therapist is supposed to have more knowledge and is being paid. Hence there is the client-therapist relationship and, as well, the various roles related to the differences in rank and power in that situation. In addition, there are differences in social and cultural rank that involve race, gender, age, education, sexual orientation, religion, health, economics, and so forth.

This rank imbalance can be an underlying, silent force that unconsciously influences the therapeutic relationship. Rank can be used consciously for the benefit of the client or abusively to put the person down. Differences in social rank can have a powerful influence on your therapeutic interactions, even if they are not stated overtly, for example, when a therapist from a mainstream part of the culture works with a client from a marginalized group in that culture.

There are two other types of rank that Eagle also identified: psychological and spiritual rank.[2] Psychological rank refers to a kind of centeredness that allows the person to remain cool in the midst of difficult psychological issues. Many therapists have this kind of detachment and, if it is used well, the client will benefit tremendously. However, if the psychological rank is expressed as a kind of superiority, it may have a downing effect on the client, causing him or her to feel less developed and less worthy. Spiritual rank refers to a person's perceived connection with god or the spirit. If a therapist has a lot of spiritual rank, some clients will come to her or him just because of this attribute. Yet, if used unconsciously, spiritual rank can make the client feel less spiritually developed, which can be quite hurtful and disempowering. On the other hand, at times the client may have more psychological or spiritual rank than the therapist. Recognizing this can be very empowering for the client.

Dona Carletta wanted to speak about very basic methods of bringing awareness into dual and multiple relationship situations, in addition to following the rules for each situation. She said that, in essence, a very heartful therapist will do all of this naturally. However, many of these situations freeze us into roles and cause us to lose our awareness. All of the following methods are geared toward supporting the *whole process* and being of service to the client.

Role Awareness

One of Dona Carletta and Eagle's helpful discoveries about following the awareness process in dual relationships is, first, to be aware of the simple fact that a multiplicity of roles exists whenever we interact with another person. Then, if the situation allows, try to be explicit about which role one is assuming in a given moment. This requires a great deal of discipline and awareness. "For example," said Dona Carletta, "in a particular situation with a client you may no longer feel like a therapist but more like an educator or teacher. In any therapy situation it is possible that the roles of therapist and student arise spontaneously as you are working together. If you are not aware of this shift, you might say to the person, 'I think you should be doing better here and you're not. Come on, it's time to wake up!' Such an exhortation will probably have less beneficial effects on the person than first being aware of what role you are in and then stating it to your client, such as, 'I'd like to say something to you as a teacher. But first, as your therapist, I need to check this out with you and see if it's OK to change the context of our relationship for a moment.' If the client agrees, you might continue, 'As your therapist, I just want to support you. And as your teacher I feel … .' Without this differentiation, the client can feel hurt by you. He or she will assume that what you are saying is a betrayal of your role as supportive 'therapist' and may feel quite upset about it."

"So," Dona Carletta said, "when dealing with dual or multiple relationships, set up a frame and be clear about what is happening. For example, imagine that you are a social activist for a particular cause, working with someone who upsets you because he or she has very opposite views on that subject. It is very important to be clear about those moments when you are speaking from the role of the therapist and when you are coming from the role or part of yourself that is an activist who is offended by what the person says or does. If these two roles are conflicted, the client could be confused or hurt and have the feeling that he has lost his therapist."

She continued with the following. "When dual roles become an important topic of focus, one helpful method, if the situation allows, is to set up spots in the room for these different roles. Both therapist and client can move in and out of these roles. The idea is that the roles do not belong to either of you but are parts of a larger field that you are in the midst of unfolding. For example, if your client suddenly criticizes you, he or she may be in the role of the teacher and you suddenly experience yourself as the student. In that case, you can make spots for the teacher, student, client, and therapist. All of these are roles in your collective field which both of you can move freely in and out of."

Dona Carletta mentioned that in this situation the person may be asking for a role switch because he or she would like to be the teacher for once, and not always the "unknowing" client. The therapist might say, "Why don't you step into my position and I'll be in yours for a while."

Dona Carletta said she and Eagle taught that if it is not appropriate to change roles or get up and move we can also do this whole process in a more subtle way by following our awareness. We can use our meditative awareness to notice when the roles arise organically in ourselves and in our clients. We might say, at one moment, "It seems to me like you are a teacher in this moment and I am the student" and at another moment, "Now we are discussing what happened and I am once again in the role of the therapist and you are in the role of the client."

Dona Carletta once again cautioned us about the complexity involved: the mere idea of multiple roles is enough to create a muddle in one's head! Many in the class thoroughly agreed! She added that in some situations, we simply feel over our head and unable to know what to do. We are lost; we do not know what is happening in the dual role situation: we lose our awareness. In all such cases, humility is always a possibility. We can be humble and say, "I don't see my way here, let's wait and see if we dream about it." Inevitably, if we fall into a dual role and lose our awareness, then rules become increasingly important; indeed, then rules are the Tao.

Dona Carletta provided one more method derived from one of the seminars that she and Eagle gave on this theme. It is an exercise that may help us when we find ourselves in a trance, unable to distinguish the various roles that are occurring. "Place your focus on your feelings and use that to help you distinguish the various roles." She led us through the following inner work exercise to practice this type of awareness.

Exercise
Role Awareness and Processing the Field

1. Think of a client you are working with in therapy who is difficult for you. Imagine yourself working with that person.
2. Now imagine or notice what role your behavior is showing and write it down, i.e.:

    teacher,
    therapist,
    activist,
    student,
    client.
3. Do the same for the client.
4. Now, choose three or four roles you think are important including the therapist role. Write down roles on paper as circles on a field and imagine them as a group process. Then process the whole field in your imagination. Just take a minute at this.
5. Imagine bringing the awareness of these various roles in with your client. Go through this imagination in your

mind. Notice the effect of consciousness versus unconsciousness of rank and roles.

6. Consider how these roles in the field are aspects of yourself and also parts of the client.

A student, Hildy, reported on this exercise. She spoke about a situation in which she felt very uneasy with a client but she was not sure why. When she imagined working with that person, she noticed that she, the therapist, looked defensive and hurt. She imagined that she was in a role of a teacher or parent who felt uncared for. When Hildy looked at the client, she noticed that this client seemed to be in the role of something like a rebel (for lack of a better word) who was yelling at this teacher or parent. The entire interaction of these two dynamic roles was submerged beneath their agreed upon "therapist-client" relationship and hence not directly spoken about by either person

Hildy imagined setting up the roles of (1) therapist, (2) client, (3) "rebel," and (4) teacher-parent and inviting the client and herself to go in and out of these various roles. In Hildy's imagination, her client took the rebel position and said she wanted to be appreciated and was not going to follow anything the teacher said. She was fed up with following anyone. After some time, Hildy, who found herself in the teacher role, wanted to listen to this rebel and learn from her. The rebel then turned shy and switched to the client role. At that moment, Hildy also switched to the therapist role. She imagined helping her client feel her own inner strength and wisdom more fully.

Hildy sighed and said that she realized she had unconsciously fallen into the "parent-teacher" role and felt defensive because of it. She began to see more clearly how these various roles were aspects of her client's process. In addition, she suddenly realized how these polarities are inside of her. She had internalized a disciplinary parent who made rules and did not allow her more rebellious and free nature to express itself. She tended to get into bad moods because of this unfinished conflict but did not know why.

To end the class, Dona Carletta slipped in a couple more points. She reminded us that the term "dual or multiple relationships" can become a stultifying term that makes it difficult to remain awake to other mysterious elements of a process as they emerge. "Keep your eyes and ears open for the irrational, spontaneous element that may occur. It may be so foreign to the topic you are focusing on that you miss it, but it may also be the jewel from which new and important experiences emerge." She also said that the tension many of us have about the issues of multiple relationships, rank, and roles is frequently eased at the point in our lives where none of the roles and none of the ranks mean much to us, where we are basically detached from them. In those moments we are able to step outside of the whole dualistic way of viewing ourselves and our clients and are more focused upon such things as eternity, a sense of community, and the future of humanity. In any case, she left us with the following exercise.

Exercise
Dual Relationships and Awareness Work (in pairs)

1. Make up a situation in which a dual relationship issue arises between client and therapist.
2. Each takes a role and acts this scenario out using any of the methods mentioned earlier.
3. Discuss what happened, giving each other detailed feedback on what was and was not helpful.

Notes

1. See Arnold Mindell's writings about rank in *Sitting in the Fire* (Portland, Oregon: Lao Tse Press, 1995), particularly Chapters 3 and 4; *The Deep Democracy of Open Forums* (Charlottesville, Virginia: Hampton Roads, 2002); Amy Mindell, "Discovering the World in the Individual: The World Channel in Psychotherapy." *Journal of Humanistic Psychology* 36 (1996)
2. Mindell, *Sitting in the Fire.*

Part Five

The Therapist's Psychology

Chapter Twenty-Nine

Working on Yourself

Noticing and processing our own issues that emerge when working with clients is essential, particularly those issues that are strongly felt and cause us to become one-sided.

After a weeklong vacation, we gathered once again for a most exciting class. Dona Carletta said that it was finally time to turn to the last part of the intake chart: the therapist's personal process. People had been waiting patiently for the opportunity to think about their own psychology more deeply. She reminded us that, while the therapist often needs help understanding the details of a particular case, even the most brilliant suggestion will be of no assistance if the therapist needs more understanding of her or his inner process. Hence, the focus of the next four classes (Chapters 29 to 32) was placed on the inner psychological work of the therapist. She hoped we would learn more about who we are, both in and out of therapy.

Once again, Dona Carletta introduced us to a new teacher. She said she knew no one who was better able to elaborate on the subject of the therapist's psychology than her dear sister, Madam Flambé. (Until this moment, no one knew that Dona Carletta had a sister.) As if she had gotten her cue to come on stage, Madam Flambé entered the room. She was a very tall and robust woman. She walked into the room in a slow, elegant way. Her head seemed suspended on top of her neck and shoulders. An aura of pride surrounded her. She wore a round purple hat with one round, red jewel centered in the front of it. She was dressed in a deep orange and flowing gown that went all the way to the ground and covered her shoes. This gave the dreamy appearance that she floated rather than walked across the floor. In fact, some people wondered whether she really had shoes, or even feet! In any case, everyone was astounded to see such an elegant figure.

Dona Carletta and Madam Flambé embraced one another, whispering and laughing about something none of us understood. Dona Carletta took a seat off to the side. Then Madam Flambé turned toward us and began to speak with an otherworldly accent, one that almost sounded, at times, as though she were singing opera. She said that this evening she wanted to discuss the therapist's inner work, particularly in connection with those difficult moments when one becomes one-sided. She said that in the second class she wanted to talk about learning styles and those moments when the therapist feels depressed or feels that she or he is a failure (see Chapter 30). Her third class would focus on the therapist's personal style of working (see Chapter 31). The fourth class, taught once again by Dona Carletta, would be devoted to deep questions at the root of therapeutic work (see Chapter 32). She said that each class would be chock full of enjoyable exercises for exploring these topics.

Signs and Signals

Madam Flambé flamboyantly and expressively began her presentation by pronouncing that there are moments, as we all know, when our processes are strongly activated while we are working with clients. No matter how detached or enlightened we might be, there are issues or feelings that can arise inside of us while we are working that take us by surprise and touch our personal psychologies. How we deal with these feelings with our clients is a matter of the moment and the particular situation.

However, there are moments when personal issues arise to such an extent that it becomes clear that we need time for ourselves, to focus more deeply on our own psychologies. As we've learned previously, if we have very strong feelings when we are with our clients and these feelings persist over time, even when the client is not there, this is a sign that it's time to work on ourselves. It is hoped, she added, that we view our work with clients as a continual source of learning for ourselves.

Madam Flambé said that working on ourselves can be crucial to our ability to be of maximum assistance to our clients. "For example," she said, "if you are in great need of love, you might be happy if a client flirts with you. However, this need for love might cause you to go unconscious, and then you miss all of the various signals and experiences that your client is bringing. Similarly, if you are dissatisfied with your personal relationship or if you do not have one but want one, you might unconsciously send out signals that confuse your client. If you are personally upset about issues related to intimacy, you may get upset about or uncomfortable with touch or sexual issues that the client brings up and potentially lose your awareness."

Madam Flambé said there were two central aspects of the therapist's inner work related to moments when therapists go unconscious and are unable to be clear about their work that she wanted to discuss. The first concerns times when the therapist's process is similar to the client's. The other has to do with moments when the therapist gets upset because of something the client does or talks about.

The Client Is You

Madam Flambé said excitedly and with high operatic tones that a most amazing discovery has come out of case supervision sessions. That is, over the years Eagle has seen that therapists most frequently get blocked with clients who are working on similar processes and edges as their own. Hence, the client and therapist are (often unknowingly) working on similar issues, fears, inhibitions, and growing edges. However, paradoxically, the similarity of our experiences seems to create a fog or a block in the therapist's awareness. Madam Flambé recalled Eagle saying that therapists tend to attract just those people they need in order to develop.

Dona Carletta chimed in and reminded us about Mary having discovered that she was working on an edge similar to her client's. She had an edge to the powerful and natural side of herself, as did Waldo. Therefore, both client and therapist were working on a similar growing point.

Dona Carletta also said that she saw this clearly in her supervision with Mary. Once, when Mary brought her situation with Waldo for supervision, she was feeling very inadequate and fearful. Every time Dona Carletta tried to provide helpful feedback, Mary seemed to slump down and give negative feedback. Dona Carletta reminded us of the class (see Chapter 20) on the client's inner power and wisdom. Mary said no to, and defeated, everything Dona Carletta recommended. In her negative feedback was the seed of her power and spontaneous nature! This dynamic mirrored Waldo's process. His power also appeared in the way he *neglected* whatever Mary suggested.

Growing Together

Madam Flambé stepped forward again and continued her discussion about the moment when a therapist is at a point in her or his development that is similar in the client. She said, "This can be either a drawback or a benefit for the client. If you are unable to grow in the way the client is trying to develop, the client may be disappointed. The person was hoping to find a model in you of someone who can go further than she or he is able to in the moment."

"On the other hand," she continued, "it could be a gift if the therapist is unable to achieve this development. The client might then experience you as an ally who is struggling with the same issues and therefore he or she may not feel so alone. At that moment, the rank differences break down and the client may feel equal with you, more understood and accompanied at that shared growing edge. You might say at that point, 'Gee, I'm shy about that too, let's grow together.'"

Madam Flambé spoke about a therapist who complained in a supervision session that his work with a client (whose issue was a lack of self-love) wasn't good enough. Any recommendation she offered to appreciate him did not work. She pointed out that the therapist and his client shared a ghost, a critic that was putting them down. She recommended that during the next session, the therapist and client together try to fight off that critic.

Madam Flambé told us to take a moment and think of a client who is problematic for us or with whom we feel blocked. She then told us to recall that person's central edges and asked us to consider whether we were working on simlar edges in our personal psychologies.

One student realized that she frequently has clients whose primary process is very feeling and easygoing and who have secondarily precise and definitive experiences about which they are shy. This student said that her process is very similar. Madam Flambe' helped her to explore her edges to her definitiveness by becoming aware of the belief systems against that way of being. She then encouraged this woman to experience that definitiveness in her body and then to get in touch with the deep essence behind it. The woman stood still and looked very intent and after a minute said the essence was a sense of "one-pointedness." She then realized that she could use that single pointedness in many areas of her life. Madam Flambe nodded and also encouraged the therapist, if the situation allowed, to either speak to her client about her own edges to this experience, or to model this type of one pointed behavior and, in so doing, provide a pattern for the client to use in manifesting her or his secondary experiences.

The Client Is Not You!

Madam Flambé continued, "So far we have learned that sometimes difficulties with a client are connected with the fact that you are going through a similar development. However," she warned, "in some situations, you may think the client is similar to you but your perception is not accurate. In those moments, it is highly likely that your awareness of your client's unique process will be become obscured.

Madam Flambé spoke about something we learned in an earlier class. "Imagine that you are convinced that a client should develop in a particular way, but the person is unable to do this or does not want to. Perhaps his or her process is heading in another direction. If, however, you continue to insist that the person change in the direction you have determined, you might consider that it is *you* who needs to make that particular change! Think about your own life and how you may be at an edge to make this particular change. In this case, the person you are trying to change is *you!* Go ahead and change yourself; then notice that this may not be the direction for your client!" There were many sighs from the room. Apparently, many people had experienced this misdirected urge at one time or another!

Advantages and Disadvantages of One-Sidedness

Madam Flambé said that all of this really has to do with the tendency all of us humans have to become one-sided—and that there are advantages and disadvantages to this tendency. She reiterated that people often come to particular therapists for assistance because of our personalities and our specific attitudes and opinions—a type of "one-sidedness" that we have toward particular life events or issues. (She differentiates these attitudes from our therapeutic styles, which she will speak about in a later class [see Chapter 31].) "However," she belted out in operatic fashion, "over time, a person will not stay with a therapist unless he or she has a meta position about these attitudes or opinions and is able to support the person's whole process!"

For example, she said, "Imagine you are personally interested in changing the world and standing against authoritative systems and your client, who has found herself in many such work situations, needs support in that area as well. This person will feel greatly understood and helped in that area, at first. However, imagine that, after some time, this woman says that she is not quite happy with the way things are going. She has spent much of her time standing against her bosses but continually loses her job. Her process has changed, and the next stage has to do with finding the value of the "boss" inside of herself, insofar as she can use the boss or authoritarian energy for her benefit. When this happens, you, the therapist, will need some detachment from your own position and biases, to open up to the evolving flow of your client's process. Otherwise, this person will eventually sense that you do not support her totality."

Madam Flambé gave us a number of questions to consider about our own attitudes and potential one-sidedness. She suggested that we discuss her questions in pairs.

1. What strong feelings and opinions do you have about social, political, or personal issues? Pick one area on which to focus. How much do you know about these feelings?
2. Ask yourself how much of a meta position you have about these attitudes. Can you talk about them? Do you feel so strongly that you tend to *fall into* these opinions and feelings and, as a result, sometimes become one-sided, without a meta position?
3. What kinds of people and processes is this part of you open to? What types of processes might these feelings marginalize, ignore, or want to repress?

Burning Our Wood

Madam Flambé acknowledged that it is not possible to work ahead of time on every issue that could arise in us during our therapeutic work. Sometimes we are simply taken by surprise and find ourselves in the thick of the soup! However, knowing some of the areas that tend to get activated is important because our ability to work on ourselves is connected with our sense of ethics and respect for our clients; we are there, first and foremost, to be helpful to our clients. This does not mean that we should change and become neutral and always open to everything that comes our way. However, what *is* important is that we have the possibility of maintaining some distance from our own attitudes so that we can be open to the entire process that is trying to unfold. Madam Flambé described a method that can help therapists work on their own one-sidedness, again noting that, when we are working with people, it is common for issues to arise that "push our buttons;" that is, we suddenly feel emotionally drawn in and compelled to fight for or against a particular issue or behavior. Such feelings might be reactions to a client's political or social beliefs, the way in which he or she treats others, the type of clothing the person wears, or any issue at all that touches us deeply.

Madam Flambé reminded us of the example of the female therapist who was upset when a male client brushed against her as he walked into the room. She felt that what he did was sexual and intrusive. In this particular case, this man was very shy and didn't know how to express his feelings. He projected onto the therapist that she had a lot of feelings, but he did not know how to gain access to his own. His inadvertent "brush against her" was secondary, an unconscious attempt to express himself. However, if the therapist has strong feelings about sexism or abuse issues, she may no longer be able to notice the man's entire process. She must, of course, appreciate and remain true to her own feelings and viewpoints, and sometimes it may be important to bring these feelings into the situation. However, if therapists do speak about their feelings too strongly, some people will feel quite hurt or embarrassed by their own secondary behavior and will not want to approach the issue again.

What kind of inner work can the therapist do? Eagle has developed a method for such inner work called "burning your wood."[1] Originally, this method referred to the issues that arise in group situations that push the facilitator's buttons. *Burning your wood* means taking time to process our reactions to "hot" issues that touch us personally. It means allowing ourselves time to open up to and consciously get into our affects and feelings, to let go and react as strongly as we feel about those issues.

"A central idea behind this process," continued Madam Flambé, "is that if you are allowed to be really free with your reactions, you may then gain some detachment from them. This doesn't mean that you will necessarily change your beliefs, but you won't be so entirely gripped by them that you lose your overview and awareness of the other person and anything that lies outside of your paradigm. The idea is that it is not until we *have* our reactions and allow ourselves to express them as much as possible that we can gain some distance from them."

That said, Madam Flambé gave us an exercise to explore burning our own wood. She said we should not worry about doing it right. The purpose is to find out more about ourselves.

Exercise
Burning Our Wood (in pairs)

1. The person who plays the therapist thinks of an imaginary situation in which someone does or says something that "pushes your buttons." Choose something that has the potential to bring up strong feelings in you, something that makes you very upset, angry, or sad or causes you to go into a kind of paralyzed trance where you feel blocked.
2. Act this situation out with your partner, who is playing the client. Notice what kind of state you, the therapist, find yourself in. Use your awareness to become aware of your body sensations, your movements, and your facial gestures.
3. At this point, your partner should stop playing the client and, instead, help you "burn your wood." Allow your reactions to surface further. Amplify your experiences by expressing them in many channels and finally finding out the very essence of what you are experiencing. What is the deep message behind what you are expressing?
4. Cherish that message and explore its effects on your body and your feelings.
5. Discuss with your partner how you might use that essential message in your everyday life. What more might you do in the world or in your own personal life to embrace or fulfill that message?

After the exercise, Madam Flambé told us to take a break, and that we would reconvene the following day. Tomorrow she would turn her attention to other central elements of the therapist's inner work and experience, namely, the beauty and the complexity of the learning process and the therapist's sense of failure. Madam Flambé bowed deeply, turned, and floated away.

Notes

1. See Arnold Mindell, *Sitting in the Fire* (Portland, Oregon: Lao Tse Press, 1995), 125-129.

Chapter Thirty

The Phoenix in the Failure

A therapist's feeling of failure can be an opportunity for greater learning and growth.

The next evening, Madam Flambé entered the room just as elegantly as the evening before, this time wearing a flowing red and gold pantsuit. She glided forward and said quietly that she wanted to speak intimately with her students. She took a deep breath and said in a dramatic tone that the process of learning to be a therapist can be exhilerating but that it can also contain moments of depression in which we feel we are not up to the task. In fact, any therapist, at any stage of her or his work, feels like a failure from time to time. Therapy is an awesome and challenging endeavor. She likened the therapist's sense of failure and, it is hoped, the rebirth that it engenders, to the symbol of the phoenix, a magnificent bird that regenerated itself after death.[1] She said she wore her red and gold pantsuit this evening to honor this amazing bird.

Madam Flambé also said that during the learning process, and later, as the therapist receives supervision, the interaction between the supervisor and therapist is crucial. Although this topic goes beyond the scope of her class, Madam Flambé said, it is an important subject to ponder.

Madam Flambé's voice became louder as she got excited about these ideas. She said, facetiously, that most people don't learn well if they are hit over the head! "Many of us suffered from this kind of teaching in school systems and are so afraid of experiencing it again that the entire interaction between supervisor and learner is quite complex." She added that the way a person learns best depends on many factors, such as her or his ability to assimilate cognitive information, her or his personal style of learning, and her or his personal psychology. Some of the students in the class remarked that they tend to learn best when a supervisor talks about how she or he had similar difficulties and was able to make a transition in her or his learning. Madam Flambé added that she felt, as Eagle does, that supervisors need to know that a learner can pick up only two or three new pieces of information at a time, at the most. The supervisor must find the therapist or learner's special method of learning and tailor her or his suggestions to that modality.

Depression and Fear of Failure

Freddy, a learner, piped up and said that after receiving feedback from a supervisor, even if he has found out some really helpful ideas, sometimes he has felt depressed. All he could hear is what he did wrong—such as missing this or that signal, not noticing the client's feedback, and so forth—and not what he could learn. Freddy said that an inner critic, who told him that he should not be doing this work at all, often plagued him. He felt he could not possibly be up to it.

Madam Flambé said that Freddy might need time to focus on his own sense of value and his feelings of being put down. As an alternative, he might need to speak first, about all the good things he has done with that client. Madam Flambé consoled Freddy by saying that it frequently takes ten years to begin to feel confident as a therapist; the sense of depression and worthlessness is a common problem that almost all therapists suffer through. Freddy was relieved to hear that bit of news!

Dona Carletta spoke up and said that another source of misery for the beginning therapist, and sometimes for the not-so-beginning therapist, is when a client decides to terminate the sessions. Most beginning therapists feel very attached to their clients, and when a client is not satisfied or leaves, the therapist is devastated and feels like a failure. For this therapist everything that happens with a client is a measure of her or his value!

Madam Flambé chimed in as she laughed hard. She shared one of her own stories. She mentioned one of her first clients, whom she kept in her room for hours until she was sure that the client had learned something! She said that one of her colleagues, Charlotta, mentioned once that when she started out as a therapist, she would phone all her clients to see if they had integrated her dream interpretations! Many others in the room who had been in practice for a while shared equally funny—and embarrassing—stories.

Madam Flambé shared Eagle's view that we should not try to get beyond who we are. In fact, life is so amazing that it is hard to have anything but humility in the face of it. His view stresses the mystery and awesomeness of process, the sense that we cannot create or mold the flow of the Tao, but only humbly follow it. Madam Flambé recalled one of her supervision sessions when a therapist spoke about feeling unsure of himself because a client was testing him to see whether he would be good enough for the client to work with. Madam Flambé said that humility can be important in such moments, possibly saying to the client, "I may not be the right person for you. Check me out and see if I am good enough for you. Perhaps we should wait for a dream to help us determine if we should work together."

Madam Flambé added that our need for clients weakens us in relationship to them. If you notice this need consciously, you might say, "I want you as a client, but I have to go slowly with my doubts." Many people will like you better if you are a bit humble; in fact, this tends to draw people toward you. Madam Flambé also said that we are all wounded healers. We have been wounded in some way, and that is exactly what makes us interested in being of help to others and, potentially, good healers.

She said that she now wanted to turn our attention to the way in which our sense of failure can be the beginning of great learning.

Plus-One, Minus-One, and Zero-State Conditions

Dona Carletta spoke up at this point about the therapist's feelings of failure, or alternatively, the desire to be perfect! In a supervision seminar that she and Eagle gave together many years ago, they focused specifically on the *mood* of the therapist as he or she is working. This mood arises from the desire either to do a good job and help the client to grow *or* from the sense of depression because the client is not developing or picking up the therapist's suggestions.

"If you are in a perfectionist mood and want everything to go well," Dona Carletta said, "and you are hungry for the client to change and grow, you are in what we call a *plus-one* condition. If you get depressed because the person is not picking up on things or following your suggestions, you are in a *minus-one* condition and feel like a failure. A detached, open, and aware state that is not attached to outcomes is the *zero-state.* The idea of the zero-state comes from an aspect of the Tibetan or Zen view of life; it is a state of emptiness and detachment from one's personal history, with no expectations, only a bare bones awareness of the present moment."

Dona Carletta added that she does not have a value judgment about any of these states. They are simply experiences that the therapist fluidly moves between as he or she works, albeit most times unaware of them. The zero-state appears when the therapist has a moment of detachment or neutrality; the plus-one state arises when the therapist is attached to a given process or result; the minus-one state appears when the therapist feels depressed because the client is not changing. She said that this minus-one state typically arises as a reaction to the crashing of the plus-one expectations!

Dona Carletta said that the minus-one state can be a blessing—if we take heed. "If you were to notice that state and amplify it," she said, "you might really give up and drop your tendency to push for results. This in turn might lead to leaving behind your ideas and intentions and re-finding the zero-state of openness, a beginner's mind. Hence, all of these are part of a flow of feelings that all of us go through and, with awareness, might be of great assistance to our clients.

Dona Carletta gave us time to try an awareness exercise based on these various moods.

Exercise
Plus-One, Minus-One, and Zero-State Awareness (in pairs)

1. One person talks about himself or herself as a therapist and tries to discern whether he or she is ordinarily closer to the plus-one, minus-one, or zero state, or some combination thereof.
2. The same person should begin to work as a therapist with his or her partner.
3. The therapist should use her or his awareness to reflect from time to time on which of the three states he or she is in. Mention this out loud to your partner, stating, for example, "I am in a minus-one state and feel that nothing I do will work" or "I am in a plus-one state and feel hopeful that you are going to develop in this direction."
4. If, after ten minutes, you, the therapist, have not noticed the zero-state arising, try to bring it in now. Pretend you can drop your personal history as easily as letting a book drop to the floor, and be open to what is happening. As you continue to work with your partner, every so often describe your partner's behavior in a bare bones way. Stay close to her or his signals and say something like, "Now you are doing this, now you are doing that. Now you are choosing to notice this, now you are choosing to notice that. Now you want me to be doing everything,

now you are following my instructions. Now I notice you are not following my instructions."

5. Continue to notice which state you are in for the next fifteen minutes while simultaneously following your "client's" process in any way that feels right for you.
6. Afterwards, consider how the awareness of these three states affected your work. Your partner should speak about how this awareness affected him or her.

Other Colleagues!

Madam Flambé came forward again and mentioned another contributing factor to a therapist's sense of failure or depression. She said that sometimes a therapist feels unhappy about his or her work with a client and as a result feels that that person would have a better experience with *a different therapist.* While this may ultimately be a good idea, the therapist's feeling can also stem from a sense of inferiority and depression. Mary chimed in and said that she had felt so upset about Waldo that the thought had crossed her mind to send him to one of her colleagues. Madam Flambé said she understood Mary's reaction and acknowledged that Waldo might get along better with someone else.

"But," she added, "we might get a lot more out of this for you personally." She then asked Mary, "Which other colleague would you send Waldo to?" Mary thought for a moment and said she would send Waldo to her colleague Mortie. "What is Mortie like?" Madam Flambé asked. Mary said that Mortie was spontaneous, strong and earthy. "Ah!" said Madam Flambé. "Aren't these the same secondary characteristics that *you* worked on with Dona Carletta? Qualities that you are not identified with yet?" Mary was surprised to realize that this was the case. "Of course," Dona Carletta said, "if you are not able to integrate these parts of yourself, then it is the client's fate to have you and your qualities as a therapist, or the person may end up leaving you for someone else. No blame. That is the way of the Tao."

Madam Flambé turned to everyone and said that Mary had just provided a wonderful example that could be of use to all of us.

She told us to take a few minutes to do a bit of inner work as she led us through the following scenario:

Exercise
The Other, Better Therapist

1. Think of a client that you feel insecure or uncomfortable with for some reason.
2. Imagine *another* therapist who you feel would be better suited to this person's needs. Or think of someone with whom you feel the client would prefer to work rather than with you. Describe that therapist and how he or she would work with this client. What is the *essence* of that therapist's behavior?
3. In what way is this essence of the behavior of that therapist a secondary process for you? How do you need that essence more in your life?
4. Imagine using that essence and energy in some manner the next time you are with this client.

Symptoms of Burnout

Near the end of the class, Madam Flambé looked as though she were pondering something deeply. She said that the sense of depression or hopelessness that a therapist might begin to feel about her or his work is sometimes connected to burnout, adding that burnout could be indicative of something very deep that is trying to take place.

She reminded us of the way Hobo had become disillusioned after losing contact with his dreaming. He experienced burnout because he became too focused on consensual aspects of his work and forgot about following his creativity and the dreaming process.

Madam Flambé listed some symptoms to watch for that may be associated with burnout:

- Not wanting to see clients.
- Feeling sleepy, depressed, or bored a lot.
- Feeling angry or frustrated with your work.
- Not concentrating well.

- Getting into bad habits.
- Having a "therapist's stiff neck."

Many people laughed because they recognized the symptom of "stiff neck." It is the common therapist's position in which the head is slightly forward and to the side and the therapist is nodding all the time. The therapist looks very understanding and sensitive. Madam Flambé said that while a compassionate perspective is very important, too much of the "helping attitude" implied by this posture can cause the therapist to feel burdened and "bled dry."

Madam Flambé said that sometimes burnout occurs because the therapist is waiting too patiently for the client to organically discover his or her process instead of suggesting to the person more directly the direction in which the therapist feels the client should go. Another possibility is that the therapist is not taking time to focus on her or himself. In this case, the therapist might feel it is not right to focus on herself or himself, perhaps believing that it is selfish to do so, not realizing that by ignoring her or his own process for too long, boredom, restlessness, and discontent are bound to follow.

Madam Flambé paused now and simply looked at the people in the class for a long time. She said she felt very close to everyone. She assured them that she, too, had been through all of the difficulties that she and Dona Carletta have mentioned. She proclaimed, "Through all of my trials and tribulations of learning to be a therapist, and in the ensuing years as a therapist, I do believe that I have gained a greater sense of myself and also a deeper reverence for the wisdom of nature. I don't know how to convince you that by going through all the difficulties, you *will* find the gold at the end of the rainbow. I can only share my feelings and hope that they are some consolation on the journey." Her statements drew people together and gave them a warm sense of their shared journey. She then glided out of the room.

Notes

1. According to the sixth edition of the on-line *Columbia ElectronicEncyclopedia* (New York: Columbia University Press, 2000), the phoenix is a magnificent bird that periodically regenerates. In literature, it is commonly used as a symbol for death and resurrection: "According to legend, the phoenix lived in Arabia; when it reached the end of its life (500 years), it burned itself on a pyre of flames, and from the ashes a new phoenix arose. As a sacred symbol in Egyptian religion, the phoenix represented the sun, which dies each night and rises again each morning. According to Herodotus the bird was red and golden and resembled an eagle."

Chapter Thirty-One

The Therapist's Style

A therapist's momentary and long-term therapeutic styles are gifts that are frequently unrecognized.

As the next evening's class began, many people were full of anticipation. They knew that Madam Flambé was going to talk about the therapist's style, and each person was eager to find out more about his or her own. Dona Carletta was not present at the beginning of the class. Madam Flambé explained that her sister had some urgent business back on her planet but would return before the evening closed.

Madam Flambé began her evening discourse by saying that, indeed, she wanted to turn the focus toward the therapist's unique style, adding that in tomorrow night's class Dona Carletta would focus on that perennial wise woman or man, the elder, who, she believes, is deeply behind and inside each one of us. She said that this evening's class would be full of exercises, and she warned us that we might be together all night! Before anyone could gasp, she assured us that we would be having so much fun that we wouldn't notice the time flying by!

"Now, let's turn to therapeutic styles," she began briskly. Madam Flambé reminded us that clients come to us in great part because of who we are and because of our style of working and therefore it is important that we *really be* who we are. Many therapists feel they should be like someone else; for some reason, she added, most people feel that way as well! And sometimes, as has been mentioned, the "other" person is a secondary process for us. "But ultimately," she said, eyeing us in her piercing way, "your individual nature, which is beautiful, is the most important gem that you have in therapy—and, of course, in life. Eagle has said countless times that you won't do process work well unless you are truly yourself."

She likened our particular styles to nature images. "Some people are like the wind, some like the stars, some like meteors," she said. "Your individuality creates the beauty and artistry of your particular way of working. It fills your original metaskill or feeling attitude, and it exudes a particular atmosphere." She continued, saying that there are as many styles as there are therapists. "My own style is quite flamboyant and expressive as you may have noticed. Some other people are very contemplative. Some are very cognitive and precise. Others are trickster-like and spontaneous. Some are extremely sensitive. Each one of us has a bit of a shamanic nature, to want to be a therapist at all."

Style and Handwriting

Before going further, Madam Flambé wanted to begin the class with a really fun and simple exercise that explores a bit about our individual styles. She said she frequently likes to do experiential exercises before talking intellectually about a given theme. And, she added, she simply was in the mood to have a good time! She giggled and said that the exercise has to do with your handwritten signature. Everyone was perplexed. She said that last night she had had a very silly dream in which everyone was doing this exercise. So, being a dreamer herself, she thought we should all try it. Here it is:

Exercise
Your Signature

1. Take a piece of paper and pen. Sign your name on the paper.
2. Look at your signature. What about it stands out to you the most? What is the most unusual, odd, or obvious part of that signature? How would you describe its quality?
3. Feel the quality of that part of the signature in your body. Make movements and sounds that go with that quality and energy. Find out the essence of that experience. What is its basic expression?
4. Now ask yourself what type of *style* this experience expresses. If you integrate this type of expression, what kind of therapeutic style would this suggest? What would you be like?
5. Turn to a partner and discuss what you learned. At another point, experiment with bringing your style into your work.

After the exercise one person shared her experience. She said that part of her signature looked wild and erratic. The letters seemed to almost jump off the page. She felt this quality in her body and made wild and erratic movements. As she did this, she was alternately quiet and then suddenly made fast, spontaneous movements. She said it felt as though she were meditating, waiting for a spontaneous impulse to arise, and then expressing it. She said that this would be a style in which she would feel quite centered, allowing her deepest intuitions to arise spontaneously. She said that this felt quite natural to her but she has been shy to live this style more fully.

Primary, Secondary and Deep Styles

After the exercise, Madam Flambé seemed ready to tell us more about her ideas. She said that the whole discussion of style is quite complex. We have many styles. One of our styles mirrors our current *primary* process, or our primary identity over a period of time.

A second style mirrors our current *secondary process,* or a secondary process that has been seeking awareness over a period of time. In addition to these two styles, we also have a third style that is deeply imbedded in and influences everything we do. She calls this the therapist's *deep and hidden* style. This style emanates from a very basic, almost mythic, part of ourselves and is characteristic of us over a *long* period of time. In fact, it is part of a long-term pattern that influences us throughout our lives. This deep style may not reveal itself fully until we have had many years of practice and have grown more comfortable with our work, yet it is always there in the background, revealing itself in subtle ways. Madam Flambé clarified that our primary and secondary styles change as we develop and grow. However, our deepest, hidden style seems to stay the same and influences all that we do.

Our Deep and Hidden Style

Now she wanted to help each of us first to explore our deep and hidden therapeutic style. Then she would turn to our primary and secondary styles. She reminded us that, just as we can look at our earliest childhood dream or memory to discover our long-term personal myth, we can look at the first dream or strong memory we had when we ourselves began therapy, or the first strong memory or dream we had when we decided to become a therapist, or both, to discover more about our deep therapeutic style. She said that our deepest style was a natural gift that each of us should cherish.

A woman in the class said she did not understand what Madam Flambé meant, so Madam Flambé asked her what she dreamed about at the time she decided to become a therapist. The woman said that she dreamed she was in the lap of her former spiritual teacher and heard a beautiful humming sound. Madam Flambé asked her what it was like to experience that sound. The woman took a moment to imagine the sound and then said that simply listening to it made her feel profoundly meditative and full of music. She then realized that this suggested a way of being with, and working with, people. She would be inward, meditative, and connected to the vibrations and music of the moment.

Actually, she started to recall how this attitude has always penetrated her life and work in subtle ways and has given her the sense of being close to her true nature. She said that she would now like to manifest it more fully and consciously.

Madam Flambé encouraged us to try the following exercise, which would help us explore our deep and hidden style. The exercise is derived from one of Eagle's original exercises on childhood dreams and personal myths. She told us we would need a large piece of paper, and she promptly produced a stack of paper and placed it in the center of the room. She wrote the exercise on the board as everyone took a piece of paper and prepared to begin the exercise.

Exercise
Your Deep and Hidden Style

Madam Flambé led all of us through the first steps.

1. Recall the first dream or strong memory you had when you began therapy or when you decided to train as a therapist.
2. Draw four squares on your paper, like a series of cartoon boxes.
3. In the first square, make a simple drawing of your first memory or dream. Don't take much time; make a simple stick-figure sketch.
4. Now *dream this first picture further.* In other words, in each successive box, let the story spontaneously unfold. Don't think about it much; allow the story to develop by drawing it in the successive boxes, like a cartoon series. Do this quickly so that it comes spontaneously; take a couple of minutes to complete the series. Come to some conclusion by the fourth box.

Madam Flambé asked us to turn to a partner and complete the following steps of the exercise in pairs.

1. Show and tell the story you drew to your partner.
2. Discuss the following:
   a. Take a guess at the style of therapy the story is suggesting and name it.
   b. How has this style been happening, or trying to happen, in your studies of, or work as, a therapist? Has this style or quality appeared in other areas of your life as well?
   c. At what point in this story progression do you feel you are today, in terms of your work as a therapist or therapist-in-training?
   d. Today, do you have any edges to this style? In the future, if you had no edges to this style, what might you look like? What kind of therapist do you imagine yourself being twenty years from now? How will you act? Make notes about this.
   e. How could this style influence your relationship to the world, not only in therapy, but also in life in general?

One person in the group spoke about her experience with this exercise. She said that when she began therapy, she dreamed she was looking at a very high mountain, at the top of which she discovered a group of shamans doing a ritual dance. In her cartoon she slowly climbed the mountain and, by the fourth box, she had joined them. When she looked at this story, she realized that, no matter how much she focuses on cognitive learning, she always seems to revert to this shamanic and trance-like experience in herself. In fact, she'd had this quality since she was a child, and it had often disrupted her attempts to act in a "normal" way. She said she also has a lot of detachment (high up in the mountains) but is shy about it. If she were to live this style more fully in her work, she said she would be able to let go of her conscious thoughts at times and follow her non-rational feelings and images. She would also use movement more in her work with people. Today she feels that she is beginning to be more accepting of this shamanic and detached part of herself and is beginning to live it in her relationships and life as a whole. When she looked at her pictures as a dream progression, she felt that she is presently somewhere near the fourth picture—almost at the top of the mountain.

The Default Button and Your Basic Gift

Suddenly Dona Carletta burst through the door. The look on her face gave the impression that she had been involved in something very important on her planet. She brushed the stardust off her clothes and quickly took her seat. However, just as soon as she sat down, she jumped up again and started to speak as if she had been in the class all along (perhaps she was telepathic).

In any case, Dona Carletta said that many of us are not satisfied with our primary, secondary, *or* deep styles and try to change them. However, we may have noticed that, no matter how hard we try to change ourselves, most of us revert to these fundamental styles. Dona Carletta said, "The woman who spoke a moment ago about her shamanic nature said that this characteristic has appeared throughout her life and frequently disrupts her attempts to be 'normal.'" Dona Carletta said that this reverting to a certain style is like the default function on a computer! "The reason this style comes back again and again is that it is basic to who you are; it is a gift that wants to be appreciated and wants to be used consciously in life. Only then will this style momentarily step to the side and allow other styles to come forward."

Madam Flambé agreed and said that she, Dona Carletta, and Eagle always emphasize that we can't really learn anything new until we appreciate our gifts. In essence, she continued, "*Every learning problem contains a gift that is unrecognized.* Hence, if you feel that you are lousy at something, this is an indication that there is a gift that has not yet been seen or valued, and this oversight is blocking you from going further. If you are able to accept and embrace this gift, many roads can open up to you. For example, if you are motherly and can't seem to get around it, there is a gift in that motherliness that has not been fully realized. It is a beautiful and crucial part of you that needs respect and consciousness. Once it is used fully and consciously, you will be able to gain access to other aspects of yourself.[1]

One therapist-in-training spoke up. She said that this sounded like a description of herself. She feels she is too kind and needs to be tougher and stronger. She said that, because of this style, she has a tendency to marginalize some of the uncomfortable feelings she has with people. Many supervisors have told her to change, and she has felt this need for a change in her personal life as well. However, no matter how hard she tries, she always ends up acting in a sweet and kind way toward people.

Dona Carletta said that this woman should appreciate this style and use it consciously. The woman asked how to make it conscious. Dona Carletta told the woman that she might say to her client, "Did you notice how motherly I am? I just noticed it, and I hope it's having a good effect." Or, "I notice that I want to intervene more strongly, but I am feeling motherly and unable to take a stand. Do you need protection? A mother?" Dona Carletta said, "When you make your style conscious and explicit, then you will be relieved from its pull and something else may emerge." She added that it is also helpful to ask, "What is the essence or very core of that style?" In this case, the essence of motherliness might be the sense of openness to all things as they arise.

Primary and Secondary Style

Madam Flambé said she was excited for us to try another quick and easy exercise to help us begin to learn more about our momentary primary and secondary styles. She learned the first part of this creative drawing method from a woman she met some years back, and she loved it.[2] She told us to grab a few pieces of paper and one of the crayons that she had brought with her. She then led us through the following experience.

Exercise
Your Style and Scribbles

1. What do you feel is your ordinary style as therapist? Write down a word that expresses this style or quality.
2. Now make a quick scribble on your paper.
3. Look at that scribble and let your mind *see* something in a part of it. Perhaps you will see the form of an animal, a face, or something else.
4. Now, take another piece of paper and draw just this section of the scribble in which you saw that particular image. Fill in the details of that picture. For example, if you saw the outline of an animal, fill in the eyes and ears, and nose, and so on.
5. Take another piece of paper and draw this new figure on it. Now imagine the environment in which this figure is embedded. What scenery surrounds this figure? What story is the figure a part of?
6. Put your papers down. Feel the quality of the figure that you drew in your body. Express this figure in your movement. As you do that, imagine what this experience might suggest about your personal life and therapy style.
7. How is this experience of your style similar to, or different from, the style you wrote down in the beginning of this exercise?

Madam Flambé clarified that the original style we wrote down may be related to our momentary primary process and the new one that came out of our drawing may be related to our momentary secondary processes. However, she said that we should take time, at another point, to find out whether these are also related to long-term patterns and deep styles. In any case, she said that scribbling is a wonderful way to create a blank access into which we can allow our dreaming process to emerge.

In sharing experiences from this exercise, one student reported feeling that she had a very clear, attentive, and helpful style as a therapist. Yet, in her drawing she saw a couch with a lethargic person reclining on it, like a couch potato! This drawing suggested to her to be more relaxed as she is working, to sit back and allow things to unfold more instead of feeling she has to be the one to "fix" everything. Another student said that she frequently feels hesitant and shy while she is working. In her drawing, she saw some very exact lines that turned into beautiful squares and geometric figures. When she felt this geometry in her body, she experienced herself being like a warrior who was very precise, clear, and analytic. As a therapeutic style, she realized she would be more exact about noticing signals and understanding the structure that her clients were revealing.

Style and Anti-Style

Dona Carletta chimed in here to say that integrating and using both our primary and secondary styles is quite a task. She cited the example of one therapist who had a very feeling type of primary style. Her secondary style was very incisive and one-pointed. Her challenge was to be aware of and use both of these styles consciously in her work. "By the way," Dona Carletta added, "Eagle also says that a therapist tends to revert to her or his primary style when the client gets to an edge. So you might want to watch for this."

Dona Carletta said that another way of understanding these two styles is to think of them as our (primary) "style" and our (secondary) "anti-style." Here is an exercise from a supervision seminar she and Eagle conducted many years ago. People gasped because they had already gone through three previous exercises but thought this sounded like fun so they proceeded.

Exercise
Exploring Your Style and Anti-Style (in pairs)

1. One person is the "client," the other is the "therapist." The therapist works with the client for ten minutes in any way that he or she likes.
2. The therapist then defines her or his style up to that point, using the following as aids in clarifying and articulating the experience. What is the quality of that style?

How does it feel in the body? Make a motion that goes along with that style, to anchor the feeling in the body.

3. Now, the therapist should ask herself or himself, "What would be my anti-style? If I were totally free just now, what style would I have?" (This is your anti-style in the moment.) What is the quality of this anti-style? How does it feel in the body? Make a motion that goes along with that style, to anchor the feeling in the body.
4. Now the therapist should experiment with using that anti-style as she or he continues to work with the client.
5. After a few minutes, while continuing to work with the client, the therapist should practice using her or his awareness to notice which of these two styles is emerging in her or himself. Alternate between styles as one or the other arises while watching for feedback from the client.
6. After twenty minutes, discuss the effect these two styles have had on the client.

After the exercise, Dona Carletta reminded us that we may not always be able to follow our various styles while we are working with people. Again, everything depends on the particular moment and our relationship to a particular person. These exercises are meant to explore and give access to many sides of ourselves and the awareness of how they arise while we are working. Generally, we tend to negate the anti-style, although, in some form, if it is present and used with awareness, it can be of great help to our work.

Music

While people were practicing the previous exercise, Madam Flambé and Dona Carletta were… dancing. This was Madam Flambé's last class before heading home, and they wanted to take advantage of it! As we finished the previous exercise, both women couldn't wait to launch into one more exercise before closing for the evening.

But it wasn't the evening! People were astounded that it was three o'clock in the morning! The previous exercise had given them a lot of energy and they had lost track of time! But when they suddenly became aware of the clock, many did feel that these women had gone a bit far.

Madam Flambé and Dona Carletta seemed unnecessarily happy, for such a late hour, and they didn't seem the least bit tired. They said they wanted to do an auditory exercise that involves music and singing. Eagle developed this musical approach many years ago. They said that, of the many ways they knew to discover your style and anti-style, this exercise was the most fun. They also insisted that this exercise could be done at any time of the day or night as a way of discovering our dreaming processes. "What better way to get to know ourselves and to learn to follow the flow of life than the use of rhythm, sound, and movement?" Who could resist?

Well, actually, the majority of people felt they'd had enough! Some began to leave the room. However, when those who were leaving heard people singing and the sounds of laughter and feet moving on the floor, they couldn't resist and came back!

Exercise
The First and Second Song

1. Think of the first song that comes to you. Sing or hum that tune to yourself. Make motions that go with it, a little dance. Notice the quality of that experience. What tempo and feeling does it have? Give this quality a name.
2. Think of a second song. Sing or hum it to yourself. Make motions that go with it, a little dance. Notice the quality and tempo and feeling of that song. Give this quality a name.
3. Consider how the first song might be closer to your primary therapeutic style and current primary process, and how the second song might be part of your anti-style and your secondary process.
4. Express both qualities or styles in one dance!

People seemed to have a lot of fun. As they grabbed their coats and hats, Madam Flambé and Dona Carletta said that the next step would be to try both of these styles while working with someone, but they would have mercy on us now and let us go home.

Notes

1. The reader may recall the exercise about the fly on the wall in the class on "That Big Flirt" (see Chapter 8). In that exercise, we observed ourselves from the perspective of a fly on the wall and noticed something about ourselves that stood out. The results of that exercise might connect to aspects of your style.
2. Many thanks to Rhoda Isaacs for developing this scribble method.

Chapter Thirty-Two

Eldership and the Biggest Questions

Each therapist has an absolute beginner as well as an ancient part within himself or herself that are wise and know that life is the greatest teacher.

As this series of classes was coming to an end, Dona Carletta was in a detached and quiet mood—quite a change from the evening before. She said she had learned over the years that you cannot push the river. She knew that people learn and develop in their own natural ways and in their own timing. Just as we try to pace the process of our clients, so too does the process of learning to be a therapist have its own flow. And she knew that all of her ideas and those of her friends were not the important ones. She recalled Eagle's continual reminder that the real teacher is within. No one on the outside could ever be as wise as your own inner process.

She decided to end her lecture series by focusing on two topics that were close to her heart. One has to do with the deepest quality behind the therapist, the elder. The other has to do with some of the big questions that face us as therapists and human beings.

The Elder

"So," she said, "What is an elder?"[1] One definition is a person who has a kind of wisdom that is connected to infinity, to history, to the universe, and to nature. Dona Carletta liked that very much. She said that many of us, or perhaps all of us, have this sort of "old soul" inside. In fact, many of us were such wise beings when we were children. This elder is involved in the momentary unfolding of life and is simultaneously connected to infinity.

She said that an elder is someone who is comfortable with her style and can go beyond it; she or he is an awareness facilitator. The elder says, from time to time, "Now this is happening, now that." She asks, "What are you aware of? What is trying to happen? Where is nature going?" This elder stands compassionately for all of the parts and, simultaneously, for the ineffable dreaming process that flows between them.

Dona Carletta was not sure how to develop or recall this inherent eldership. Some people have it and maintain it throughout their lives. Most grow into it over time. Other people develop it through years of their own inner work. Some develop it naturally, after having worked with others and having lived through many facets of human experience.

Your Ninety-Year-Old Personality

Dona Carletta told us that she began working as a therapist when she was in her mid-twenties. She often came home after a long day of work and wished that she were older. She yearned to be at least ninety years old. She thought she would have more experience, more perspective, more detachment—and, she hoped, more humor. She would have grown more into herself and her own comfort as a therapist. She knew that being an elder did not depend on age, but she imagined it would come to her later in life.

One day, she realized that if she had this fantasy of being ninety years old, it must be a secondary process happening right now. In other words, this pattern she longed for was *already happening* inside of her, but she was not yet fully aware of, or identified with, it. She developed an exercise to find out more about this part of herself and to help others experience their elder within as well. She led us through the following inner work.

Exercise
The Elder Within

1. Describe yourself today. What kind of therapist are you? How do you feel about yourself?
2. Imagine that you grow older and are now ninety years old. Imagine yourself as a therapist at that age.
3. What kind of person and therapist are you as this ninety-year-old? Are you a mystic, a monk, a basket weaver, a clown, a scholar, a fool, an artist? Describe the qualities of this person to yourself. Do you remember figures in your life who have exemplified these qualities?
4. Are you in touch with these qualities in yourself? Have you had a sense of yourself growing into this elder recently? Have you had dreams about it?
5. Now assume the posture of this ninety-year-old person. Sit like her or him. Make little movements that she or he would make. Begin to speak like that person; then imagine being a therapist and working with people from that new state.
6. Give this part of you a name.
7. Consider the difference between the ordinary you as a therapist and this ninety-year-old part.

Some people spoke about their experiences of the exercise. One woman said that she imagined when she is ninety years old that she would use artistic and theatrical methods in her work. Another felt as if she were a martial artist who would suddenly come out precisely with insights and then pause until another insight occurred. Another student said she would carry a kettle and constantly go into the mysteries of the universe. Another person said he would be like a cave dweller; he would stay deep inside and speak only occasionally from deep within.

Dona Carletta reminded us that we should not criticize ourselves for *not yet* being at this stage. She said that flowers, fruit trees, mountains, and stars grow slowly and in their own time. She said that this part of us is there anyway, deep within all we do, and that part of the elder's compassion has to do with accepting ourselves *as we are now.*

Dona Carletta continued the exercise and said that we should now try to work with a partner for a few minutes as this ninety-year-old person. She said that we should notice how this way of being is similar to, or different from, our ordinary ways of working. She gave us fifteen minutes per person.

After the exercise, Dona Carletta told us that when she first tried this exercise many years ago, she imagined herself at ninety years old being inwardly focused, like a mystic. With the permission of one of her clients, she tried this. She put fabric over her head and stayed deep inside and simply spoke aloud mystical thoughts that came into her head. That session turned out to be the most healing and satisfying one yet, for both the client and Dona Carletta. Today, Dona Carletta said she feels a great deal closer to this experience.

The One Who Knows Nothing

To throw us off balance, Dona Carletta tossed in another interpretation of the elder. She said that sometimes she and Eagle feel that the best spiritual teacher or elder is really an idiot or a fool, someone who knows very little! In Taoism, the true sage knows nothing; she or he simply follows the Tao. Knowing a lot can get in the way of having a beginner's mind and observing what is unfolding. She said that, ultimately, nothing we have learned is of any importance except the simple use of awareness.

Someone asked how to *unlearn* what we have learned. He felt he had so many thoughts in his mind, and he could not get rid of them! Dona Carletta said that the therapist-in-training usually goes through typical stages of learning. She reminded us of the Zen proverb that goes something like, "Before Zen a mountain is a mountain. During Zen a mountain is no longer a mountain. After Zen a mountain is a mountain again."

"What does this mean?" the man asked. Dona Carletta said, "First, the therapist is just himself, with his own personality and style and perhaps a few tools. Later, those tools get more complicated. He tries to learn a million different things. He puts his individual nature to the side to learn many skills. Finally, as his skills become more familiar and fluid, he can drop the focus on what he is doing and once again become his natural self. His methods become fluidly integrated with his style, and this forms the seamless fabric of his work. In this way, we need not be the *knowing* therapist, but instead, someone who uses her or his awareness to follow what is happening.

A Heroine or Hero of the Unknown

Dona Carletta added, "Eagle told me once that the elder also has the quality of being a hero or heroine of the unknown. This means that to be a good therapist, you need to adapt to where the client is, but *also* to discover the dreaming that is in the midst of unfolding. This dreaming is usually very different from the person's conscious thoughts. In essence, you are intervening in a person's or a society's culture—and that is a huge step to take! Therefore, it takes great courage to step beyond the bounds of the known world and bring in the unknown," Dona Carletta said. "On the other hand," she added, "we do not need any courage at all if we are an elder whose sights are set on eternity and who knows that nature is the guide."

Big Questions

Dona felt that it was important to end this series of classes by engaging us in a discussion about the big questions that therapy raises. What is the role of the therapist? What is our real task? What do people need? What is therapy about? How much responsibility do we have? She said she was aware that we would need a lot more time and much thought to approach these deep philosophical issues. She also said that each of us has our own answers to these questions and must take the time to ponder them for ourselves because they are the spiritual backbone of all that we do.

Before going further, Dona Carletta asked us to think about this question: "Why am I, or why do I want to be, a therapist?" The answer to this question motivates us but is frequently an unconscious force that simply drives us from its background position. "If you are not connected to your deep visions and reasons for being a therapist, it will all seem like rote exercises and you will begin to feel insecure. You will feel you have no center on which to turn. Without a connection to these deep principles, we are like a wandering sailboat bobbling on the open seas with no one sailing it."

Dona Carletta said that a few weeks ago she had stumbled upon some notes from a seminar of years ago in which Eagle spoke about this theme. "Now, let me share some of my notes from Eagle's short lecture on this subject," she said. "Although these notes are somewhat outdated, they still ring true for me. Therefore, I want to speak about them with everyone."

What Is Your Goal?

Eagle approached the whole question of goals. What is our goal as a therapist? Is it to follow the process that's happening or to be a therapist? He warned that if we are too focused on being a therapist and healing people, we might miss the process that nature is presenting. We run the risk of remaining fastened solely to consensual views of success and outer pressures. He said that for him, ultimately, our role is to take care of the relationship between our everyday lives and the relationship to the divine, the ever-mysterious flow of nature.

He said that perennial philosophies have asked questions about goals from the point of view of happiness. What makes life rich? In this case, he said, the question would be, "Can I help the person live a happy life?" Zen masters and shamans like Don Juan[2] (the Yaqui shaman described in Carlos Castaneda's books) focus on the *path of heart.* In other words, is the person following the heart in all that he or she is doing in life? In the world of therapy,

Jung said we should become a stone: our original self. But he also added that, of course, people have lots of therapeutic issues to work on as well.

Preparation for Death

Another viewpoint is that therapy is a preparation for death. Eagle spoke of the elder who maintains a sense of eternity while working. He said that he often imagines how the client will feel just near death when he or she asks the big questions such as, "Did I live my life completely? What haven't I done what I would like to do?"

For some ancient cultures, such as Egyptian and Tibetan cultures, the developmental focus lies more on the preparation for what comes after death. In some religions, such as Buddhism, the goal of life is to be absolutely present in the moment and, by practicing that now, we prepare for death. Eagle said that the closer we are as therapists to the sense of death, the more able we are to step out of time, to have a grand overview and allow the whole process to express itself.

Who Is the Client?

Who is our client? Most of us assume our client is the individual who is coming to see us. However, even this viewpoint may change according to each situation and individual and the state of the world. Eagle said that sometimes he thinks of the client as the individual who is sitting in front of him, and sometimes he thinks of his client as the *whole system or environment* that the person is living in (as many systems theorists also contend). He speculated that the future of psychotherapy will include the concept of "the client" as the whole world and will focus strongly on changes occurring in culture.

Developmental Ideas

Someone in the class asked whether process work has a developmental aspect to its theory. "Well, yes and no," Dona Carletta replied. "On the one hand, Eagle has said that there is no place to go and that nothing has any *meaning*. We are simply living in the stream of process and trying to follow and unfold it with as much awareness as possible. In other words, what develops over time is our awareness. On the other hand, he has said that there are typical stages people go through and these are viewed variously depending upon our therapeutic orientation. For example, Jung looked at development in terms of two halves of life: from focus on the personal to the worldly and spiritual, or, in Jung's terminology, from focus on the shadow, anima, or animus to the Self."

Eagle described phases of development that are not necessarily linear in direction. They can come and go and cycle; they appear and reappear at different moments during our lifespan and overlap onto one another. Some of the phases he described are connected with Don Juan's teachings. He said that, of course, since we are all human, both the therapist and the client go through these phases during their lives. He also stressed that these are *phases* of development; they are not goals. The only goal that is ever something one should hold to is awareness, or even awareness of awareness, which means that sometimes we can consciously allow ourselves to go unconscious. Dona Carletta named some of these phases:

- In the *therapeutic phase*, the person's focus is concentrated on personal history, abuse, pain, parents, social systems, and so on.
- The *warrior phase* occurs when the person's focus turns toward flexing her or his abilities to meet the unknown inside and out. This is the time when the person is discovering and wrestling with the unknown and gaining enrichment from it.
- In the *seer and near-death phase* the person experiences himself or herself living as a Yogi—as a dead man or woman in life. At this stage in life, the feeling of detachment and eldership begins to take over by itself. The "therapeutic" paradigm starts to drop off, and a new paradigm begins. Those who only needed therapy will leave at this point.

- Some people go on to another phase, the *awareness phase*, in which they learn about awareness and wholeness. At this point, the work transforms and the person begins to look at everything as a process. Personal history issues that cycle and problems that trouble us do not go away but are experienced as processes rather than problems. The person begins to worship process, to mother it, to love her or himself, and to focus on all things that come into her or his awareness.

At this point, relationship work with the therapist may become important. You are both "in the bathtub together," learning to live wholeness from moment to moment with someone near you. The elder continues to grow from this stage; someone who is open to what is happening and who also may begin to have the sense of caring for the community and larger world around him or her.

Why Go to Therapy?

Dona Carletta recalled that, years ago, someone asked Eagle an interesting question. "If people are always in the midst of process, why do they even bother to go to a therapist?" Eagle offered the following thoughts. He said that, yes, people are always in the midst of their processes, but most of them identify only with one side and are not aware of the other parts of themselves. This can be a great source of suffering. A therapist can offer this wider perspective.

People frequently come to therapists to gain affirmation for where they are in their lives at the moment. They are asking for validation of where they are in their process as human beings in the flow of life. Also, a therapist can give a sense of contentedness by offering someone a view of where the person is in the present moment and where he or she may be heading. People come to a therapist to gain help in living a path of heart, to get along with nature in their own special way.

Closing

With that, Dona Carletta ended this series of classes. She glanced out of the window at the setting sun and breathed deeply as the mystery of the nighttime approached. She took her chair and moved it forward so that it was closer to the group. As she sat down, she paused for a long while, looking around the room at everyone. She thanked all of us for being present over these past weeks. She felt she had grown closer to everyone and that she was as much a learner and beginner as each and every student. She felt that we, as her students, were also her teachers and that wisdom and insights we brought made the experience very rich for her. She smiled warmly to us and said she would leave the rest of our learning, for the moment, up to our inner teachers, our own dreaming… the source of all wisdom.

Notes

1. For his conception of the elder, see Arnold Mindell, *Sitting in the Fire* (Portland, Oregon: Lao Tse Press, 1995); *Leader as Martial Artist* (Portland, Oregon: Lao Tse Press, 2000).
2. See Carlos Castaneda, *The Teaching of Don Juan: A Yaqui Way of Knowledge* (London: Penguin, 1970); *Journey to Ixtlan* (London: Penguin, 1974); Arnold Mindell, *Shaman's Body* (San Francisco: HarperCollins, 1993/1996).

Bibliography

Arye, Lane. *Unintentional Music: Releasing Your Deepest Creativity.* Charlottesville, Virginia: Hampton Roads, 2001.

Biedermann, Hans. *Dictionary of Symbolism: Cultural Icons and the Meanings Behind Them,* trans., James Hulbert. New York: Penguin (Meridian), 1994.

Castaneda, Carlos. *Journey to Ixtlan.* London: Penguin, 1974.

———. *A Separate Reality.* London: Penguin, 1973.

———. *The Teaching of Don Juan: A Yaqui Way of Knowledge.* London: Penguin, 1970.

Cathey, Randee. "The Dreaming Facilitator." Thesis for the diploma program, Process Work Center of Portland, Portland, Oregon, 1998.

Columbia Electronic Encyclopedia. 6th edition [online], http://www.infoplease.com/ce6/ent/A0838843.html. New York: Columbia University Press, 2000.

Erickson, Milton. *The Nature of Hypnosis and Suggestion.* Vol. 1 of *The Collected Papers of Milton H. Erickson on Hypnosis,* edited by Ernest L. Rossi. New York: Irvington, 1980.

Goodbread, Joseph. *The Dreambody Toolkit: A Practical Introduction to the Philosophy, Goals and Practice of Process-Oriented Psychology.* 2nd ed. Portland, Oregon: Lao Tse Press, 1997.

———. *Radical Intercourse: How Dreams Unite Us In Love, Conflict and Other Inevitable Relationships.* Portland, Oregon: Lao Tse Press, 1997.

Hauser, Reini. "A Message in the Bottle: Process Work with Addictions." *Journal for Process-Oriented Psychology* 6 (1994-95): 85-90.

Jung, C. G. *The Structure and Dynamics of the Psyche.* Vol. 8 of *Collected Works,* 2nd edition. Princeton, NJ: Princeton University Press, 1969.

———. *Two Essays on Analytical Psychology.* Vol. 7 of *Collected Works,* 2nd edition. Princeton, NJ: Princeton University Press, 1967.

Kalff, Dora. *Sandplay: A Psychotherapeutic Approach to the Psyche.* Santa Monica, California: Sigo Press, 1980.

Mindell, Amy. *Coma: A Healing Journey.* Portland, Oregon: Lao Tse Press, 1999.

———. "Discovering the World in the Individual: The World Channel in Psychotherapy." *Journal of Humanistic Psychology* 36 (1996): 67-84.

———. *Metaskills: The Spiritual Art of Therapy.* Tempe, Arizona: New Falcon Press, 1994. Reprint. Portland, Oregon: Lao Tse Press, 2003.

———. "Moving the Dreambody: Movement Work in Process-Oriented Psychology." *Contact Quarterly* 20 (1995): 56-62.

———. "Working with Movement in Process-Oriented Psychology." *Internationale Zeitschrift für Musik-, Tanz- und Kunsttherapie* 2 (1989): 103-112.

———. (by Amy Sue Kaplan). "The Hidden Dance: An Introduction to Process-Oriented Movement Work." Master's Thesis, Antioch University, Yellow Springs, Ohio, 1986.

——— and Arnold Mindell. *Riding the Horse Backwards: Process Work in Theory and Practice.* New York: Penguin, 1992. Reprint. Portland, Oregon: Lao Tse Press, 2002.

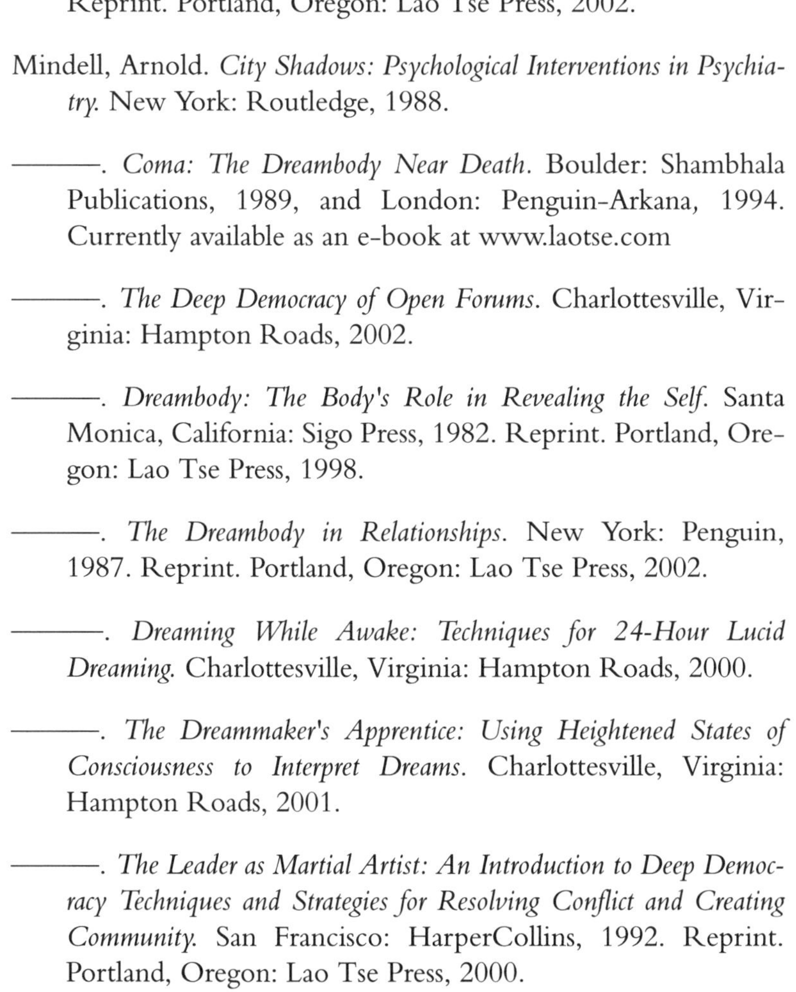

Mindell, Arnold. *City Shadows: Psychological Interventions in Psychiatry.* New York: Routledge, 1988.

———. *Coma: The Dreambody Near Death.* Boulder: Shambhala Publications, 1989, and London: Penguin-Arkana, 1994. Currently available as an e-book at www.laotse.com

———. *The Deep Democracy of Open Forums.* Charlottesville, Virginia: Hampton Roads, 2002.

———. *Dreambody: The Body's Role in Revealing the Self.* Santa Monica, California: Sigo Press, 1982. Reprint. Portland, Oregon: Lao Tse Press, 1998.

———. *The Dreambody in Relationships.* New York: Penguin, 1987. Reprint. Portland, Oregon: Lao Tse Press, 2002.

———. *Dreaming While Awake: Techniques for 24-Hour Lucid Dreaming.* Charlottesville, Virginia: Hampton Roads, 2000.

———. *The Dreammaker's Apprentice: Using Heightened States of Consciousness to Interpret Dreams.* Charlottesville, Virginia: Hampton Roads, 2001.

———. *The Leader as Martial Artist: An Introduction to Deep Democracy Techniques and Strategies for Resolving Conflict and Creating Community.* San Francisco: HarperCollins, 1992. Reprint. Portland, Oregon: Lao Tse Press, 2000.

———. "Process Work with Addictions, Altered States, and Social Change." Lecture given at the *11th International Confer-*

ence on Spiritual Quest, Attachment and Addiction. Eugene, Oregon: International Transpersonal Association, 1990. Find transcript of lecture at:
http://www.aamindell.net/publications_frame.htm

———. *Quantum Mind: The Edge between Physics and Psychology.* Portland, Oregon: Lao Tse Press, 2000.

———. *River's Way: The Process Science of the Dreambody.* London: Routledge & Kegan Paul, 1985

———. *The Shaman's Body: A New Shamanism forTransforming Health, Relationships, and Community.* San Francisco: HarperCollins, 1993/1996.

———. *Sitting in the Fire: Large Group Transformation through Diversity and Conflict*. Portland, Oregon: Lao Tse Press, 1995.

———. *Working on Yourself Alone: Inner Dreambody Work*. New York: Penguin, 1991. Reprint. Portland, Oregon: Lao Tse Press, 2002.

———. *Working with the Dreaming Body.* London, England: Penguin-Arkana, 1984. Reprint. Portland, Oregon: Lao Tse Press, 2002.

———. *The Year I: Global Process Work with Planetary Tensions*. New York: Penguin-Arkana, 1989.

Reid, Howard and Croucher, Michael. *The Fighting Arts.* New York: Simon and Schuster, 1983.

Reiss, Gary. *Changing Ourselves, Changing the World*. Tempe, Arizona: New Falcon, 2000.

Richardson, Alan and Hands, Peter. "Supervision Using Process-Oriented Psychology Skills." *Supervision in the Helping Professions: A Practical Guide*, edited by M. McMahon and W. Patton. Melbourne: Pearson Education Australia, 2001.

Sanbower, Martha. "Deep Democracy: A Learning Journey." Thesis for the diploma program, Process Work Center of Portland, Portland, Oregon, 2000.

Strachan, Alan. "The Wisdom of the Dreaming Body: A Case Study of a Physical Symptom." *Journal of Process-Oriented Psychology* 5 (1993): 53-59.

Straub, Sonja. "Stalking Your Inner Critic: A Process-Oriented Approach to Self-Criticism." Unpublished thesis, Research Society for Process Oriented Psychology, Zürich, 1990.

Tart, Charles. *Waking up: Overcoming the Obstacles to Human Potential.* Boston: Shambhala (New Science Library), 1986.

Van Felter, Debbie. "Heroin Addiction: From a Process-Oriented Psychological Viewpoint." Doctoral thesis, William Lyon University, Zurich, 1987.

Index

M

N

O

P

R